almanacs 647 Hudson
2 flights up 2

JOY LA: 42818

[illegible]PPY HEARTH AND HOME [illegible] CO.

The Dai[illegible]
and Improved Form.

The Desk Calendar [illegible]

The Busi[illegible]

ALMANAC

OF USEFUL FACTS, ADVICE, INFORMATION AND FIGURES;

REPORTS, ESSAYS, SAYINGS, WRITINGS ON THEORETICAL AND PRACTICAL PROBLEMS OF SCIENCE, ART, LITERATURE AND EVERYDAY LIVING, CONTAINS USEFUL HELP AND ASSISTANCE FOR MAN OR BEAST AND SOMETHING THAT SHOULD BE IN EVERY HOME.

1942

HELLO

People

ART WORKS

Steven Brower
& Nora Guthrie
with contributions from Billy Bragg and Jeff Tweedy

Woody Guthrie

RIZZOLI
NEW YORK

THIS BOOK IS DEDICATED TO:

Sam & Dave's Corner Store at Beach 36th St & Mermaid Avenue, Brooklyn, New York—Woody's suppliers of fine construction paper, watercolors, crayons, inks, chalk, glue, paste, paper, pads, pencils, as well as phone calls, newspapers, milkshakes, ice cream, and egg creams. And some stuff for the kids too.

and to

Marjorie Mazia Guthrie and Cathy Ann "Stackabones" Guthrie, savers and saviors both.

First published in the
United Statesof America
in 2005 by Rizzoli
International Publications, Inc.
300 Park Avenue South
New York, NY 10010
www.rizzoliusa.com

Design: Steven Brower

2004 2005 2006 2007/
10 9 8 7 6 5 4 3 2 1

Printed in the United States

ISBN: 0-8478-2738-0

Library of Congress Catalog Control
Number:
2005927398

FOREWORD

Most folks think Woody and me started collaborating when Nora brought us together to work on the Mermaid Avenue project. Truth is we had already been secretly songwriting before Nora and I had even met.

A friend of mine used to work at the Smithsonian Institute in Washington D.C., in the Folkways Archive. She kept telling me I ought to come by sometime and take a peek in some of the boxes of Woody Guthrie material they had. It wasn't the photos she wanted me to see, nor the lyrics, nor letters; it was his drawings.

One time in May 1991, I had a few days off between Baltimore and Charleston, West Virginia, where I was due to play a show for striking mine workers. Seemed like a good time to pay a visit to Woody.

And what a shock I got. As I looked at the cartoons and kids' drawings, the illustrated songs and stories, the wildly impressionistic watercolours and the finely executed portraits, I realised that I didn't really know Woody Guthrie at all.

I'd read the books and sung the songs, I'd seen the photos and heard the records, but there was something of Woody in his drawings and paintings that I'd never seen before.

There was a sensuality here, not just in the flowing lines and curving colours, but in the subject matter too. Lovers caressed and bodies entwined. A naked woman took up the whole frame of an illustration, her full figure a blur of shimmying movement. Across the lower part of her body, Woody had written the words "You woke up my neighborhood."

A week later I was in Athens, Georgia, recording with REM. When guitarist Peter Buck asked me if I had any lyrics for a tune he'd written, Woody's phrase came to mind. We wrote and recorded the song there and then, music by Buck, lyrics by Bragg, inspiration by Woody G.

These illustrations offer us a unique insight into Woody's consciousness and show him to be much more than the political songwriter of legend. I hope you find them as inspirational as I did.

—Billy Bragg

THIS MACHINE
KILLS FASCISTS

PREFACE *Nora Guthrie*

In 1992 I began unpacking boxes and boxes of my father's materials: notebooks, diaries, song lyrics, manuscripts, photos. All were being collected and housed in the Woody Guthrie Archives in New York City. I was always aware that my father created artwork that often accompanied his music. A few pieces decorated our walls at home, but most of it was packed away in boxes and file cabinets. I must admit, though I had seen some of it, I had never really looked at it.

I had seen small reproductions of line drawings in his autobiography *Bound for Glory*, but I had never seen the originals. I was delighted to discover that they were much larger and statelier than the comparatively puny reproductions.

I had seen reproductions of his watercolors published with song lyrics, but I had never seen the originals. The reproductions were usually black and white. I was surprised to find that many of the originals were in color.

I had seen some cartoons published along with writings, but it wasn't until I found the originals that I learned that they were often part of a much larger series and the complete set was often broken up, leaving the lone cartoon out of context.

But the biggest surprise came when I counted them up. There were many more than I ever suspected. Hundreds of drawings, cartoons, illustrations, and watercolors were discovered, many in the most unusual and unlikely places. Large artist's pads, accountant's books, and marble school notebooks contained wide brushstroke watercolors, illustrating everything from lyrics to daily events. Children's composition notebooks were filled with political cartoons done in crayon. Letters and diaries contained detailed pencil-and-ink drawings elaborating his thoughts. Watercolors on construction paper were found among his piles from the 1940s, a period in which he was home much of the time with his children and writing most of his children's songs, which were released on Folkways Records. Sheets of onionskin legal paper contained voter registration posters and topical cartoons. Small pocket notebooks contained portraits and tiny figures drawn while traveling the roads, trains, and subways. Altogether, more than six hundred individual pieces were organized and entered into the Woody Guthrie Archives database from our family collection alone, while hundreds more seem to "litter" correspondence, diaries, notebooks, and even postcards. Many more are presently housed in the Smithsonian Folkways Collection in Washington, D.C., originally part of the collection of Asch Recordings, where Woody did most of his recording during the 1940s. One can't help but be astounded by his sheer output.

My father's artwork was always around the house. The easy strokes, curves, and wiggly lines were fun to look at. The colors were simple and the content straightforward.

Pete Seeger once confessed that when he first heard "This Land Is Your Land" he thought it much too simple. "Not one of your best songs" he told my father. And yet it is that simple song, chock-full of content, that has outlasted and outperformed most of the others.

I feel the same way now as I look at my father's drawings. So much is revealed in their simple lines: much about himself, much about the life he lived, and much about his understanding of the people and the issues that surrounded him. The more I look, the more I see.

His style of drawing mirrors his style of living: fast, spontaneous, impulsive, self-taught, and straight from the heart. They are all about energy. They capture both his personal energy, or vibration, and the pulse of everything he saw around him.

In 1996 I was called upon to curate a traveling exhibition for the Smithsonian Institution. Working closely with designer Jim Simms, who shared my fascination with Woody's artwork, we were able to include much of it in the show. The reaction from the public confirmed what we felt. Many people wrote that the artwork was the most surprising and exhilarating part of the exhibition. At that point, I decided that I had to do a book devoted solely to Woody's artwork.

In doing this book, I wanted to learn about how Woody and Art met: when, where, and why.

Then, I wanted to strip away Woody's public persona and go back in time, to before his story became legend.

And finally, I wanted to cut the umbilical cord that always tied his art to his songs or writings. Woody rarely separated the two. His songs, his writings, and his artwork all seem to be deeply entwined in his creative process: watercolors that can be found layered on top of his lyrics; diary entries brimming with accompanying cartoons; poems and notes framed by colorful brushstrokes; record album covers painted over with his own creations.

Although Woody didn't seem to separate the two—his language and his art—I wanted to. Just for a brief moment, I wanted to see what he might be saying to us with these drawings in addition to the more

Portrait of the artist as a young man.

Nora, Joady, Woody, and Arlo, Coney Island, New York, 1951.

obvious message of his words. I wanted to give his art some breathing room so that I might see what more he was trying to convey. There is something unique in art. It contains the elusive and subtler qualities of human beings. A river that words cannot ride. What more might be revealed from Woody Guthrie's images and imaginings that his words and music couldn't, or that his songs inevitably overshadow?

I began by going back to the books, back to the stories, and back to my memories. Then, I went into my own intuitions.

I found out that Art was my father's longtime friend. Art had accompanied my father on every road he ever traveled. Yet Art had never been formally acknowledged as anything other than something of a bastard child—something he dabbled in between writing "great"songs.

I now know that Art was Woody's first muse, staying ever-loyal to him, appearing both as inspirer and teacher.

I also now think that through his work with the visual arts, he learned and retained many lessons and ideas that were to become the founding principles years later in his job as a songwriter: how to develop a disciplined focus to retain the details of a story; how to create an effective "image," or account, of a story; how to see through a first impression to find a more compelling truth at work; how to "color" a story with a personality, a point of view, a sense of humor or tragedy. And finally, he learned how to view what was happening right in front of him as worthy of being expressed as "art." If one could find the art in daily life, one could find the artist deep within. If a person really had something to say about the life happening around him, he would eventually and inevitably find a unique voice within to say it well. I believe that Woody first found his expressive identity in art and then used that knowledge to become a great songwriter.

His discovery of and enduring friendship with Art began when he was a young man. Having lost most everything else that gave meaning and structure to his life, he found Art lying dormant at the dark bottom of the pit.

> **I knew that my trail would be a story that whirls, and a song that spins in the middle of the sun, a hunt for the universe on the points of our needles. I knew the tale would be a freewheeler, a quick starter, but a high running, circling chorus that keeps on repeating over and over, and would sing every song to be sung under the one tune and the one name and would shake under the fires and gates and furnaces, a track that would go everywhere.**

Tracks Behind a Leaky Mind

In 1925 thirteen-year-old Woodrow Wilson Guthrie found his life was in utter disarray. His home in Okemah, Oklahoma, had burnt down; his older sister, Clara, had died in a separate fire; and his mother, Nora Belle, had been carted off to live the rest of her days in an insane asylum. His father, Charlie, seriously injured in yet another suspicious fire, had moved to Pampa, Texas, another oil boomtown, to recuperate. Charlie had lost all the family's money, and their middle-class lifestyle, a few years earlier in a series of real-estate failures and foreclosures. Woody and his three brothers and sister were scattered about to live with any kindhearted friends or neighbors who would take them in. In 1929 he decided to join his father in Pampa. But the chaos of their world was worsening.

Struggling to survive the oil boom bust and the dust storms incessantly ravaging its farms, the hard-struck town of Pampa wasn't able to hold itself together much longer. "The hard-working people just stumbling about bothered with mortgages, debts, bills, sickness, worries of every blowing kind. . . . People hunted for some kind of an answer. The banker didn't give it to them. The sheriff never told anybody the answer. The chamber of commerce was trying to make more money . . . the people asked the preacher, and still didn't learn much where to go or what to do."

After years of living more like a street rat and less like a human being, Woody began searching through Pampa's local library for answers. He was looking for something to do, something to be, and something to hope for.

"I scratched around in the books. I carried them home by the dozens and by the armloads, on any subject, I didn't care which. I wanted to look into everything a little bit, and pick out something, something that would turn me into a human being of some kind. . . . My head was mixed up. I looked into every kind of an 'ology,' 'osis,' 'itis,' and 'ism' there was. It seemed like it all turned to nothing."

Determined not to unravel, Woody decided there was one place left that he had not scoured for hope: within. He committed to look to himself for guidance and for independence from his hopeless circumstances.

"I wanted to be my own boss. Have my own job of work whatever it was, and be on my own hook. . . . My whole life turned into one big question mark. And I was the only living person that could answer it."

Two self-portraits. TOP: 1938. BOTTOM: 1944.

At nineteen, he found an unexpected friend, and some fresh hope, in a hidden talent: Art.

In his autobiography, *Bound for Glory,* Woody describes his new obsession with art:

> **For the next few months I took a spell of spending all of the money I could rake and scrape for brushes, hunks of canvas, and all kinds of oil paints. Whole days would go by and I wouldn't know where they'd went. I put my whole mind and every single thought to the business of painting pictures, mostly people.**
>
> **I made copies of Whistler's "Mother," "The Song of the Lark," "The Angelus," and lots of babies and boys and dogs, snow and green trees, birds singing on all kinds of limbs, and pictures of the dust across the oil fields and wheat country. I made a couple of dozen heads of Christ, and the cops that killed Him.**
>
> **Things was starting to stack up in my head and I just felt like I was going out of my wits if I didn't find some way of saying what I was thinking. The world didn't mean any more than a smear to me if I couldn't find ways of putting it down on something.**

This newfound friend wasn't relegated to or concerned with the principles of the "high" arts. This friend could go anywhere and everywhere with him, and do anything:

> **I painted cheap signs and pictures on store windows, warehouses, barns and hotels, hock shops, funeral parlors and blacksmith shops, and I spent the money I made for more tubes of oil colors. "I'll make 'em good an' tough," I said to myself, "so's they'll last a thousand years."**

It's unclear whether he ever formally studied art (it is speculated that he enrolled in a mail-order art course) or whether his skills were acquired by trial and error or by imitation. In any case, Art became the means by which Woody could survive his circumstances and think positively about his future.

He also found it was a way to participate fully in his life, rather than feel like another victim of the day's damning events. With

Art, he could help his community—whether it be simply making the local store signs prettier, or creating pictures that would decorate people's walls.

But the most important discovery he made was that as an artist he had a voice. The images, feelings, and ideas that were simmering beneath the surface, once expressed, could bring smiles, even laughs to his despondent townsfolk. And as an artist, he could also help change things, even if, at such a young age, he was simply able to improve the moods of his neighbors. In a time of feeling powerless, Woody began to sense that art gave him some small degree of power. Using the tools of a pencil or paintbrush he could help people, and even change them. His increasing awareness of this was to become the most enduring discovery of his life, one that would unfold and solidify in his work years later when he took pen to paper as a songwriter. Art could effectively make things better.

An interesting serendipity was also taking place at this time. Woody's uncle, Jeff Guthrie, was also living in Pampa. He played music around the house with family and neighbors. Uncle Jeff began to teach Woody how to play a guitar. Playing music for hours with his relatives gave Woody a sense of familial closeness that he had thought was irretrievably lost.

It also fortified his sense of community, and its continuity, in a town that was being eroded daily by the devastations of the dust storms and the Depression. As each day went by, farmers that had worked their lands around Pampa for generations were being forced to leave their homesteads to look for work in the fruit orchards of California to survive. More and more families were seen packing up their belongings and heading down Highway 66. Woody knew them all.

Woody turned to art—drawing and painting—out of which he forged a personal identity and a newfound purpose. And he turned to music to stay tied to family. The melding of these two experiences would eventually blossom into a style of songwriting that layered traditional, roots, and religious music (Woody's immediate experience with his family and local community representing "what is") with art's "impressionistic" political and personal vitality (Woody's intuitive sense of a much larger human experience representing "what could be"). However, during this time, Woody's art and music remained separate, but equal, experiences.

As Woody got better at playing the guitar, he began performing at local events. Experimenting with a new idea he picked up from his art, that of self-expression, he began writing new lyrics to traditional tunes. He mused over the comparable economics and potentials of the two:

> **I got to going out a couple of nights a week to the cow ranches around to play for the square dances. I made up new words to old tunes and sung them everywhere I'd go. I had to give my pictures away to get anybody to hang them on their wall, but for singing a song, or a few songs at a country dance, they paid me as high as three dollars a night. . . . Canvas is too high priced, and so is paint and costly oils, and brushes that you've got to chase a camel or a seal or a Russian red sable forty miles to get. A picture – you buy it once, and it bothers you for forty years; but with a song, you sing it out, and it soaks in people's ears and they all jump up and down and sing it with you, and then when you quit singing it, it's gone, and you get a job singing it again.**

And, "On top of that, you can sing out what you think. You can tell tales of all kinds to put your idea across to the other fellow. . . . I seen there was plenty to make up songs about."

Using the points of both needles, Woody continued to put his ideas down on paper. But now they appeared in two separate forms: as artwork and as song lyric. In both art and lyric, politics was an endless source of material. With both he often mimicked the homespun humor of his then hero, Will Rogers. He created both topical cartoons and songs based on the daily news and events.

At times, two forms began to merge and take shape; one of his earliest songs, "So Long, It's Been Good to Know Yuh" includes both a strong cartoonist's visual description of the townsfolk's plight as well as the creation of a musical canvas, on which he could paint words.

By 1937 things were as financially bleak as they could be. Now married with two children and living in a small, run-down shack in the shriveling town of Pampa, Woody received a letter from his Aunt Laura in California. "Texas is so dusty and bad, California is so green and pretty. You must be twenty-five by now, Woody. I know I can get you a job here in Sonora. Why don't you come?" Woody jumped at the invite. "Yes, I'll go. . . . This is a right nice day for hittin' th' road. 'Bout three o'clock in the afternoon . . . I pulled the crooked door shut as best I could, and walked one block south to the main highway leading west."

Contrary to popular mythology, it was with paintbrushes in hand, not a guitar, that Woody Guthrie hit the road for California. He had hocked his guitar the week before. It would be too cumbersome to travel with.

He wrapped his paintbrushes in an old piece of cloth and shoved them into his back pocket. He would work his way to California using his art brushes for barter, wryly identifying himself as a "sign painter." He painted bold, fresh signs for shop windows, flop houses, and churches. He decorated menus at restaurants, truck stops, and soup kitchens. He painted posters and advertisements on truck's sides. He accepted any kind of painting work he could get—it was his art skills that he brokered for a night's room and board.

Woody's eyes were witness to the "hard travelin'" of hundreds of thousands of "Okies" migrating west along the highways. These pictures were to be forever embedded into his psyche: the sight of their clothes layered with dust, their bodies often limp with hunger, the old cars loaded down with possessions and children. And his ears took in their language, the words they spoke, and the stories they told. Ultimately, it would be his songs that painted the defining portraits. But at the moment, on the road, he still identified himself as a "sign painter."

An incident occurred on this first journey to California that, in retrospect, seems to have cinched his destiny with songwriting while severing any immediate future in art. Woody was hitchhiking with a group of young men when their car ran out of gas. Stalled and hungry, Woody jumped out of the car and headed off down the street looking for some sign painting work that would get them some food. He describes the day in *Bound for Glory*:

> **I heard one of them holler, "Meet you right here at this spot in an hour and no later."**
>
> **I yelled back, "Okie doke! Hour! No later." And I walked down through the town. I peeled my eyes for an old sign that needed repainting, or a new one to put on. I stuck my head into ten or fifteen places and got a job at a shoe store, putting a picture of a man's shoe, a lady's shoe, and: Shoe Repairing Guaranteed. Cowboy Boots a Specialty.**
>
> **I had left my brushes in the seat of the car, so I made a hard run up the main street. I got to the spot, puffing, grinning, and blowing like a little**

horse, and looked around – but no boys, and no car . . . . It was gone. So were my pardners. So were all of my paint brushes.

Woody continued on his way to California without his paint-brushes, his "meal ticket." Forced to find an alternative means of surviving, he started playing borrowed guitars at roadside saloons in exchange for some grub. He sang all the old songs that reminded the migrating families and workers of home, always guaranteed to bring good tips. And using his uncanny ability to come up with a quick line, he would create a new lyric written on the spot just for the situation and just for that audience. Much like his ability to quickly improve an old store window, he discovered that he could just as quickly sing and create songs with the same satisfactory outcome: he would get fed.

Within weeks he was settled with his family in Los Angeles and got a job singing with his cousin, "Oklahoma Jack Guthrie," on the radio. Trailing along with actors involved with agitprop theater, he visited the migrant camps—overpopulated and unhealthy makeshift shelters that were sprouting up all around the orchards. It was a desperate sight.

It was in Los Angeles where he was to meet political activists for the first time: Communist party organizers, writers, actors, filmmakers, and radio producers all involved in progressive politics. In particular, Woody was drawn into the more immediate efforts to organize the migrant workers.

He managed to land a radio show on KFVD in Los Angeles, where he began writing and performing his own songs in earnest. Reporting what he was witnessing, he created both music and art. "Dust Bowl Refugee," "I Ain't Got No Home," and "Do Re Mi" painted the scenes with lyrics. "Woody Sez," a column he wrote and illustrated for the left-wing newspaper the *People's World*, was accompanied by his cartoons, which left no topic of the day uncommented upon.

His life was taking on a new role. And with moderate success, his work as a songwriter and musician was being chiseled in stone by the necessities of the day. But still Woody continued to draw. It was now as natural a part of him as songwriting was to become in the next decade.

Over the next ten years Woody Guthrie would become known for his music. In 1940 he came to the East Coast and New York City, where he first recorded and performed his songs. However, as his work in music increased, he remained insistent that he illustrate his own recordings and liner notes. His writings, essays, and news articles were, for the most part, always dotted with illustrations. His autobiography, *Bound for Glory*, published in 1942 in New York, abounds with detailed pen-and-ink drawings, visual records of the people he grew up with in Okemah, Oklahoma, and Pampa, Texas, and those he met on his journey to California and his visits to the migrant camps.

Woody would often begin working on a song by using a line he'd overheard someone speak. That line might become the core thought of the chorus. ("So long, it's been good to know yuh.") Then, with an illustrator's eye, he would begin to build the scene: who was there, what they were wearing, what they said, what the mood was, a description of the location, what exactly happened. ("A dust storm hit and it hit like thunder, It dusted us over and covered us under, Blocked out the traffic and blocked out the sun, Straight for home all the people did run.") He would continue to do this for as long as necessary until he sensed he had painted an accurate picture of the event, the people, and the setting. ("A song should be as long as the story you're trying to tell.")

Once he felt he got the story right, he would then either elaborate or summarize, purposefully adding his own subjective impression, a comment, or his personality. ("The preacher could not read a word of his text, So he folded his specs and took up collection!").

When he completed what he thought was a good representation of both the objective and subjective elements, he would often go to his art tools to complete the experience by drawing or painting over the lyric. There's almost a sense of this being a kind of personal ritual: a comical baptism of sorts, a magician's wave of hand, announcing the moment when the new song takes on its own life.

Conversely, he would sometimes first draw a picture and then, as if trying to pull out a specific idea that lies dormant in the art, he would work more as midwife and start writing words to a lyric or a thought over the art.

Music and art are always at play, often teasing each other for dominance or collaborating with each other in purpose. In Woody's creative equation, one was never far from the other.

Composing children's songs in the 1940s, Woody continued to use art as a means of enhancing his lyrics. Often created with watercolors on construction paper, his pictures are wild and carefree as if made by a child's own hand. (I wonder, too, if it was a means by which he could go back in time to reinvent his own childhood, an era stolen by so many tragedies.) With his recordings and songbooks, he is both musical and visual Pied Piper, leading children with quirky drawings and musi-

Woody in 1953.

cal instructions to bouts of giggling and every style of silly behavior. "Put your finger in the air" is both a poster-art for empowering children, as well as a song written as a father's playful game.

Woody's handwriting is also evidence of his constant sensitivity and aesthetic understanding of the visual world: at times perfectly elegant, with pen ink color intentionally chosen for effect; at other times wild and out of bounds, the letters themselves evidence of a life often lived on the outskirts of town, or in praise of some juicier passions thriving outside the borders of acceptable behavior. His handwriting always mirrors his persona, representing in its very size and manner of line the role he was playing or the job he was doing at the time: the street rat, the disenfranchised, the angry, the child, the uneducated, the lover, the radio show performer, the writer, the businessman—all self-portraits via "the points of our needle."

In all his work, you can't help but sense a proud nod to the people he met along the way, who, like himself, had little or no formal schooling. It winks at our "youngest citizens," as he called them, who had yet to learn how to read. Woody needed to make his artwork, as well as his music, readily available to all. You can hear him say, "Well, if you can't or don't want to bother reading, well, you can just look at my idea! Or just listen to it. Either way you'll get the jist of what I'm sayin'!"

I wonder sometimes what would have happened had that car not driven off with Woody's brushes and he had been able to continue his journey to California with paintbrushes in hand. Would he have found work as a sign painter, illustrator, or professional cartoonist? Would he have hooked up with other visual artists, rather than musicians?

I think he ultimately found words to be the expression of choice—it was, after all, words that he began searching for in the town library of Pampa, Texas, in 1929. I think had he not been stricken with Huntington's Disease in the 1950s, the illness to which he succumbed in 1967, he would have developed more as a writer.

But I also know he would have continued to illustrate these writings by his own hand—ensuring that by giving us as much of himself as he could, with every talent he was given, he would leave no idea misunderstood. He left behind many tracks, many trails and clues—through songs, through writings, and through art—just to cinch his deal with us: to make sure we get it.

The pictures you see here are simply what Woody saw. Whether they be portraits, abstracts, illustrations, or cartoons, they are all true.

They were all seen at one time or another, in one way or another. They are all representations of the life that was happening around him—on his streets, in his home, in his mind. And like his songs, which are ballads and journalistic in essence, so, too, are his artworks.

They were created with whatever he had in his hand, or in his pocket, or on his desk, or in his house at the time. He never abandoned artwork if he didn't have "proper" supplies. He used whatever was available to him: a pencil and pad on the road kept in his pants pocket; pen and ink and whatever paper was laying on a friend's desk; watercolor and construction paper always in supply for his children in the home; even gift-wrapping paper; and paper towels swiped from public bathrooms in army barracks and hospitals. All could be used for painting, drawing, and writing.

For me, this book is a toast to Woody's first muse, Art. This is the right day, the right time, to reflect on how Art nurtured Woody Guthrie the songwriter. To formally acknowledge her as his first real Muse and first true friend—one that continued to travel with him anywhere, everywhere, and who would do anything.

Had fortune and destiny worked a slight shift of the hand, it's very possible that Woody Guthrie might have become a visual artist. And this book might just as easily have been an episode uncovering the unknown songs of Woody Guthrie, rather than his unknown art.

Toward the end of his life, the advice Woody was to give every young songwriter that came to see him was his own truth: "All you can write is what you see."

For Woody, it's all about what you see. And the tracks you leave behind.

WRITING:
Tracks behind
a leaky mind

SELF PORTRAIT
Woody Guthrie

A PHOTOGRAPHER WITHOUT A CAMERA

I would like to paint you a picture with strokes of electricity.

Steven Brower

There is no hard evidence that Woody Guthrie ever formally studied art. There are hints that he took correspondence courses, art supply lists that one would assume were made in class, instructive notes on shadow and form, and postcards from an art museum. What we do have are thousands upon thousands of pieces of art, line drawings, and color and form—some just barely squiggles, two oil paintings, brushwork, pen-and-ink illustrations, political cartoons, portraits, children's art, and a handful of pastels—that speak to us from ledgers and notebooks, decaying construction paper, and sketchbooks. Lost, more than likely, are hundreds more, distributed to friends and family, left behind in his many travels, sold to survive, gone. What remains is evidence is that Woody Guthrie was a visual artist.

In fact, it was in the visual arts that Guthrie first began to express himself creatively. Growing up in the frontier towns of Okemah, Oklahoma, and Pampa, Texas, he displayed a flair for cartooning and caricature, utilized frequently to amuse his classmates. Throughout his life he continued to paint, draw, sculpt, pot, letter, and design, often earning a living as an advertising designer, portrait artist, sign painter, illustrator, and landscape artist. He was as passionate about his artwork as he was about everything else he created and experienced.

Guthrie's approach to creativity was a symbiotic wedding of art and text. Did the images support the lyrics, or vice versa? There are no clear distinctions. Sometimes the artwork was created first, with text overlaid, and other times he created the lyrics and then illustrated them. Pictures were created to reinforce words; words pictures. Within this yin-and-yang relationship Guthrie created a dynamic, uniquely integrated art form, in which one is not complete without the other.

Still, to date, little has been seen of Guthrie's total creative output. Although his art has been published in conjunction with his writings, usually poorly, there are hundreds of pieces that exist independently. It is all assembled here for the first time, displaying surprising depth, variety, and a highly refined understanding of composition and expression. And just as Guthrie himself defied classification—as a folksinger, writer, poet, entertainer, radio personality—so, too, does his art.

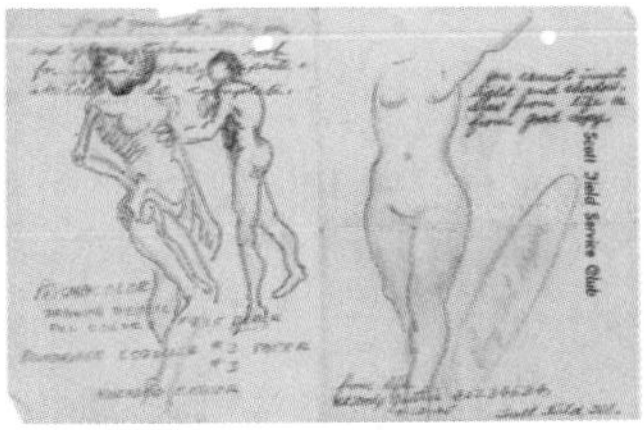

ABOVE: Notes from art classes made during Woody's U.S. Army enlistment. The extent of his enrollment is unknown. ACROSS: During World War II, Woody joined the merchant marines, traveling on Liberty ships bringing supplies, ammunition, and troops to Europe and North Africa. His unfinished novel, *Sea Porpoise*, was based on his experiences. Among his illustrations for the novel, Woody created his own icon.

It is at once illustrative, abstract, socially conscious, bawdy, comical, and serious. With a wide spectrum of media Guthrie created art that stands on its own merits and is an integral part of his overall creative métier.

Beginning as a commercial artist, Guthrie first earned money as a sign painter, displaying a facility for the vernacular typography of the day. He would also paint large murals on storefronts, signed simply "Woody." One, advertising Cudahy Bacon, led to a job offer from a Cudahy executive passing through. He'd illustrate various products and submit them to companies, receiving job offers, cash, or food in return. He would also draw caricatures of bar patrons, receiving money or drinks as payment. While on stage entertaining he would even draw cartoons to keep audiences amused.

Concurrently, he began painting in oils: landscapes; portraits of Lincoln, Jesus, and family members; as well as copied classics, such as Gainesboro's *Blue Boy* and *Whistler's Mother*, which he then sold or swapped (once for a Martin guitar). He would spend his days painting and nights playing music.

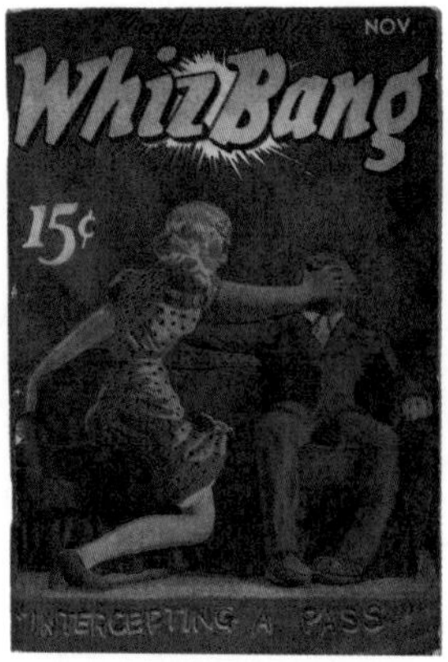

A cover and cartoon from *Captain Billy's Whiz Bang* magazine.

Art historian Ellen G. Landau sees in Guthrie's early work a similarity to that of Thomas Hart Benton, and there is no denying there is a relationship both in their equalitarian, worker's view of the world, and the elongated stylized figures. However, I think we can find Guthrie's influence somewhat closer to home. As an adolescent in Okemah he was a fan of the popular *Captain Billy's Whiz Bang* magazine, published by Fawcett. Begun in 1919 as a mimeographed pamphlet, by 1923 it boasted a national circulation of 425,000. The humor magazine, somewhat risqué in content, accompanied articles with cartoons and illustrations by the leading artists of the day. There is a striking similarity between Guthrie's early work and these depictions of a slightly darker side of American life, with people inhabiting saloons and speakeasies during the prohibition.

More significant still is the influence of Will Rogers on the impressionable Guthrie. Rogers—radio personality, entertainer, movie star, rope-twirling monologist, writer— was born in Oklahoma in 1873. He began as a columnist for the McNaught Syndicate in 1923, and his wry observations of politics written in the simple vernacular of the West were picked up by more than one hundred newspapers within two years. The number swelled to some four hundred by the early 1930s, and it is estimated that more than forty million people read his daily column. Rogers's columns railed against the corruption of bankers in favor of the plight of everyman, and the hypocrisy of the elite. He was not a visual artist himself, and his essays were accompanied by single-panel cartoons that illustrated the editorial content. And although the illustrators varied, one mainstay was Nate Collier. Collier, born in 1883, was a popular cartoonist of his day, and the one most associated with Rogers, having illustrated Rogers's first book *The Illiterate Digest*, published by the A. L. Burt Company in 1924. With his economical use of line, hatching, and white space, as well as comical characters, Collier appears to have influenced Guthrie right along with Rogers's prose. Into the bargain, Collier created a pen-and-ink doppelganger for Rogers, in due course something Woody would do for himself as well. When Guthrie was to begin a column of his own, his cartoons would accompany his essays, in a much looser fashion than Rogers or Collier—one that was unmistakenly Guthrie.

The argument could be made that Guthrie was simply working the current cartooning style of the day. There is as much a relationship between his playful renderings to both animated cartoons of that period and syndicated newspaper comic strips as to anything else. Whether this was a result of correspondence courses, or studying art and cartooning books at the Pampa Public Library, is unknown. Nevertheless, there are clues left behind. In one of his notebooks in 1942, Guthrie created "Rubberface John" who guides "Railroad Pete," a surrogate for Guthrie's unborn child, through various facial expressions. This was a parody of exercises in how-to-draw books of the day, such as *Draw Comics: Here's How—A Complete Book on Cartooning* by George Leonard Carlson, Whitman Publishing Company, 1933.

In any event, Guthrie used his talent as a means of survival. After he hit the road in 1937, he reflected back on his journey as a sign painter and artist:

> **The thousands of days, the hundreds of towns, the miles of paint spread, chalk and pencil lines drawn on windows, on boards, walls, building, fences, on rooves. On trucks. In sun so hot it knocked me over, wind so hard it pushed me down, cold so cold it made me shake and caused my brush to fall out of my hand. I used my brushes to make the bread to go with the beans. . . . I painted for service stations and got candy, beer, wine, oil, tires, patching and a little jingling money. . . . I painted fence signs for farmers, desk signs for clerks, name plates for officers, silver dust signs on windows of any sort of store. I learned what eats at the paint along the salt sea and alikily desert, up the wet mountain and under heavy shade**

TOP: Nate Collier's illustrations for Will Rogers's *The Illiterate Digest.* Courtesy of The Will Rogers Memorial Museums, Claremont, Oklahoma. BOTTOM: Facial expressions from *Draw Comics: Here's How—A Complete Book on Cartooning.*

trees. I had to work a thousand tricks to get the job and a thousand more to make it stick.

Now living in Los Angeles, Guthrie began his column "Woody Sez" for the *People's World*, on May 12, 1939. A four-page tabloid-sized publication in standard newspaper format, the *World* combined the news from overseas and of the latest union struggles with reviews of fashion, film, radio, sports, and art. The publishers thought enough of Guthrie's work to allow him a place for teaser art on page one. These self-contained, single-paneled cartoons worked on their own merit, as well as guided readers to the subsequent column on page four. Often, Guthrie's was the only art on the front page. Occasionally it would be joined by fairly restrained caricatures of political figures. In contrast, his lively and witty art added life to the otherwise solemn gray of page one.

His essays on page four, which were illustrated more often than not, shared the page with such contemporary political illustrators as William Gropper and Fred Ellis, and on occasion the single-panel cartoon "The Ruling Class" by Redfield. Perhaps Gropper, from time to time, most resembled Woody's pieces in line and content, but overall his work displays a studied execution, whereas Guthrie's remained folksy and immediate. Additionally, Guthrie supplied art for ads announcing his friend Ed Robbins's radio show. Eventually Guthrie would contribute eighty-two cartoons in all to accompany "Woody Sez" in the *People's World* and the *Daily Worker*.

Some of Guthrie's most pointed social and political cartoons of this period were left unpublished, contained in small blue notebooks that were ironically entitled "Progress." Here, in sequential fashion, everything was grist for the mill: the economy, the environment, exploitation of the worker and farmer by unjust landlords and bankers—all infused pointedly with humor.

It has also been suggested that there was a relationship between Guthrie's early work and the art of James Thurber, a *New Yorker* essayist, cartoonist, and social satirist. And while it is true that on occasion there is more than a passing resemblance between Guthrie's cartoons and some of Thurber's expressive and playful line work, as well as its symbiotic relationship to his written word, Thurber's humor and art are decidedly "uptown"—something Guthrie would have avoided at all costs. Not surprisingly, Guthrie, by 1940 living in New York, was weary of high society and all of its entrapments and elitism. This carried over to his view of the art world, as he relayed in a "Woody Sez" column:

Illustrations by James Thurber. Originally published in the book *Is Sex Necessary?*

New York is a big town for painting pictures. Least, they call em pictures. Some of em look like you didn't get done with em.

Call em modern paintings. But I'm glad to see em in fashion. It makes everybody a artist. I mean when you can't get no other kind of a job; why you get a hold of you some paint and you're a artist.

I always did think that all of us was good for something – and now I see what it is. We're painters.

And if you can't tell what our pictures are sposed to be, we take down the $5 tag and put up a $50 one.

Paint – splatters on!

In actuality Guthrie had more than a passing interest in the art world. While living in Los Angeles, he would visit the Los Angeles County Museum of Art with radio show singing partner Maxine Crissman ("Lefty Lou from Ole Mizzou") and explain to her how paintings work (for example, he told her one had to stand several feet from a painting to understand impressionism). In New York, visitors to the Almanac House, where Guthrie was residing, included such art stalwarts and innovators as Rockwell Kent, Jackson Pollock, and Willem de Kooning.

On September 23, 1944, Woody visited the Art Institute of Chicago, where the work of Cézanne, Gauguin, Kandinsky, Monet, Picasso, Seurat, Toulouse-Lautrec, and Van Gogh was on display in the permanent collection. Guthrie chose two postcards from the museum to send to his wife and daughter, which he wrote while in the gallery. One featured Pierre Puvis de Chavannes's *The Fisherman's Family*, the other *Le Guitariste* ("The Old Guitarist") from Picasso's Blue Period, chosen for its subject matter and expressive quality ("God, I wish we could go on some kind of trip together. You can look at this and see how me and my guitar feel for you.") As luck would have it, a more traditionalist painting was also on display, one that perhaps had some significance to Guthrie. Grant Wood's *American Gothic* was widely regarded as a folk symbol of a bygone America, even at that time. One could not find a greater antithesis to Guthrie's image of rural Americans than this idealized, dour-looking couple. Where they are humorless and stoic, Guthrie's people grimace, spit, and smile. Where Wood's characters are static, Guthrie's explode off the page in motion, dancing, fighting, unquestionably alive.

Wood's couple looks a bit vexed, with brows furled, and Guthrie's people are ultimately bound for glory. There is even a visual reference to Wood's painting in the published version of *Bound for Glory* at the end of Chapter 17, but in contrast to *American Gothic*, Guthrie's couple stands with arms around their daughter, trees in the background, connected to family and environment.

During 1942 Guthrie worked on his illustrations for his autobiographic novel. Working in a tighter, somewhat more traditional illustration style than the earlier cartoons, Guthrie completed more than fifty illustrations, only twenty-one of which were used in the book, and those were reduced greatly on the page. He had intended to create the cover as well, but the publisher assigned this task to someone else. Still, these illustrations and his self-portraits contained within went a long way toward creating Guthrie's public persona.

Bound for Glory also marks the first printed appearance of "Railroad Pete." A capped, ski-nosed character, a precursor of the "Where's Waldo" cartoon figure, Pete represented Guthrie and Marjorie's unborn child, who, in 1943, was in reality born Cathy. Then again, this caricature, who appears as early as 1942 in Guthrie's notebooks, may also serve as his own alter ego: comical, determined, and persevering. Pete's visage would continue to appear in Guthrie's work, even in abstraction in the later years.

"Railroad Pete."

In fact, Guthrie's interest in abstraction began this same year. Perhaps because he had to work in a representational style to illustrate the book, or simply out of his restless, inventive spirit, Guthrie began to consider other approaches to art. On one side of a sheet of paper, dated August 29, 1942, he wrote:

> **My sketch on the other side of this sheet is one of my proudest and most original.**
>
> **I started out to fill a page as full as I could of just lines, that is, lines that could conflict with one another.**
>
> **I tried hardest to keep from drawing any one certain way or any certain object. I noticed a few times that I drew a box, a flower, a face, a circle, ovals, by mistake, and I drew a house. And 2 cactus and a tree and a piece of pipe, (all from force of the copying habit) then I said I would use conflicting lines to decompose or to attack the objects. And every line I used I asked "does it look like a shape or a design of any earthly plan or object!" If it did I drew other splotches,**

blotches and lines, dots, dashes, to erase the object, the design pattern.

Now the result of this whole page is all of the attacking of line against line. And when I looked at it I said here is my one, my only, real original drawing. To me, if not to everybody, it looks like conflict. I know all of this is childish and simple but try it. It is more fun than you'd think.

Incongruously, a tentative representational portrait in pencil joins the writing itself. In any event, this early interest in abstraction is significant, in that it marks a change in overall approach to his artwork going forward, and perhaps lays to rest the belief that his abstract renderings were only a result of Huntington's Disease. Instead, I suggest, it represents his growth as an artist, and increasing introspection. Guthrie had accomplished much in the public realm; his personal notebooks embody art intended not for publication but as a means of self-expression. As was the case with Guthrie, there are never any absolutes or straight paths, and he would continue to work in several styles over the next years. He also diligently signed almost everything, which speaks to the fact that he was aware of the importance of this work to his overall oeuvre, whether he anticipated this work to be viewed by the world at large or not.

His interest in art and modernity extended beyond painting. In his notebooks he worked on architectural plans for a dream house for himself and his family, designs that are decidedly Bauhaus-inspired, to be constructed of "glass and steel frames." In later years he would take to listening to the avant-garde music of John Cage. He performed in Sophie Maslow's *Folksay*, an offshoot of the Martha Graham Dance Company (his soon-to-be second wife was also a Graham dancer). His philosophy was one of simplicity, yet he didn't really adhere to the "less is more" credo. He created thousands upon thousands of pages of writing and artwork, much of which featured his expansive, Joycean prose, and his themed-based artwork went on for entire notebooks.

Guthrie's interest in the arts may have been the result of a heightened awareness of his own childlike sense of wonder and play after Cathy was born in 1943. Both in songwriting and art, Guthrie seemed to have a heightened awareness of the creative freedom of childhood. There is a direct correlation with the lighthearted animated stick figures and his singsong children's music of this period, both culminating in the album *Woody's 20 Grow Big Songs*, completed with Marjorie after Cathy's death in a tragic fire in their Mermaid Avenue apartment in 1947. Guthrie viewed his young daughter, and children in general, as true, unfettered, natural artists, whose lead was to be followed. "The best kind of artist you can be is when your art runs out of you just like it runs from kids." Of Cathy, he wrote:

> **Marjorie and me said when Stacky was first born that we wouldn't break our necks and Cathy's too, trying to teach her any vast nor any deep theories or feelings about art, books, movies, nor about songs nor music, but that we would try our level best not to block, bar, hinder any of these things when they did bubble up in Miss Stacky. . . . While most dancers and singers are somewhat down stumbling with their intellects, Cathy is already out and down, on and gone, gone over to that genius place and left every chain and shackle, every lock and key, cage and pen, every hall and wall. . . . Watch the kids. Do like they do. Act like they act. Yell like they yell. Dance like they dance. Sing like they sing. Work like kids do. You'll be plenty healthy and feel pretty wealthy, and live to be wise, if you put these songs or any earthly song, on your radio, record player, or on your lips, and do like kids do. I don't want kids to be grown up. I want to see the grownups be kids.**

And on another occasion:

> **And it flew across my mind when I watched the seat of your britches dance into the front room that I would do right well for myself and the whole human race if I could put down on paper, film, clay, canvas, wax, metal, or on some windier material, the song you sang for me, and the way you sang it.**

This fascination with the artistic abilities and insight of children extended to others as well. In a letter to Alan Lomax on May 2, 1950, while staying with friends in California, he wrote:

> **To just sorta halfway give you a rough idea of the Peakly Pinnacle so far hit out here in the ant world from B.C. down to Ensenada, I'm shooting you herein a real genuine firsthand Plutonium sine sketch by that best folky artist of them all,**

Steve Haggerty. I take the liberty here of calling him Stevie, although his real name is really Stephen Haggerty. His kid friends and mama and papa all call him by some different sound and nickname up and down these Hills around the 26th postal zone here, and you always hear all of Steve's callers yell at him by some different nickname to match how mad or how glad they feel at him when they call. He hasn't quite been around this human race for six years yet and he sure knows most of what is wrong with us and how to fix us up. Only trouble is he can't get any listeners when he tries to tell us how crazy we are – but – and so – well – he grabs up his flakey pencil and knocks off a few dozen pictures a day to hang in front of our eyes till doomsday to try to make us feel and think. Steve's one and his biggest grenade to shimmer the art world is his new hatched idea to let the customer or the receiver name each picture to suit. He tells me that full too many a loft and gallery pile full of pictures, pictures, pictures where the personal technique is okay but where the title ruins the whole picture.

When Guthrie shipped out with the merchant marines during World War II, his creative impulses continued, between gun drills and chores. He often drew caricatures of the men on board. In addition, as is described by shipmate and friend Jim Longhi, when Guthrie was assigned to set up the mess hall, the crew entered, only to discover the following scene:

Not a table was set up – two minutes before chow time, and not a plate nor a fork was in sight Woody was standing before the menu blackboard, chalk in hand, putting the finishing touches on the most ornately decorated menu imaginable. The dishes, written in a beautiful flowing script, were framed by birds, flowers, mermaids, and black and white children playing together . . . chow bell rang, and the first rush of diners took their seats.

Woody, still decorating the menu, called over his shoulder, "I'm your new messman. I'll be right with you." The gunners watched dumbfounded as Woody put a last delicate touch on a lovely mermaid's breast. There wasn't a sound of complaint about the unreadiness of the messroom. Woody

stepped back to examine his handiwork, head cocked to one side, and then turned to the men and said, "All right, men, what'll it be?"

Guthrie's stance against fascism was not to be taken lightly. The same passion he expressed for the downtrodden, the helpless, the exploited during the dust bowl and the Depression, to which he dedicated his work and life, was now applied to winning the war overseas:

All art and all industry and all work and all play, in these days, should point to the defeat of fascists the world over . . . art is a weapon and as deadly as steel cannons or exploding bombs. Art should not be pacifist nor mystic, but should send fighting people to the field of battle filled with the clear knowledge of what the real enemy is, and what the people of the world are [fighting] towards.

Woody making a "Hoodis" in the backyard of his Mermaid Avenue apartment, July 1947. He created sculptures out of assorted found objects and junk.

During the same trip, Guthrie began construction of an "Anticyclone and Ship Speeder Upper Aerodynamic Wind Machine," a Rube Goldberg–esque creation, built from whittled and sawed wood, with a makeshift propeller, which was then fastened to the mid-ship rail for the stated purpose of pushing the ship "just a little bit faster" (and the unstated one of raising morale). Eventually entitled "Hoodis" by Guthrie's toddler son Arlo ("Who's this?" he would ask), it would be the first of many fanciful art constructions created out of found objects. Rather than viewing these in an absurdist Dada milieu, Guthrie instead chose to explain them in a more directly utilitarian fashion:

A Hoodis "goes to show you that you can take all of your ugliest things, your brokest and worn outtest things, and stick them together the ways mama nature does her leaves and her stems and her weeds and her grassblades, and make out of your trashiest things your very nicest and prettiest of flowers."

Sadly, no Hoodises survive.

Cathy's death devastated Guthrie. Still he continued to create. In notebooks he wrote and painted, using vibrant colors to either emphasize the words or let them stand on their own merit. He expressed his anguish on these pages. Where good-humored books were dedicated to her during her lifetime, this expressionist outpouring took on a darker appearance. Terms used earlier in political pieces, such as "Conscious of Guilt," referring to the convicting judge and jury from his unpublished Sacco and Vanzetti series (the album would appear with woodcuts by Antonio Fransconi), now reappeared as an expression of his own pain. It is believed that the stress of this event exacerbated the onslaught of symptoms of Huntington's. As he worsened, Guthrie took to creating poems, prose, and art with the theme "I Ain't Dead" running throughout. Other early phrases, such as "All Work Together" took on a sardonic turn, with his formerly humorous characters carrying a casket. He drew angels (one entitled "Pritty Near"), people vanishing off the page, rendered in dry brush. Railroad Pete makes a last appearance, abstracted, as "Arlo's Funny Man."

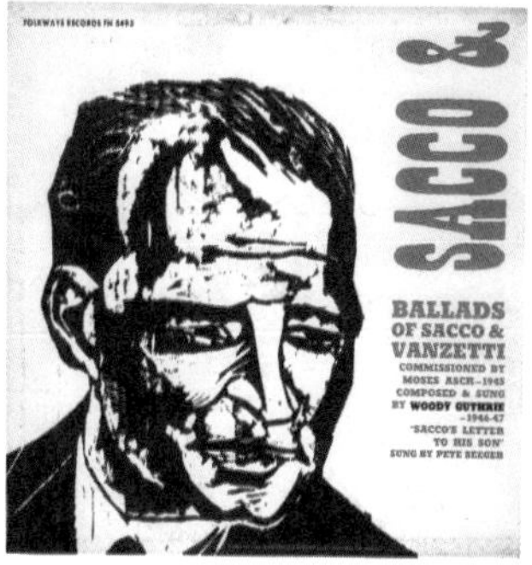

Ballads of Sacco & Vanzetti album cover art by Antonio Fransconi.

Still, Guthrie continued to use his art as a political vehicle. One notebook in particular, entitled "Southern Whites only," explodes page after page with watercolored expressionism, an indictment of the racism and the Ku Klux Klan he encountered while staying with friend Stetson Kennedy in Florida during 1951. There also was an increase of erotica to be found in the work, something that always was present from the earliest days, but was now more explicit, depicting couples in coitis, sometimes using titles from songs ("Jealous Love").

The remarkable thing about Guthrie is how much he continued to create as his health deteriorated. The survivor of a disproportionate amount of tragedy throughout his life, he now faced his greatest challenge, and his need to make something out of nothing, to express a positive vision of the world and remain active, was ever-present. In this work there is still humor, and messages of peace and wonder. If his strangely abstracted modernist portraits and figures were indeed a result of his increasingly unsteady perception of the world, these artworks stand as an even greater artistic accomplishment. In the face of adversity, he continued to express his experience through color and form. Similar to a bedridden Matisse, who held a pointer while directing assistants where to cut paper that he could no longer reach, Guthrie refused to let illness get in the way of his art and allowed his illness to guide his creation. If he were simply "nothing more nor nothing less than a photographer without a camera" as he once described himself, then he was steadfastly recording his journey, for himself, for us, for posterity.

As with any true artist, there was a certain amount of compulsion contained within, the need to create at all costs. As late as 1957, after having been hospitalized for his illness for three years, Guthrie, poet, writer, radio personality, defender of the powerless and disenfranchised, sign painter, artist—when his body was failing but with a determined look in his eyes—still managed to take pen to paper, to create outlines of barely recognizable forms, decorated with stars, typically incorporated with the now barely legible written word, which he then filled in with scrawling pencil. It was his way of saying never, ever give up, never surrender: "I ain't dead yet."

A hand-drawn card announcing his 1939 column "Woody Sez." The words "I ain't dead yet" were possibly added in 1947, when Woody became aware that he might have inherited his mother's illness, Huntington's Disease.

ACROSS: One of Woody's early lyrics from a typed songbook written in Pampa, Texas, in 1935. He collected traditional and original lyrics in a loose-leaf binder, which he used for performances on a local bootleg radio show and at various community performances.

IF I WAS EVERYTHING ON EARTH

If I was a merchant rich enough
I tell you what I'd do
I'd bawl out all my customers
And fire the hired help, too.

If I had a bank on Wall Street
I'd fill it up with gold
And dump it in the ocean
And we'd all go dig some more.

If I was king of England
I'd make them talk to me
'Stead of actin' high falootin
Like some picture shows you see.

I'd turn out all the prisoners
And put in all the rich
But it dont look like my cowboy life
Will ever come to sech.

If I was president Roosevelt
I'd make the groceries free
I'd give away new Stetson hats
And let the whiskey be;
I'd pass out suits of clothing
At least 3 times a week
And shoot the first big Oil Man
That killed the fishing creek;
If I owned all of Hollywood
I'd hire each living soul
To be a great big movie star
And give 'em homes of gold;
And not one single nickel will
This nation e'er be worth
Until you make a guy like me
'Bout everything on earth.

May, 1935
Woody Guthrie,
408 South Russell St.,
Pampa, Texas

Woody Guthrie
408 So Russell St.,
Pampa, Tex.,
May, 1935

HOW HE LOOKS AT THINGS

You know what a artist is don't you? A artist is a person that got out of a job so blame long they learnt to do something else.

By 1935, twenty-three-year-old Woody Guthrie was earning his living as a creative entity. Painting advertising murals on the sides of stores and signage by day and playing music by night, he was able to eke out a modest living for himself, his young wife, and infant daughter. To say he was self-trained would not be entirely accurate: he was a voracious reader, having worked his way through the Pampa Public Library, and one can only assume this included everything pertaining to art. Most likely he studied through correspondence courses as well.

He would stretch his own canvases, which he would then cover in gesso. On these he would paint landscapes or portraits of President Lincoln and Jesus, which he would then give to family and friends. For money he would create window placards in calcimine paints for local merchants. When these materials proved scarce he would continue to create with whatever was at hand: on newspapers, napkins, even on tablecloths and wallpaper.

On stage he would continue to intertwine the disciplines, using the popular vaudevillian chalk-talk device of drawing cartoons as a means to keep the audience entertained. By all accounts, Woody was at his happiest while he was creating.

Around this time Guthrie began the lifelong practice of recording his art in notebooks and journals. The earliest of these attest to his burgeoning political consciousness, lampooning the oppressors of the day: bankers, landlords, big business, and corrupt politicians. Already in evidence is the combination of humor, politics, and erotica that would mark his creations throughout his life.

Many of his drawings from this period appear to adhere to the conventional cartooning wisdom of the day ("you begin with a circle . . .") but at the same time display a sophisticated understanding of sequence and composition. There is nothing indecisive or hesitant about these cartoons. Beautifully composed, they reveal no pencils beneath the inks, no sketches beforehand, simply pen put directly to paper.

At the very same time, Guthrie was spending time in art museums, as evidenced in the inscription on the back of the Adobe landscape painting represented here on page 38:

"This is adobe art, painted of open air, clay and sky. Imagined in front of the Santa Fe Art Museum when an old lady told me "the world is made of adobe", and I added, so is man"

—Woody Guthrie

Perhaps the only two paintings that survive are by no means remarkable, other than the fact that Guthrie painted them. His Lincoln portrait looks like it might be the product of one of the correspondence courses, although it is not without a certain charm. It is purported to have been painted for Mrs. Todd, the librarian at the Pampa Library, who was a supporter of Guthrie's intellectual growth during his teen years. Although she was not related to President Lincoln's Mrs. Todd, it is alleged she is the inspiration for these portraits, of which only this survives (see page 39).

The landscape painting too is not extraordinary in and of itself, yet it is significant because it hints at Guthrie's understanding of impressionism and perhaps cubism, even at this relatively early stage. It also allows us a glimpse of what could have been, had Guthrie taken a different road and ventured purely into the visual arts. The likelihood of this is finite, though, because he never headed purely into anything, but rather was a creative force that spilled out in all directions.

His understanding of the visual is incorporated in his lyrics. He painted pictures with words, filled with descriptive rhythms and colors:

As I was walking that ribbon of highway
I saw above me that endless skyway,
I saw below me that golden valley,
This land was made for you and me.

When the sun come shining, then I was strolling
And the wheat fields waving, and the dust clouds rolling,
A voice was chanting as the fog was lifting,
This land was made for you and me.

Conversely, his time spent in art museums found its way into his choice of songs to perform as well, as in the traditional "A Picture From Life's Other Side."

In the world's mighty gallery of pictures
There's scenes that are a painted from life

Scenes of youth and of beauty
Scenes of hardship and strife
Scenes of wealth and of plenty
Old age and a blushing young bride
Hanging on the world, the saddest of all,
Is a picture of life's other side.

Now in Los Angeles in 1939, Guthrie began his column for the *People's World*, the communist party's newspaper. *People's World* announced the column in this way:

Woodrow Guthrie or just plain Woody, as he is known to thousands of radio listeners will be a daily feature in The People's World from now on.

Woody calls himself a hill-billy singer. He is one of the 200,000 people who came from the dustbowl looking for work and a little food – the people who have picked the fruit and the crops of California – lived in shanty camps, been beaten and driven about by the bank-landowners.

But Woody came with a guitar on his back and with an eye and an ear sensitive to the suffering of his own people.

He sings songs every day over KFVD from 2:15 to 2:45 and has many thousands of listeners and people who write him letters. He writes these songs himself.

And Woody has gathered a great deal of homely wisdom from his people. Every day he will speak to you on this page in his own way about how he looks at things.

Here his cartooning took on a looser fashion, painted in ink with brush, for a more spontaneous feel. Again, there is no evidence of pencilwork beneath, nor sketches: these small gems arrived fully realized on the page. While the single-panel cartoons on page one were consistently rendered as line art, the art that accompanied his essays on the editorial page varied in style, often using wash to add tones.

Art as subject found its way into his "Woody Sez" writings as well, not surprisingly mixed with social concerns:

Stayed a few nights with a artist and painter by trade, and he's got a mighty good picture of a lynching a hanging on my

right wall. I mean my right hand, and it shows you one man, a Negro man, already hung for excitement and entertainment, and another'n being drug in and beat up with clubs and chains and fists and gun – and so naturally I caint think up no jokes for today. This painting is so real I feel like I was at a lyching, and it somehow or other just takes all of the fun and good humor and good sport out of you to set here and realize that people could go so haywire as to hang a human body up by a gallus pole and shoot it full of Winchester rifle holes just for pastime. It reminds me of the postcard picture they sold in my home town for several years, a showing you a negro mother, and her two young sons, a hanging by the neck from a river bridge, and the wild wind a whistling down the river bottom, and the ropes stretched tight by the weight of their bodies and – the rope stretched tight like a big fiddle string. Aint no telling how many will march by the songs that have whistled through the ribs of the poor lynch victims.

Never one to sit still, either literally or figuratively, Guthrie gave up his radio show and headed to New York City in February of 1940, while still contributing his column and art to the *People's World* and later to *Worker's World Daily*. And just as he changed locales, his illustration style would again undergo a metamorphosis. Woody was not about to be reigned in, even by style, nor would he produce what was expected.

Life has got a habit of not standing hitched. You got to ride it like you find it. You got to change with it. If a day goes by that don't change some of your old notions for new ones, that is just about like trying to milk a dead cow.

If you're too bull headed to change your old notions for the ones that come up every morning, you belong over in the herd with the ones that are herded around like cattle.

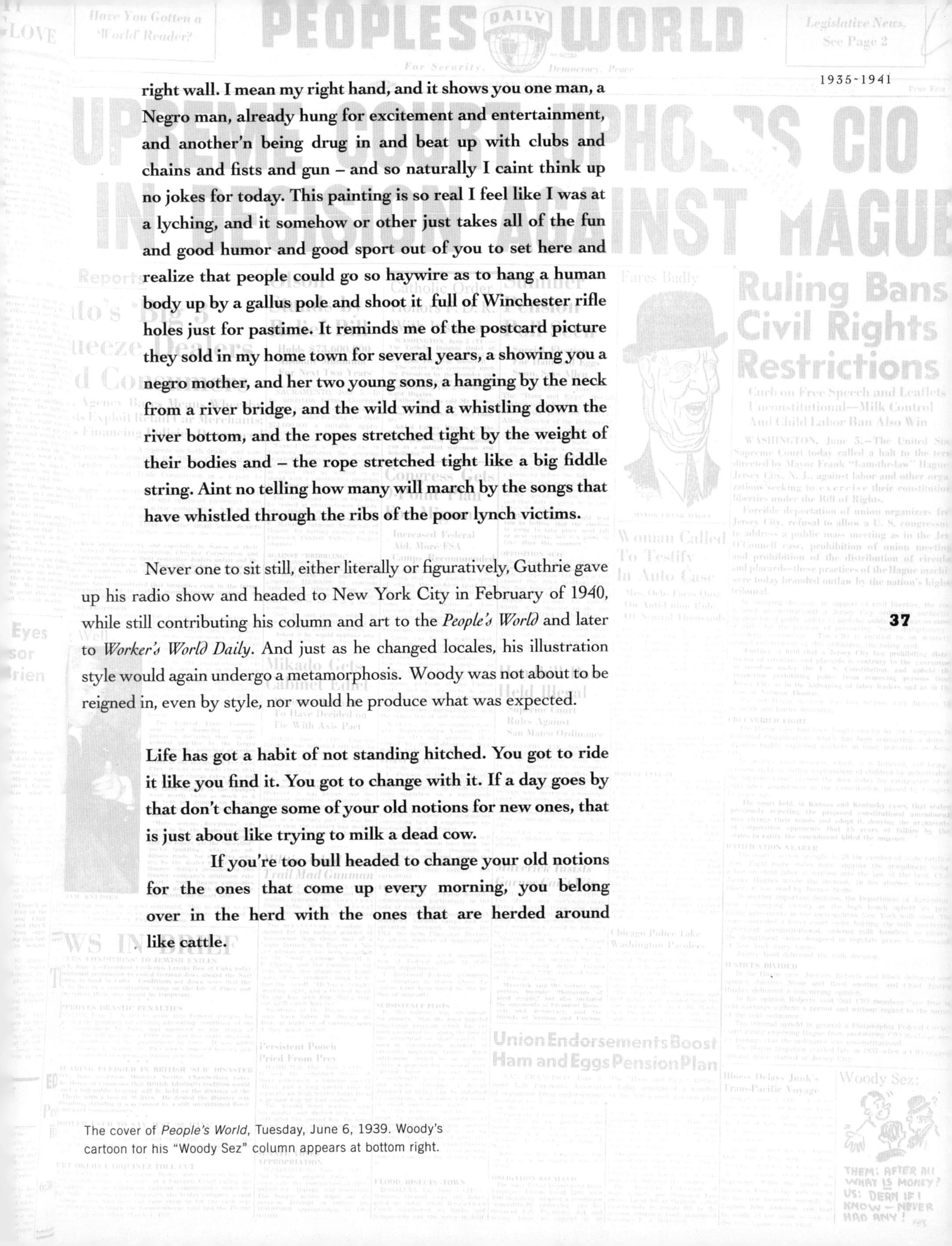

The cover of *People's World*, Tuesday, June 6, 1939. Woody's cartoon for his "Woody Sez" column appears at bottom right.

Woody originally worked in oil on canvas, creating more traditional and conventional paintings: portraits, Christ images, reproductions of historic paintings, landscapes, and various images from nature. ACROSS: Perhaps his visit to the Santa Fe Art Museum in 1936 at the age of twenty-four inspired this impressionistic approach to an adobe landscape. BELOW: Mrs. Todd was the librarian at the Pampa Public Library in Texas, where Woody moved in 1931. She introduced Woody to many new ideas, including the arts. This is one of a series of portraits he did of Abe Lincoln, possibly to honor his local "mentor" who bore the same surname as Lincoln's wife, Mary Todd.

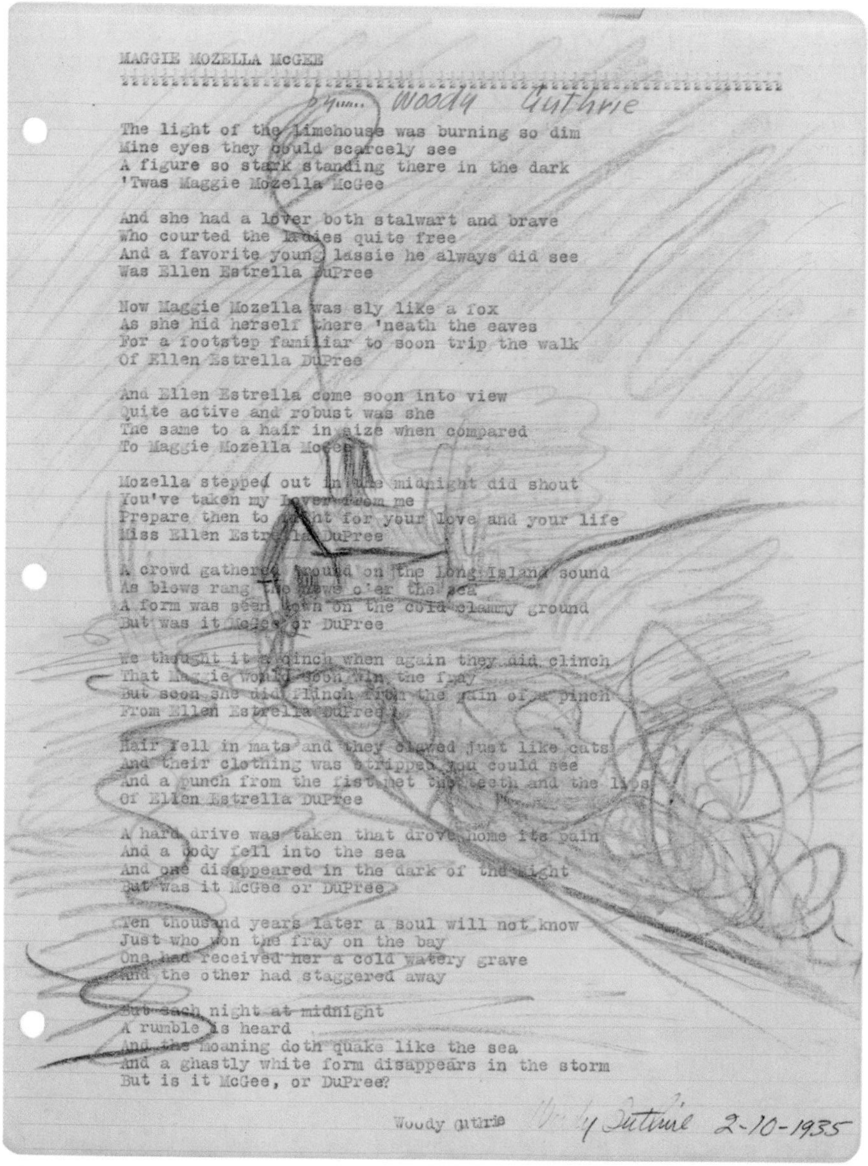

MAGGIE MOZELLA McGEE

by..... Woody Guthrie

The light of the limehouse was burning so dim
Mine eyes they could scarcely see
A figure so stark standing there in the dark
'Twas Maggie Mozella McGee

And she had a lover both stalwart and brave
Who courted the ladies quite free
And a favorite young lassie he always did see
Was Ellen Estrella DuPree

Now Maggie Mozella was sly like a fox
As she hid herself there 'neath the eaves
For a footstep familiar to soon trip the walk
Of Ellen Estrella DuPree

And Ellen Estrella come soon into view
Quite active and robust was she
The same to a hair in size when compared
To Maggie Mozella McGee

Mozella stepped out in the midnight did shout
You've taken my lover from me
Prepare then to fight for your love and your life
Miss Ellen Estrella DuPree

A crowd gathered around on the Long Island sound
As blows rang the news o'er the sea
A form was seen down on the cold clammy ground
But was it McGee or DuPree

We thought it a cinch when again they did clinch
That Maggie would soon win the fray
But soon she did flinch from the pain of a pinch
From Ellen Estrella DuPree

Hair fell in mats and they clawed just like cats
And their clothing was stripped you could see
And a punch from the fist met the teeth and the lips
Of Ellen Estrella DuPree

A hard drive was taken that drove home its pain
And a body fell into the sea
And one disappeared in the dark of the night
But was it McGee or DuPree

Ten thousand years later a soul will not know
Just who won the fray on the bay
One had received her a cold watery grave
And the other had staggered away

But each night at midnight
A rumble is heard
And the moaning doth quake like the sea
And a ghastly white form disappears in the storm
But is it McGee, or DuPree?

Woody Guthrie Woody Guthrie 2-10-1935

An early Guthrie lyric, illustrated in crayon, from his 1935 loose-leaf songbook. At this time, he was performing locally in Pampa, Texas.

In 1937 Woody landed a radio show with his cousin, Jack "Oklahoma" Guthrie, which later became "The Woody and Lefty Lou" show. At its height, the show received more than ten thousand fan letters from "Okies," a derogatory term used to describe the hundreds of thousands of dust bowl families heading west to California in the 1930s. Many of Woody's best-known songs—"Talkin' Dust Bowl Blues," "Do Re Mi," "Dust Bowl Refugee," and "Vigilante Man"—were written for his "Okie" audience in response to their letters, and were first performed on this show.

Having lost their farms in the greatest natural disaster that ever hit the country, these farmers flooded Route 66, looking for work in the California orchards. Woody traveled the same road and witnessed the injustices and hardships these families experienced. They were turned away at the California border if they didn't have $50 on them, and were often harassed by vigilante groups, encouraging them to turn back.

BELOW: A page from Woody's playlist for his radio show, 1937.

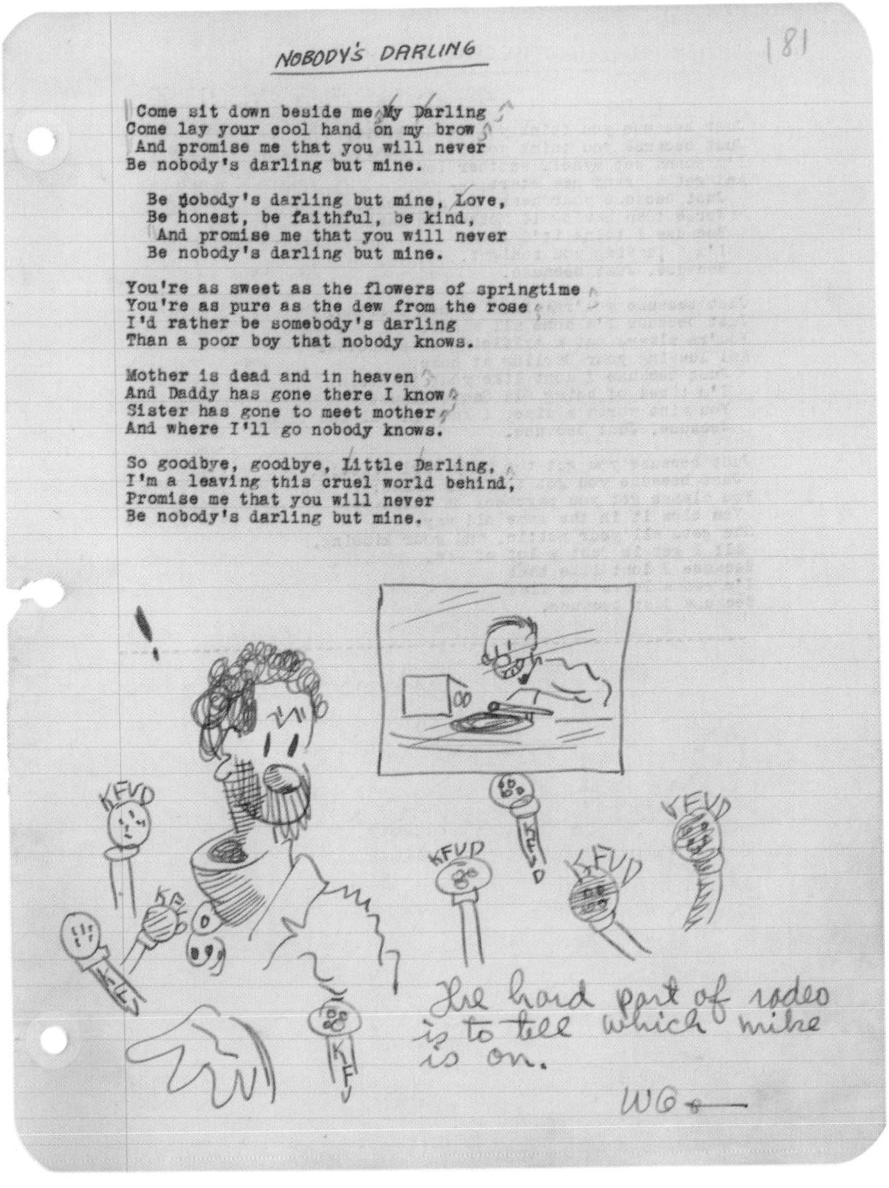
NOBODY'S DARLING

181

Come sit down beside me, My Darling
Come lay your cool hand on my brow,
And promise me that you will never
Be nobody's darling but mine.

Be nobody's darling but mine, Love,
Be honest, be faithful, be kind,
And promise me that you will never
Be nobody's darling but mine.

You're as sweet as the flowers of springtime
You're as pure as the dew from the rose
I'd rather be somebody's darling
Than a poor boy that nobody knows.

Mother is dead and in heaven
And Daddy has gone there I know
Sister has gone to meet mother
And where I'll go nobody knows.

So goodbye, goodbye, Little Darling,
I'm a leaving this cruel world behind,
Promise me that you will never
Be nobody's darling but mine.

In 1938, Woody created two notebooks of cartoons dealing with the political and topical issues of the day. In Los Angeles, he had been introduced to many activists— actors, filmmakers, writers, and directors—all involved with progressive politics. He traveled with them to the migrant camps, creating agitprop theater and writing songs to support the cause of organizing the workers into unions. The art in these notebooks reveals his increasing interest in politics, and the social issues surrounding elections.

LOOK UP!

In 1938, Culburt Olson became the first Democrat to be elected governor of California in forty-four years. The single act that probably endeared Olson to Woody Guthrie was his pardon of Tom Mooney, one of his first acts as governor. He supported Franklin Roosevelt's New Deal and even tried to push for an expanded New Deal in California. Olson championed many of the issues Woody did.

SOAP
LARD
MILK
SUGAR
WHAT HE DONE ABOUT IT!

A major architect of the New Deal during the Great Depression, Harry Hopkins created such programs as the Federal Emergency Relief Administration (which provided millions in welfare money to the needy), the Civil Works Administration (which provided temporary jobs for the unemployed), and the Works Progress Administration (an agency that pumped money into highway and building construction, reforestation, and other public works).

GREED
THE MAN WE DONT WANT
IN OFFICE !!

JUSTICE
THEY AINT NO SECH!
I TELL YOU THE SIGN PLAINLY SAID "VOTE TWICE FOR OLSON".

HERE IS THE NEW SLIGHT SLATE

(SLIGHTER INFORMATION ADVANCES DEFECTIVE DEMOCRACY)!

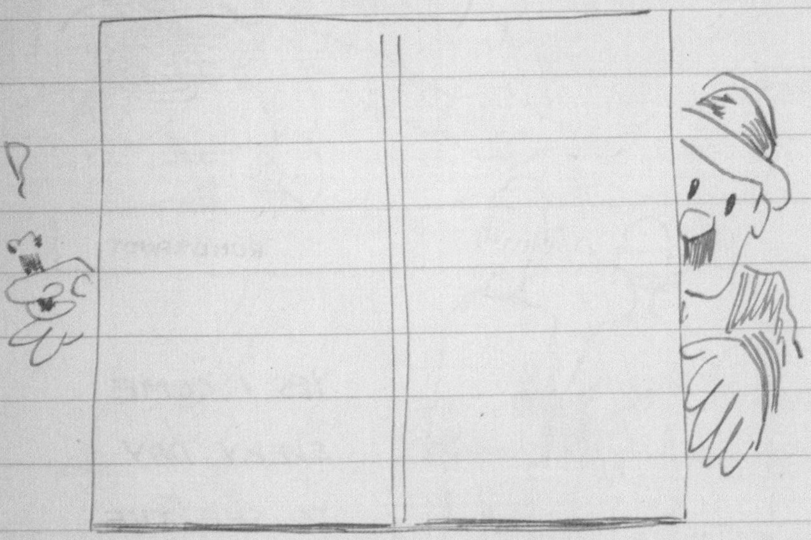

SO GOOD IT AINT TRUE!

SO SLIGHT YOU CAINT TELL IT!

SO HIGH YOU CAINT READ IT!

SNIFF AN YOU'LL SMELL IT!

A NEW NAME FOR THE HEARST PAPER.! A HITLERIZED NEWSBOY.

THERE IS ONE CONSOLATION LEFT — THE CHILDERN THAT ARE RAISED IN THE SUN WILL ALWAYS BE THE BRIGHTEST!

51

IT'LL ALL HAVE TO BE REWRITTEN, MISS HIPPS, AND RAISE THE PENSION FROM $35 EVERY WEDNESDAY TO $36.00 EVERY FRIDAY.

YOU CANT DO THIS JOB
TILL YOU JOIN THE UNION!
LOCAL 365
"IF YOU JOIN THIS
UNION YOU CANT
TAKE THAT JOB!"
?

Fletcher Bowron was elected as mayor of Los Angeles in 1938, after he won a landslide recall election against the openly corrupt Frank Shaw. He served as mayor until 1953, being one of the longest serving mayors of Los Angeles ever. He washed the municipal government clean of corruption and was known as an honest man.

A
B
NO YOU AINT HIT THE TEXAS DUSTBOWL YET, THIS IS ONLY JUDGE BOWRON SWEEPING L.A. !

IT'LL TAKE
A GOOD MAN
MR. BOWRON!
THE OLD MAN OF THE MOUNTAINS

Woody's first wife, Mary, joined him in Los Angeles with their three young children: Gwendolyn, Sue, and Bill. Many of the local landlords refused to lease apartments or houses to families with children. A father himself, Woody was sensitive to the issue and created a number of pieces highlighting this discriminating practice.

POWER PLANT
GARRISON REVENUE ACT
WOOD IT WORK ON A CANNIN' FACTORY?

CIVIL RIGHTS
THEY'RE SAFEGUARDED ALL RIGHT!

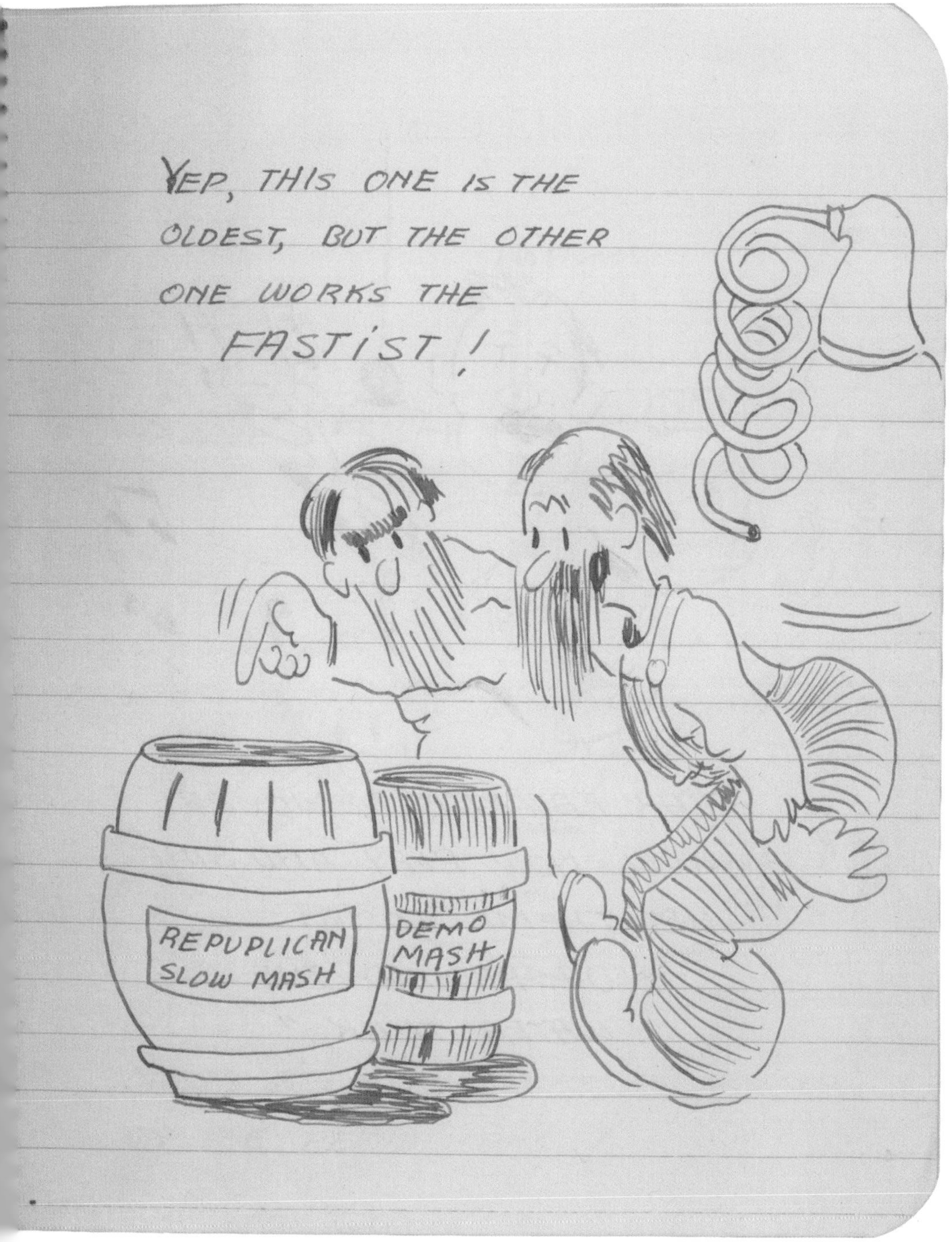
YEP, THIS ONE IS THE OLDEST, BUT THE OTHER ONE WORKS THE FASTIST!
REPUPLICAN SLOW MASH
DEMO MASH

GET THESE REPUBLICAN GOGGLES
OFF OUR PEOPLE SO'S THEY
CAN SEE WHAT'S GOIN' ON !

Woody created many single-paneled cartoons and illustrations to accompany his column for the *People's World* daily newspaper in Los Angeles. "Woody Sez" first appeared in 1939. Basing his humor on Will Rogers's popular "Will Says" column printed in the national newspapers, Woody was free to write his own alternative wry comments on issues of the day: the Stock Market, the price of tobacco, farm foreclosures, and other national or political news stories.

BANKERS
WE PLEGE OUR ALEGIANCE TO OUR FLAG...... AN TO WALL ST., FOR WHICH IT STANDS.....ONE DOLLAR, UNGETTABLE .....

I TELL YOU JOHN 3 OF THEM ARE MISSING!

HITLER UND CO.
FRESH PICKED APPEASMENT PLANS 98¢

YA GOTTA PICK A LOT OF COTTON TO SMOKE A 5¢ CEEGAR!

Woody Sez:
ITS THE NEW DEAL OR NUDE DEAL!
(For more of Woody Sez, see page 1.)

Woody Sez:
TEACHER
OUR SCHOOLS
They caught him a teaching!
WOODY

I'M TOO SOBER TO FORECLOSE ON A WIDOW!

A 1939 poster art series created to organize voter registration to support progressive candidates.

Woody Guthrie
AND DON'T COME BACK
TILL YOU
REGISTER
TO VOTE

THIS IS THE HAND

PUNCHIN' TH' CLOCK

SUN DOWN

ND BAWLS WIFE OUT !

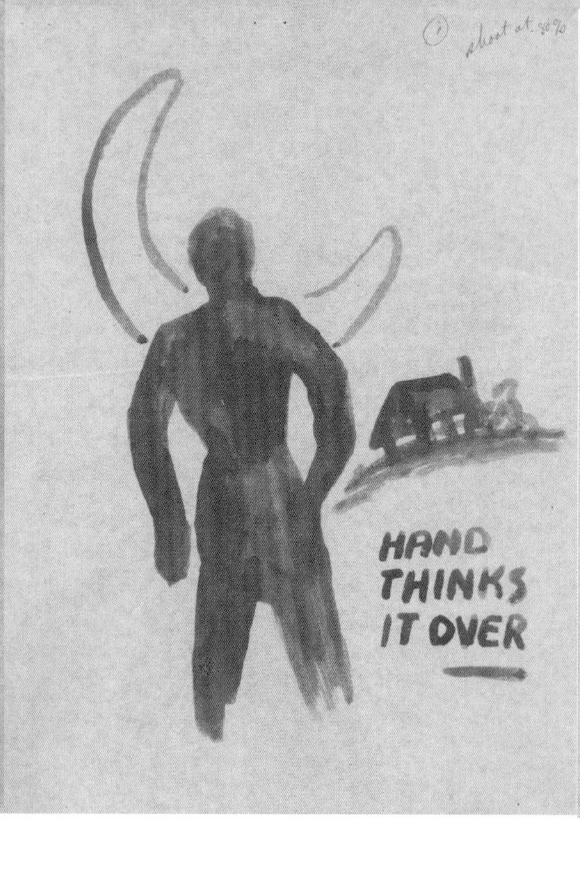
HAND THINKS IT OVER

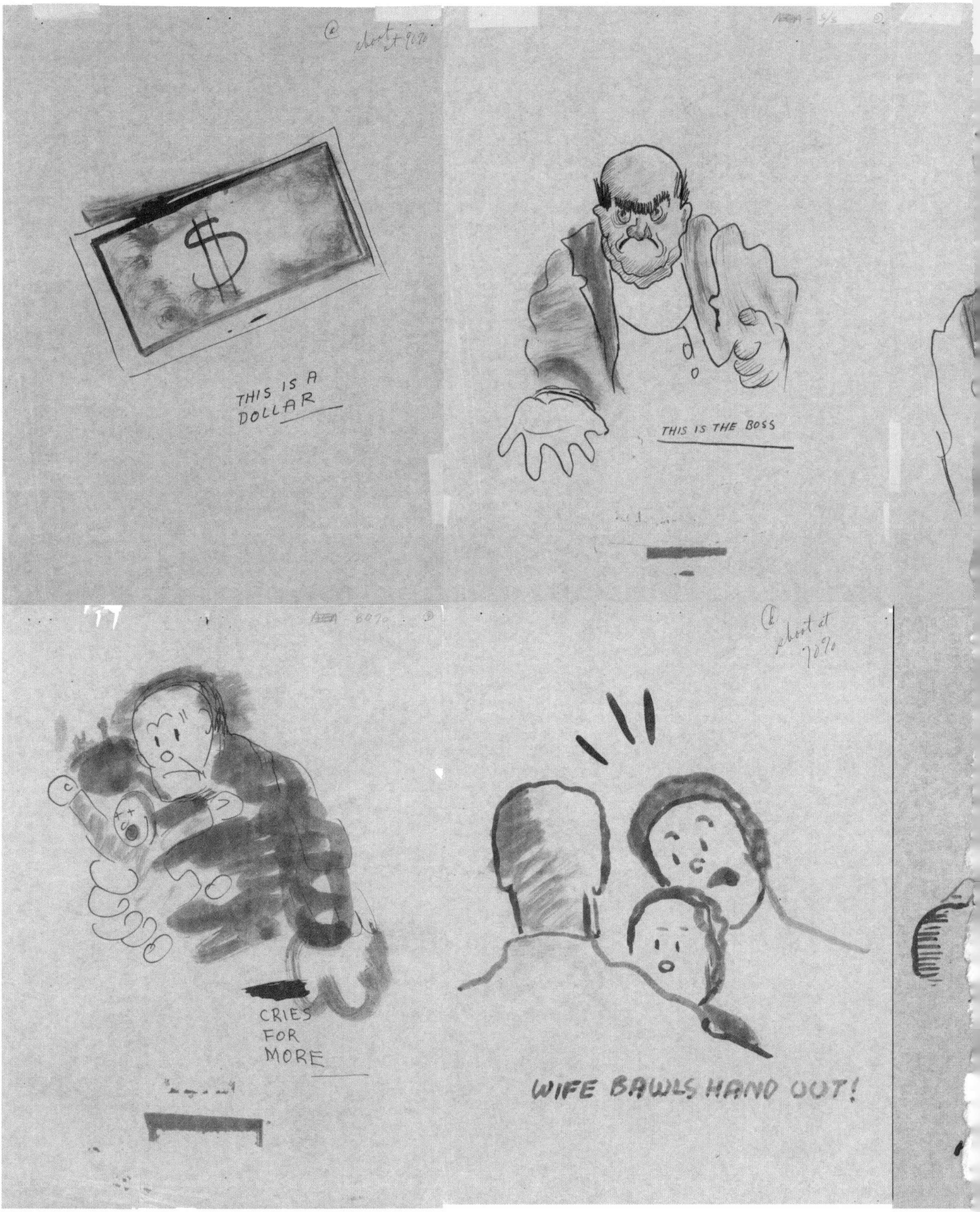

shoot at 90%
THIS IS A DOLLAR
THIS IS THE BOSS
CRIES FOR MORE
shoot at 70%
WIFE BAWLS HAND OUT!

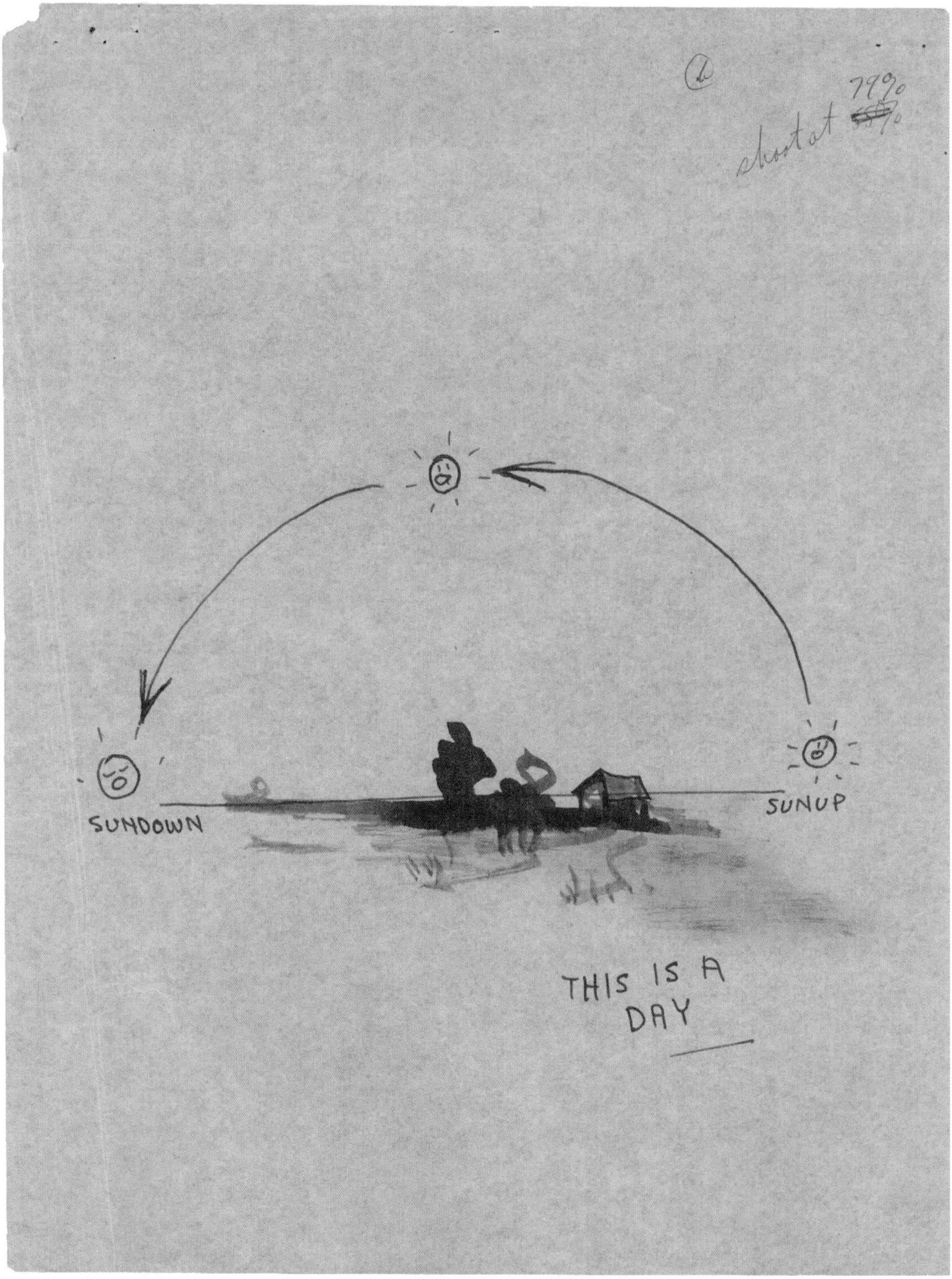
shoot at 79%
SUNDOWN
SUNUP
THIS IS A
DAY

JOIN

HAND BUYS
LOAF OF BREAD

HANDS
KIDS
EAT
BREAD

HAND IS CHARGED WITH TRYING TO
OVERTHROW U.S. GOVERNMENT!

When Woody arrived in Los Angeles in 1939, he was "discovered" by many of the left-wing and progressive political figures and artists, who introduced him to the leftist movement. Traveling alongside such actors as Will Geer and friend Cisco Houston doing agiprop theater in the migrant camps in California, Woody was appalled by the plight of the migrants and sided with the message of the organizers. He often used his artistic and music talents for the cause. It's possible that this series "Join the CIO" (Congress of Industrial Organizations, a precursor of the AFL-CIO) was created as a handout.

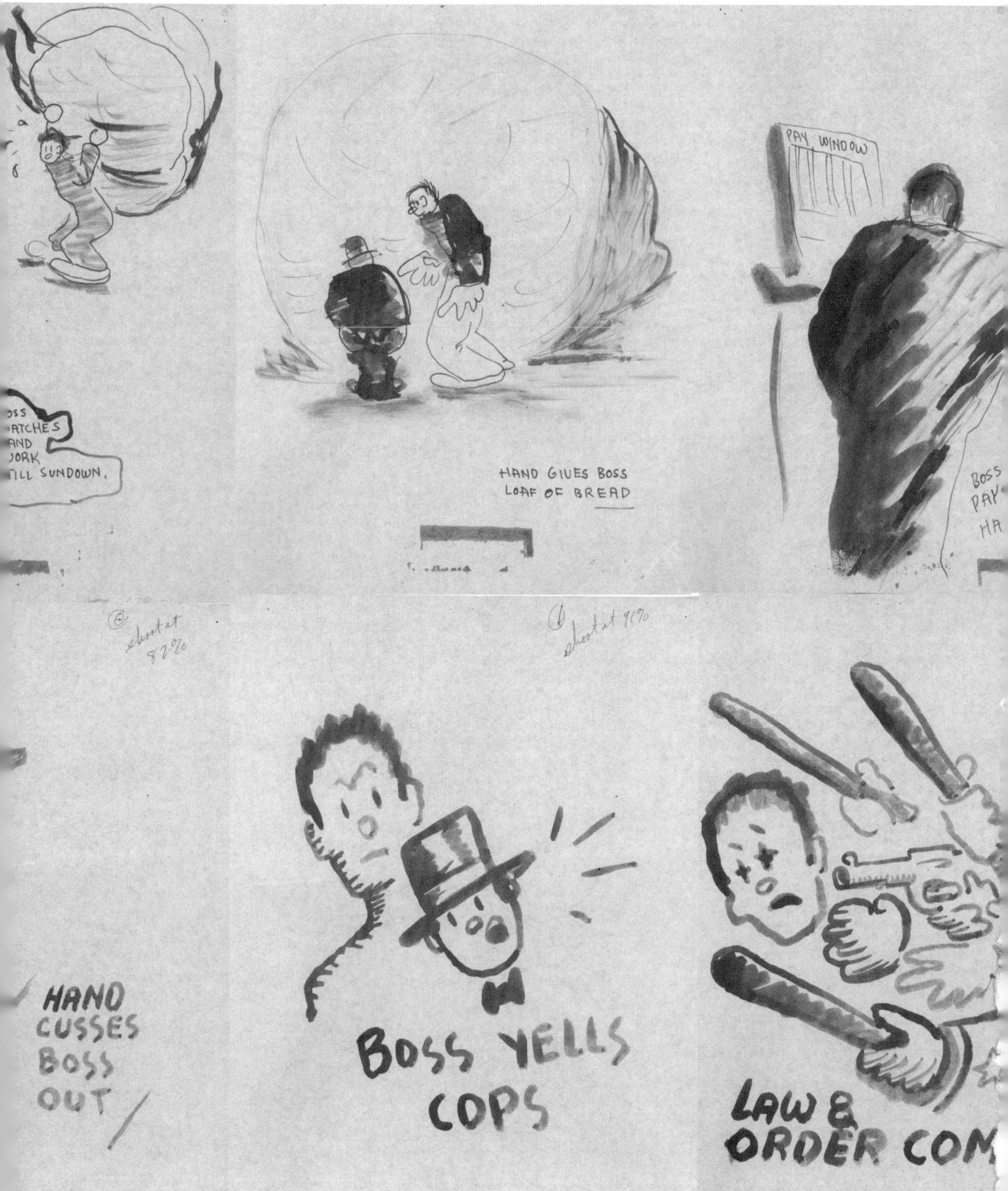
OSS
ATCHES
AND
ORK
TILL SUNDOWN.
HAND GIVES BOSS
LOAF OF BREAD
PAY WINDOW
BOSS
PAY
HA
shoot at 82%
shoot at 91%
HAND
CUSSES
BOSS
OUT
BOSS YELLS
COPS
LAW &
ORDER COM

A portrait of persons unknown. On the wall is what appears to be an artwork by Gordon Frieson, who sometimes sang with the Almanacs.

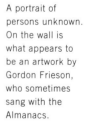

Woody arrived in New York City in 1940 on an invitation from a friend, actor Will Geer. Geer had come to New York from Los Angeles to star in "Tobacco Road," a play opening on Broadway. Upon Woody's arrival, he was introduced to the Almanac Singers, a group of musicians who were living communally in a loft on Hudson Street. These sketches depict various members of the Almanacs, who were the 1940s precursor to many of the folk groups that emerged in the 1950s: The Weavers; Peter, Paul and Mary; and others. TOP LEFT AND BOTTOM: Lee Hayes. CENTER: Sis Cunningham. OPPOSITE PAGE: Millard Lampell.

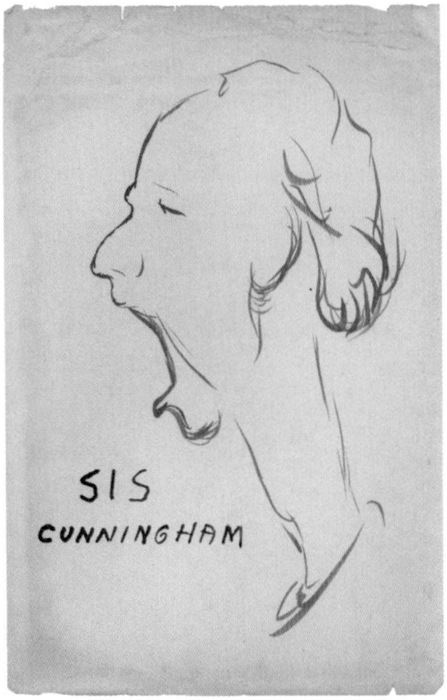

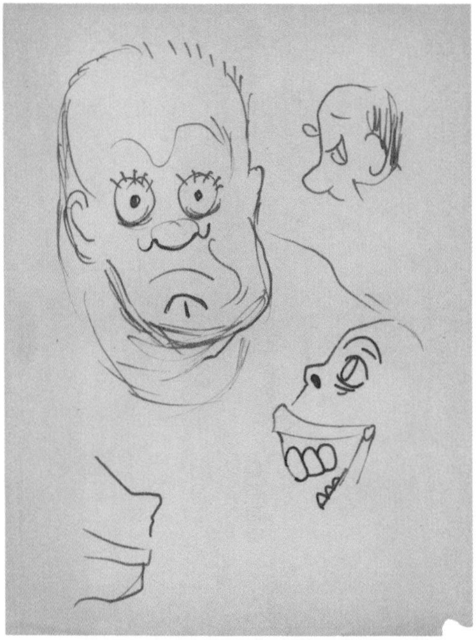

HOWDY!

HERBERT HIGH, ACE AVIATOR, offers his services in the capacity of search director if it should develop that a geographic survey has to be made to recover the Almanac Singers copy of their manuscript, Hard Hitting Songs. It seems that a traveling organizer, writer, and orator, speaker, and talker, Millard Lampell, wabash cannon ball graduate, was entrusted with and lost the songs.

Pages from a humorous, tongue-in-cheek newsletter Woody created that covered the daily activities and topical concerns of the Almanac Singers.

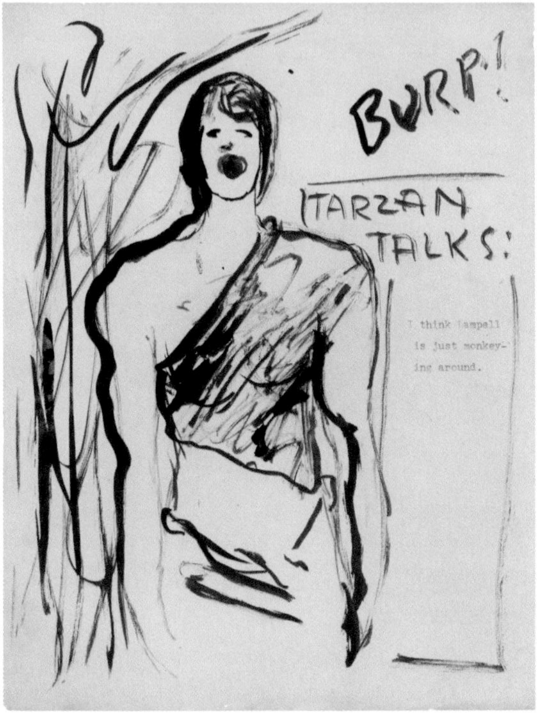

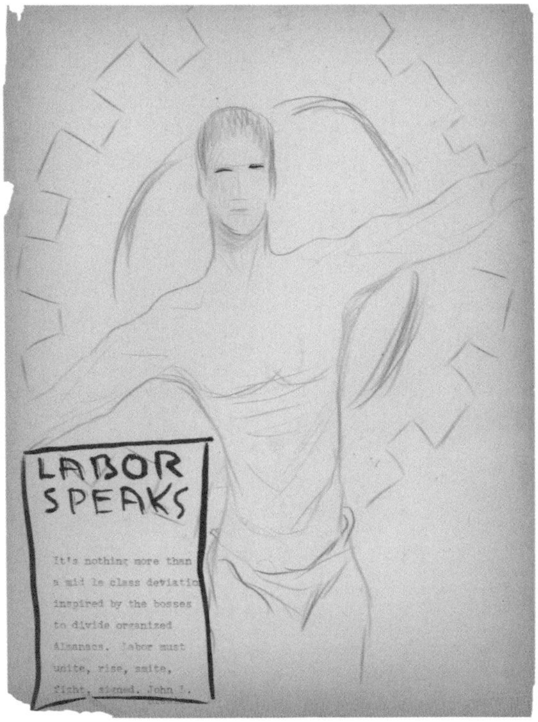
LABOR
SPEAKS
It's nothing more than
a mid le class deviatio
inspired by the bosses
to divide organized
Almanacs. Labor must
unite, rise, smite,
fight, signed. John L.

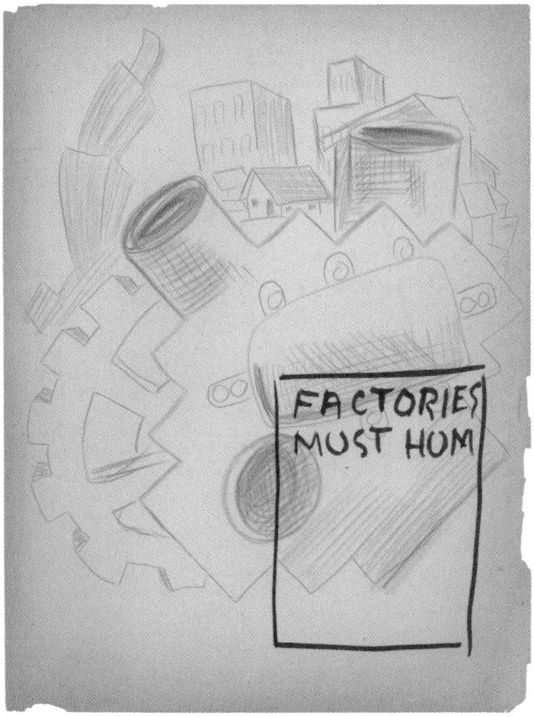
FACTORIES
MUST HUM

CORA JACKSON BOWERS, authoress, writeress, and a lot of other esses, is betwee a rock and a hard place, but an interview with her at her typewriter disclosed that she is still optometrist about it.

You see, it all happened the other day, when after a visit to the Almanac House, a talk with Mill Lampell, a rag chewing with Peter Bowers, and two short conferences with Dick and Rosie Dawson, Cora decided to change the entire plot, plan, technique, approach, production, and presentation of her latest 15 radio scripts, worked out with the help of one John Spraddle Smyth, and formerly titled 'Days and Nights in Both Countries'.

However, it was disclosed in a cablegram to the sister republics that they couldn't get their days and nights to coming together, so something had to be done that would interest, amuse, tickle, and teach the school kids. So Cora grabbed her telephone and called the editor (Ed) of the Daily Almanac. She could not hear what the Ed.(Editor) was saying in both countries, because of the meowing of the friendly (and how) Almanac Cat. She misunderstood the telephone conversation completely, and wrote a script called 'Screaming Cats in Both Countries'.

Her show sold. The contract read as follows: Party of the first part will be called party of the first part, party of second part, part and half or two parts --- that for the next three years, the Foamy Soap Company, will present the show.

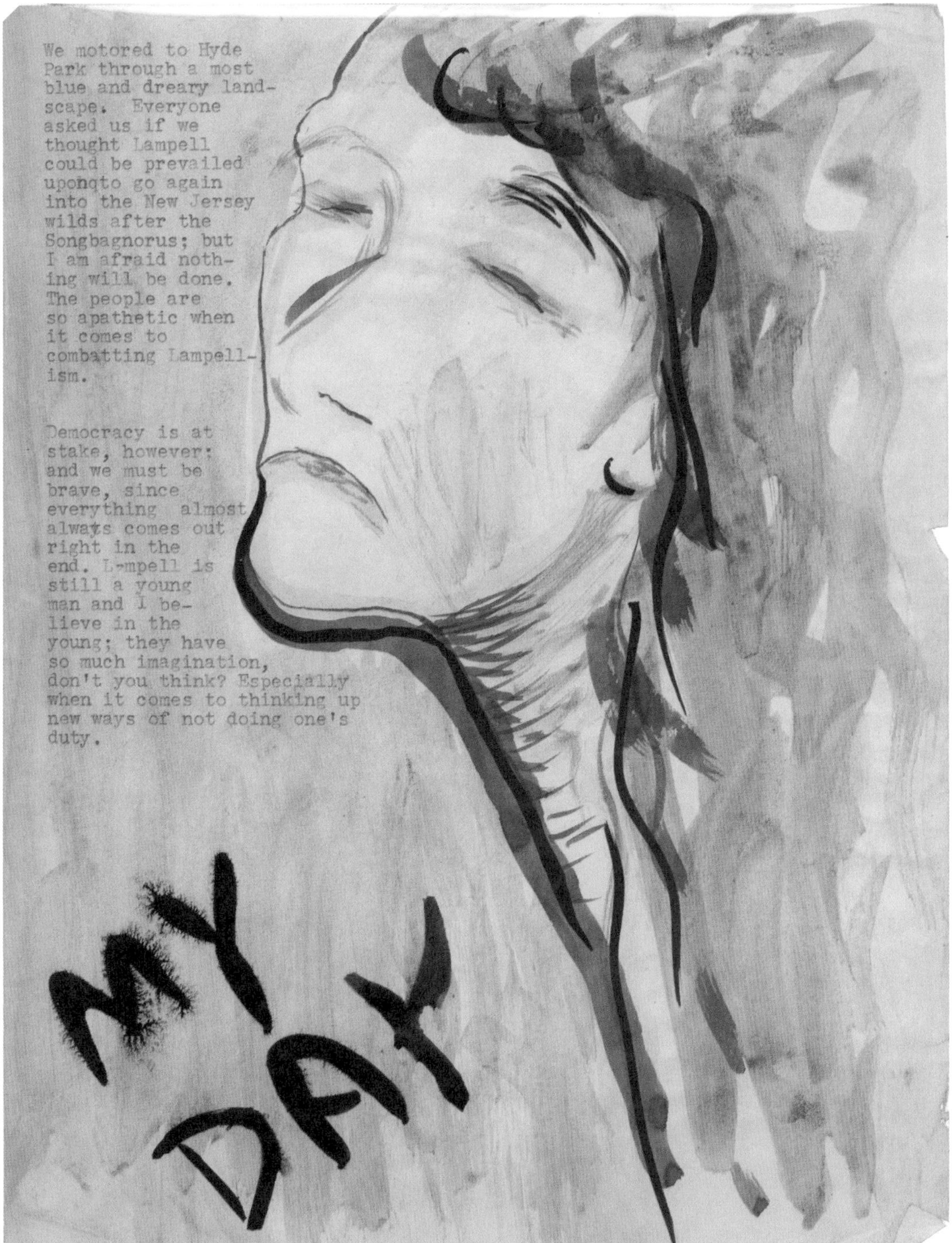
We motored to Hyde Park through a most blue and dreary landscape. Everyone asked us if we thought Lampell could be prevailed uponqto go again into the New Jersey wilds after the Songbagnorus; but I am afraid nothing will be done. The people are so apathetic when it comes to combatting Lampellism.
Democracy is at stake, however; and we must be brave, since everything almost always comes out right in the end. L-mpell is still a young man and I believe in the young; they have so much imagination, don't you think? Especially when it comes to thinking up new ways of not doing one's duty.
MY
DAY

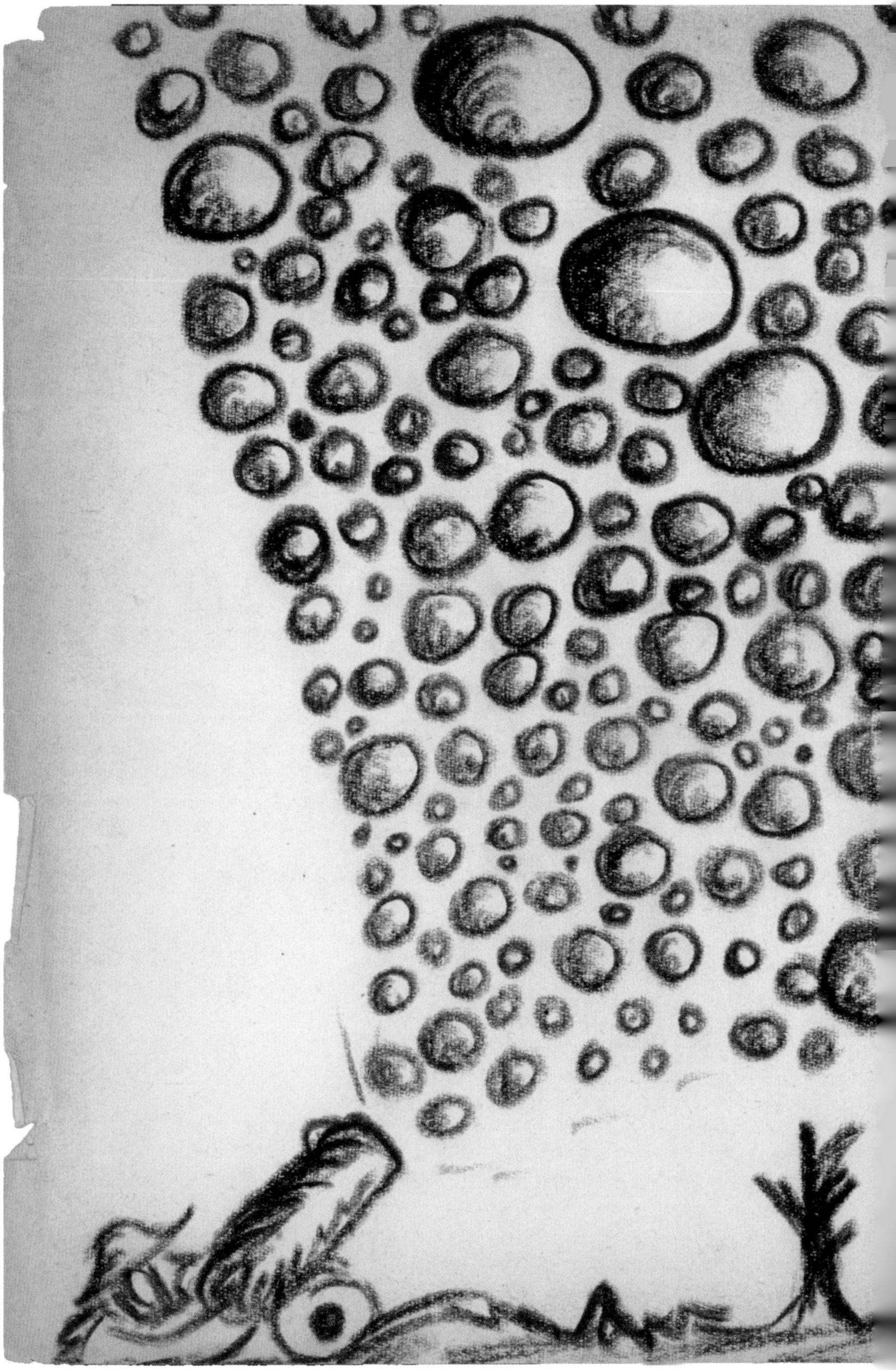

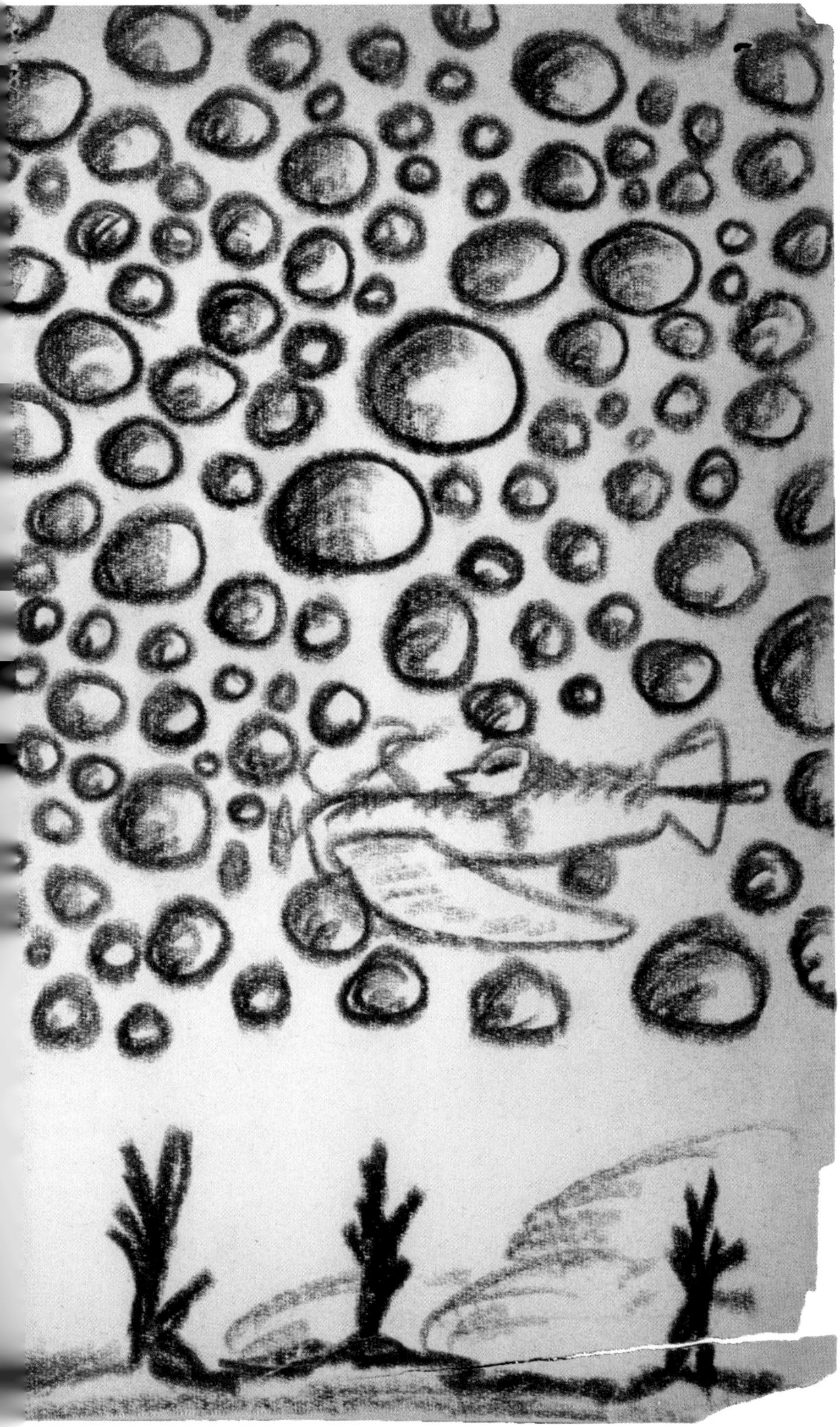

PAINT YOU MY SONG

When I first got to New York and looked it over, with this nice salty air to chew paint off, I figured that I was looking at a sign painter's paradise.

In 1942 Guthrie was completely ensconced in New York City. At first he resided at the Almanac House, a.k.a. "The Loft," in Greenwich Village, with other like-minded folk musicians, including Pete Seeger, Lee Hays, and Millard Lampell. Guests included artist Rockwell Kent and writer Dashiell Hammett. Woody would position himself at the table, typewriter or pen in hand, and create throughout the night. The others would wake to find him curled up under the table, with pages of writing and art scattered around the tabletop and floor. Some pieces would flow into the wastepaper basket; others would be stacked up in no particular manner. Roommate and fellow Almanac singer Hays said, "Woody always reminded me of water over a dam, just an unstoppable creation." It would take the resolve of his new paramour, Marjorie Mazia, a dancer with the Martha Graham Dance Company, to begin to organize both the work and the man.

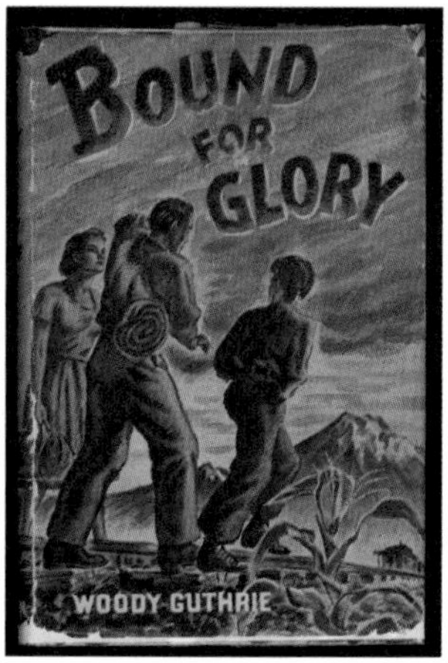

First edition of *Bound for Glory*, with cover art by Woodi Ishmael.

His newfound organization led to a request for Guthrie to write his autobiography, originally known as *Boomchasers* but eventually entitled *Bound for Glory,* to be published by E. P. Dutton. He tore into the project with the same dedication and obsessive creativity he demonstrated with his overall oeuvre. Once he completed more than twelve hundred single-spaced manuscript pages, he began working on the illustrations to be included throughout. Here the work shows a departure from the earlier cartoon style that was featured in his "Woody Sez" column. In fact, these images are closer in style to the Collier art that accompanied Will Rogers's syndicated strip, and for the most part are rendered in a more traditional pen-and-ink illustration style. The styles he employed throughout are somewhat inconsistent, some utilizing a heavier, looser brush line, others a finer, more studied pen line. Some appear more rushed, others more careful. Two in particular (pages 88 and 89) stand up to any great illustration of the day, and once again give us a glimpse of Guthrie's potential for a career in illustration, had he desired one (or had he desired a career). Although he was originally intended to illustrate the cover, he sadly did not get the commission, and we are left to wonder what might have been, as no cover sketches survive.

Critical reviews were overwhelmingly positive for *Bound for Glory*. The *New York Times* wrote "There certainly hasn't been anything like it before, an ecstatic, breathless, jutting geyser of scrambled words" and the *New Yorker* concurred: "Some day people are going to wake up to the fact that Woody Guthrie and the ten thousand songs that leap and tumble off the strings of his music box are a national possession, like Yellowstone or Yosemite, and part of the best stuff this country has to show the world." Nevertheless, not all were as kind to his illustrations. In *Book* the reviewer observed: "The illustrations by the author are pretty bad and add nothing to the book's flavor. But it is a fine narrative job."

After the book's publication Guthrie continued to wed imagery, lyric, and prose, and explore the social ramifications during this period. His vision of an egalitarian society was framed within art in his essay of November 29, 1943, "All Artists," and he saw little difference between art forms, as all led to the betterment of the world:

> **Now if people who read books and go around making speeches, if they are called political organizers, so are we who stare into music books and play instruments, so are we who try so hard to sing, so are we who mould the clammy clay, the wild colors of paints, so are we political organizers.**
>
> **We are politicians too, that bend with our shovels and hoes and rakes, that dig the oil, the ores, the chemicals, the minerals, the dusts, powders, we who blast the flames to mould our alloys, our crops of troubled medals, so are we dancers; we bend, don't we?**
>
> **So are we actors. We fret and walk and puff and strut, we laugh, cry, moan, and sing—**
>
> **Singers are we all. Singing farmers. Singing miners. Lumberjacks. Truck drivers. Cabbies. Dock Workers. Singing longshoremen. Dancing newsboys. Speaking barbers and hairdressers. Talking doctors. We are all preachers and artists and makers of sad and silly mistakes.**

Not one to rest on his laurels, Guthrie would never again return to the more studied style of art contained in *Bound for Glory*. Afterward his work took on a looser, more immediate fashion. He was also on the move, and mobility leant itself to a rich and liberated body of work. Still, 1942–43 was a watershed period for him, what with his book about to be published and the arrival of Cathy Ann in 1943. His popularity as a performer at union halls and leftist events took him far from home, and thus he rendered plaintiff cartoons on the fronts and backs of postcards sent home.

The war in Europe also called, and he would soon ship out to sea with the merchant marines. As always, he continued to record his experiences in journals, and to use art as a means to entertain himself as well as his crewmates. Railroad Pete was also enlisted into the cause, and would soon be defeating Hitler in typical comic fashion.

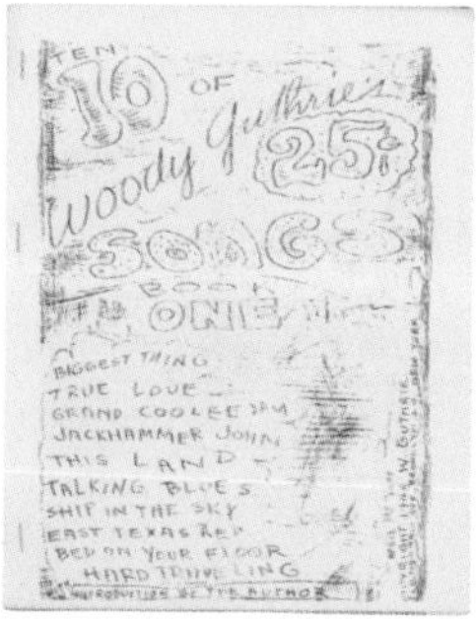

The unadorned mimeographed cover of *Ten of Woody Guthrie's Songs—Book One*, 1945.

At the end of the war Guthrie returned from three tours of duty and settled back into life in Coney Island. Marjorie and Woody borrowed a mimeograph copier from the Martha Graham offices and created a 25¢ songbook to promote his short-lived new radio program. The cover was drawn in a loose fashion, featuring handwritten type. Woody would personalize each copy with comic characters painted in red and blue dyes on the front. Never repeating himself, he came up with dozens of variations, one after the other, creating one hundred in all. Unfortunately, he never got to distribute them.

"Fatigued," Woody in uniform while stationed at Fort Dix, NJ, his first day in the army, May 9, 1945.

On May 5, 1945, the U.S. Army, perhaps as a result of his political affiliation, drafted Guthrie and stationed him in Texas, once again separating him from his new family. He tried to give the experience a positive spin, enrolling in an art course while there. He painted signs for the army and threw himself into learning the Teletype with the same determination he had in his approach to everything else. Finally discharged in late December 1945, he returned to Marjorie and Cathy Ann in Coney Island, New York, and resumed his creative output. Now recording for Moe Asch at Folkways Records, he would be asked to illustrate small booklets published within the LPs.

During this period Guthrie became increasingly aware of symptoms similar to the ones his mother had experienced years before. Still nameless, his condition would be yet another obstacle to overcome, and he continued to create art, write, and perform. He would complete entire series in one sitting, dashing off art in stream-of-consciousness fashion. For the first time we also see artwork in sketchbooks, one to a spread, sans words.

He began work on a songbook to accompany one of several LPs he recorded for children, alternately entitled *Work Songs to Grow On* and *Woody's 20 Grow Big Songs*. Through his daughter he experienced the childlike wonder of the world, and his art reflected this in his kinetic, colorful stick figures, moving cars, and funny animals. He also began illustrating song lyrics and poems written by Marjorie's mother, the Yiddish playwright and poet Aliza Greenblatt.

He would fill sketchpads with pencil sketches of Cathy, whom he dubbed Stackabones, as well as mother and child, and other children at play. He illustrated and designed covers for the LPs, although these went unpublished, the commission having been given to popular designer and illustrator David Stone Martin.

On the side of one of his many sketches for the *Grow Big* covers, Guthrie tried his hand at instructions for the printer, which evidenced an understanding of the printing process, but was perhaps a true printer's nightmare:

Cover of a sketchbook entitled *What a Beautiful World*, a collection of drawings based on the writings of Aliza Greenblatt.

> **Bleed one inch (all around).**
> **Background:**
> **A gray, light wash of pink Reddish**
> **and Orange, Or any Light, Gay Tone,**
> **Letters will be of same wash tones, As the background,**
> **a part of it, will raise out of the background coloring**
> **A good greenish white and yellowish green would be**
> **good—Try all tones of green...WG**

In 1947 the tragic death of four-year-old Cathy Ann in a fire in their apartment devastated the Guthries, and the resulting stress perhaps brought on increased symptoms of his Huntington's Disease. His art became broader during this period, decidedly more abstract and colorful. Strange Picassoesque faces made their appearance, and increasingly erotic renderings appeared alongside childlike flights of fancy. His writing and art would now become completely seamless, and even the outwardly unconnected prose featured some form of brushwork above or below the writing. Marjorie and Woody completed *Woody's 20 Grow Big Songs* in 1948, dedicating it to Cathy Ann and their new baby, Arlo Davy. It was not until 1992 that this work would be published by HarperCollins, and even then it was not quite what was originally intended.

The illustrated cover for *American Folksay Ballads and Dances* by David Stone Martin.

As this period wore on, Guthrie would express his sadness not only overtly, but using dry brush to render figures and faces that barely made it onto the page. His humor took on a darker turn, so "The Jolly Miner" of the song by the same name, is anything but.

His earlier, exuberant self-portraits were now reduced to brushstroke and dry ink. He was beginning to fade from public view, and perhaps felt himself fading away as well. Still, Guthrie was never one to quit, and much more art was yet to come.

TROUBLE
AINT WORTH NOTHING
SO I WONT
CHARGE NOTHING
TO FIX IT.
The trouble buster
BRING TROUB ME
NO FEE

In 1943, E. P. Dutton & Co. published Woody's autobiography, *Bound for Glory*, which included his original illustrations. Uncharacteristically, Woody created pencil sketches, which he likely submitted to the publisher for approval. He would ink the pencil sketches afterward. Although he created sixty-six pieces for the book in total, only twenty were ultimately included, and these were much reduced in size. Woody created these images from memory, and each depicts a particular person, place, or situation in his life. Some are images of his family or childhood friends left behind. Street scenes depict the various towns he lived in or traveled through. Others are his impressions of the many homeless families and hobos he met migrating to California and bear witness to their difficult circumstances. His own self-image, curly headed and usually with a guitar nearby, appears throughout the book. BELOW: An illustration dealing with radio censorship. Woody stands up to the sponsor.

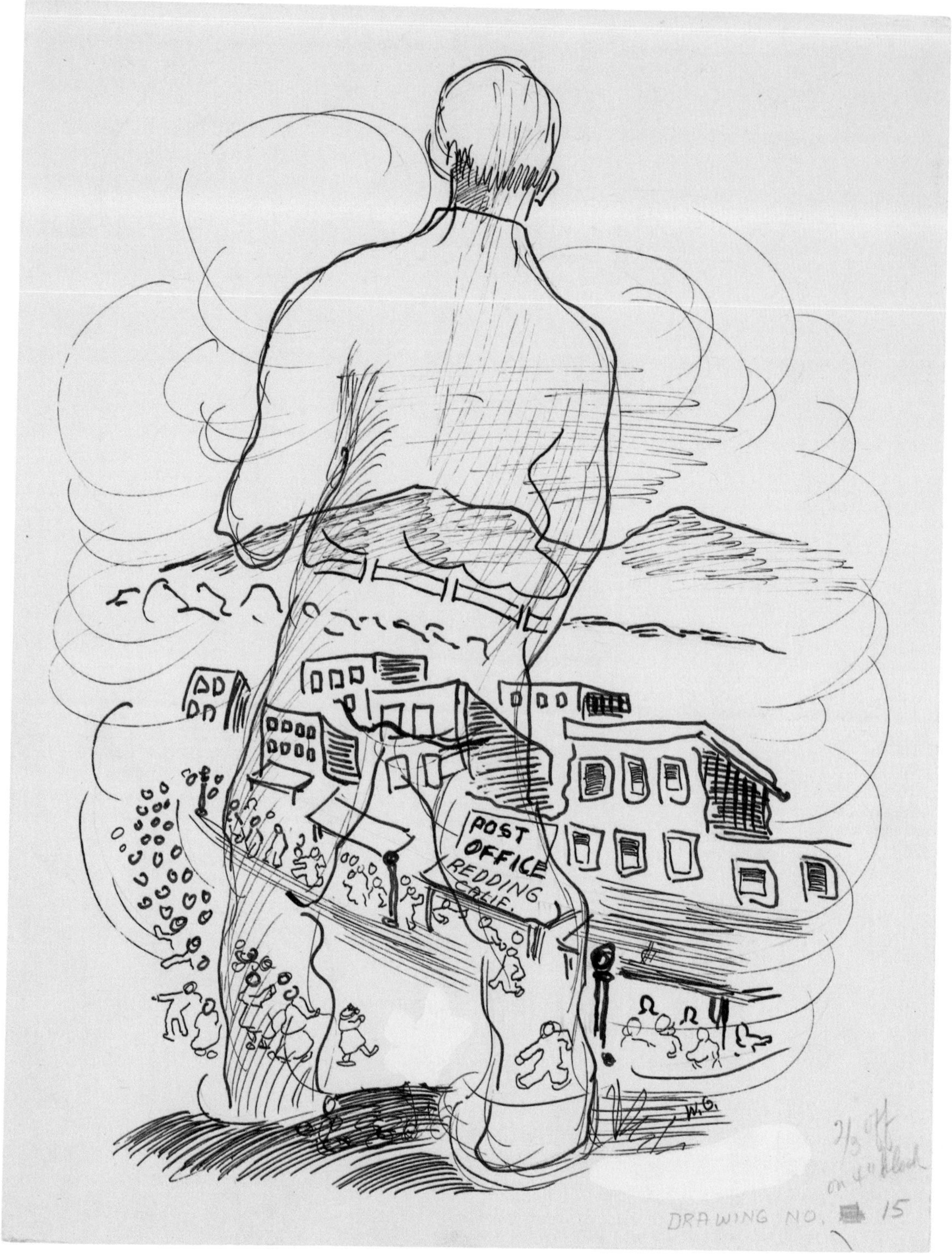
POST
OFFICE
REDDING
CALIF.
W.G.
DRAWING NO. 15

Dream.

woody guthrie

Riding the boxcar to California.

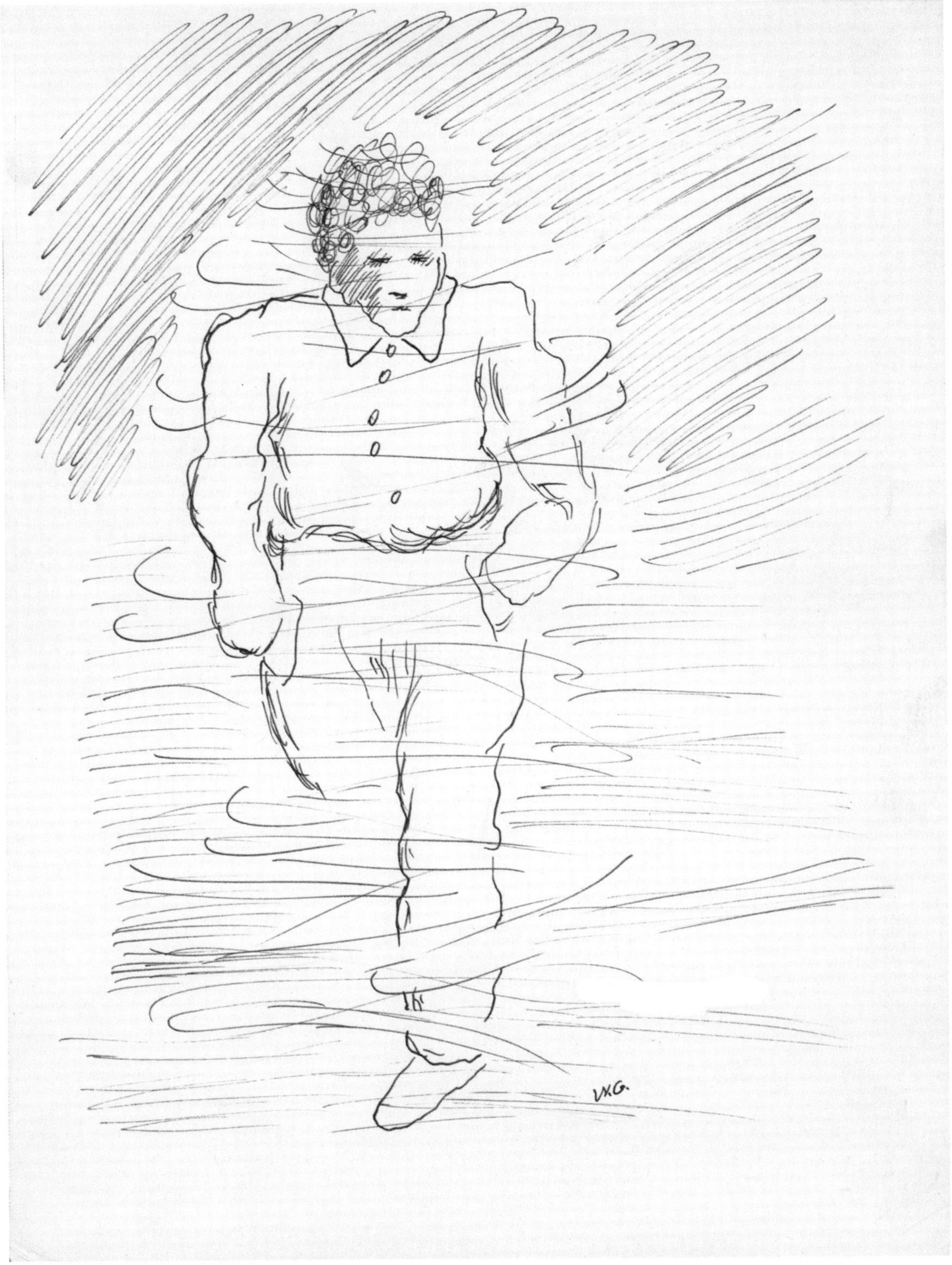

Walking in the Wind.

BOTTOM LEFT: *Rounded up in Tracy Calif.* RIGHT: Two versions of the same art for *The Extra Select Girl*, both with and without Woody. It is possible this was the result of comments from the editor or art director at the publishing house.

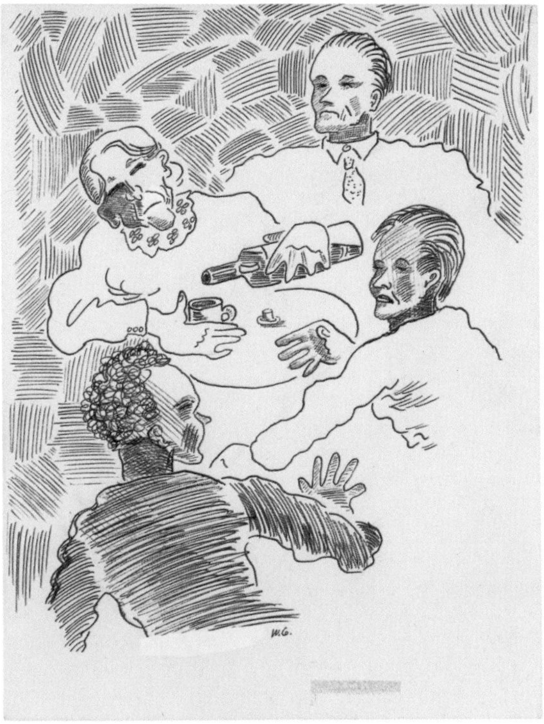

ABOVE RIGHT: *It must be broke down and sad.* LEFT: *Old Women of the Barge.*

Rare pencil sketches, possibly submitted for approval. THIS PAGE: *War Tank!*

97

Woody's take on local politics during the boomtown years in Okemah during his youth, *Election Day in Okemah, Oklahoma*.

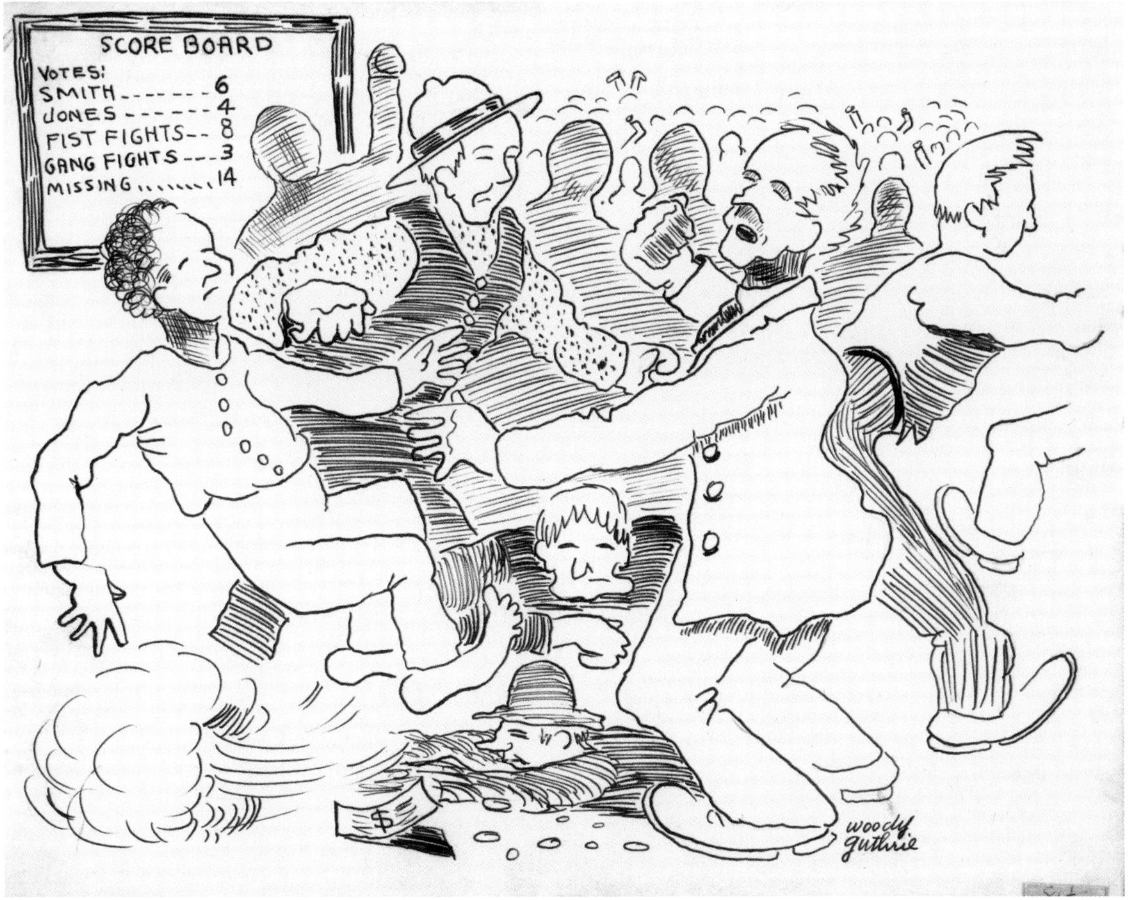

Woody's images of Okemah as a boomtown during the 1920s. THIS PAGE: *Big Jim Fight*. NEXT PAGE: *Boomtown*.

OWL
ROOMS
WIDE AWAKE
SERVICE
HOME ALL NITE
UNDERTAKER
HOCK & SHOP
FLOP
BEDS
BEER
TWO BITS
BEEF
CHILI 15¢
POOL
BUY LAND
woody guthrie

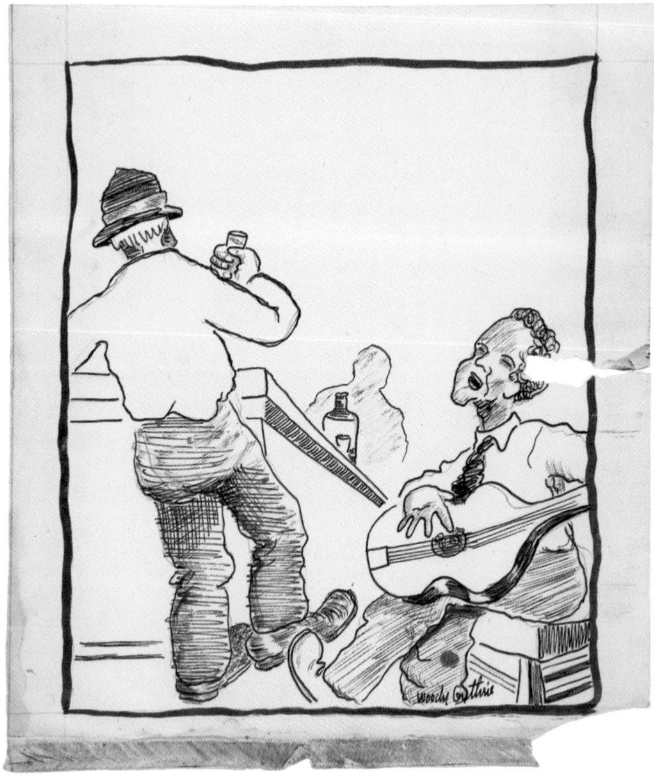

Uncharacteristically, Woody renders the same image three times, perhaps an indication of how seriously he approached these illustrations. The one at top right is the published version. NEXT PAGE: *Cyclone Destroys London House.*

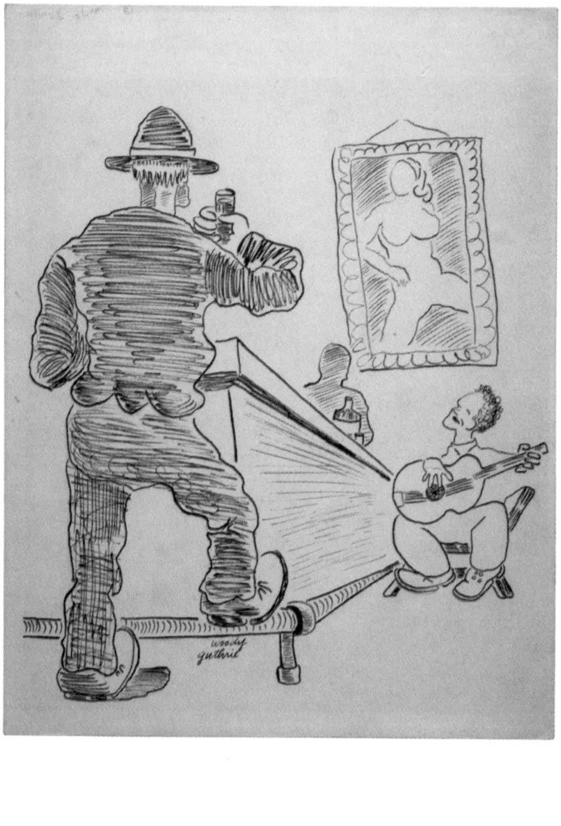

36.8
Woody Guthrie

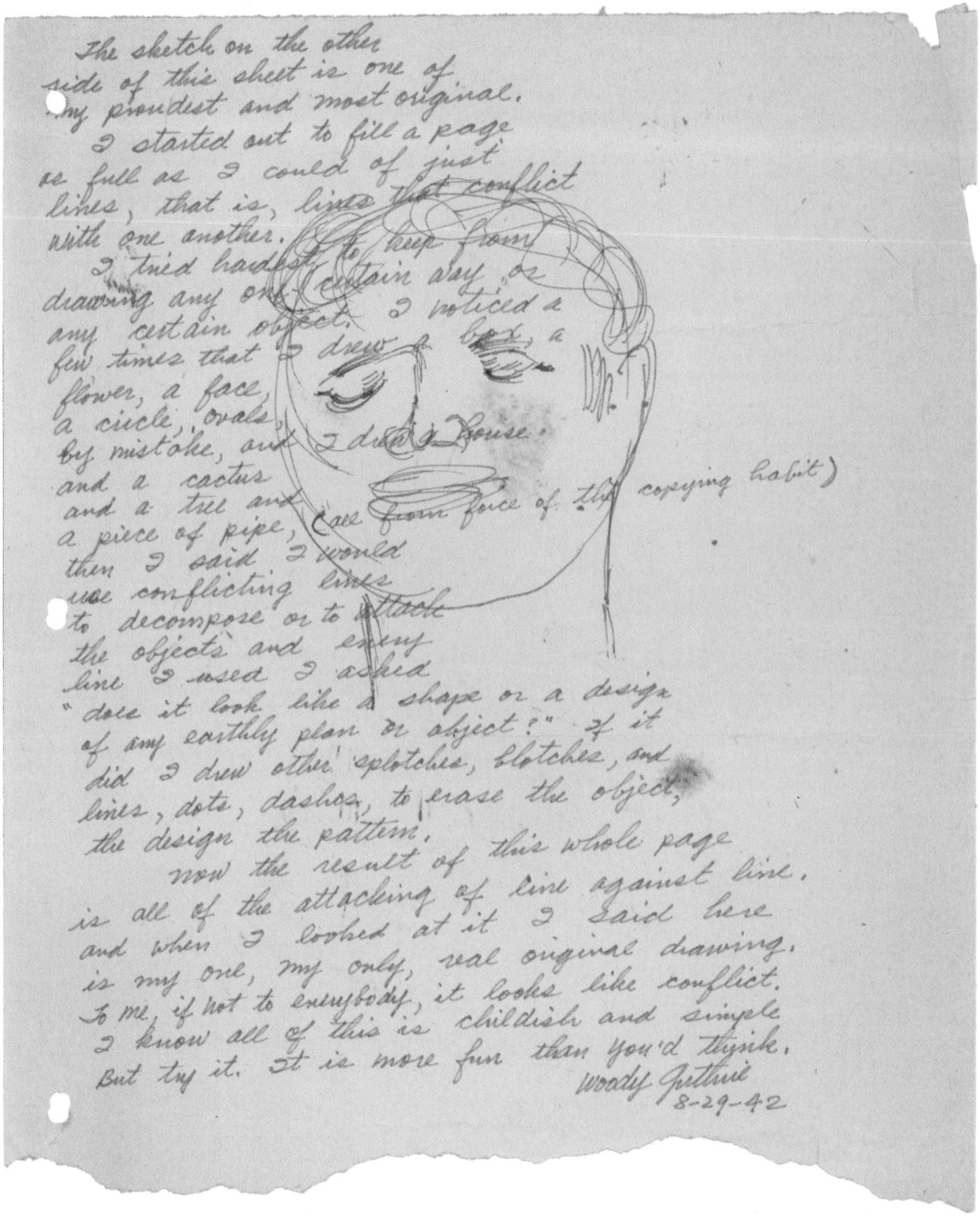

The sketch on the other
side of this sheet is one of
my proudest and most original.
I started out to fill a page
as full as I could of just
lines, that is, lines that conflict
with one another. To keep from
I tried hardest
drawing any one certain way or
any certain object. I noticed a
few times that I drew a box, a
flower, a face,
a circle, ovals,
by mistake, and I drew a house
and a cactus
and a tree and
a piece of pipe, (all from force of the copying habit)
then I said I would
use conflicting lines
to decompose or to attack
the objects and every
line I used I asked
"does it look like a shape or a design
of any earthly plan or object?" If it
did I drew other splotches, blotches, and
lines, dots, dashes, to erase the object,
the design the pattern.
Now the result of this whole page
is all of the attacking of line against line.
and when I looked at it I said here
is my one, my only, real original drawing.
To me, if not to everybody, it looks like conflict.
I know all of this is childish and simple
But try it. It is more fun than you'd think.
Woody Guthrie
8-29-42

The front of a letter to Marjorie Mazia, in which Woody discusses his burgeoning interest in abstract art.

The back of the same letter illustrates his attempt to "decompose" or "attack" any familiar objects by using "conflicting lines."

In 1942, Woody met Marjorie Mazia, a dancer with the Martha Graham Dance Company in New York City. Although both were married, they began living together in Marjorie's apartment on Fourteenth Street. Here Woody wrote many songs and began writing *Bound for Glory*, with Marjorie helping as editor, proofreader, and musical notator. An avid diary writer, Woody chronicled every aspect of his life in journals. In them, he could contain his thoughts, new lyrics, things to do, and images from the day. The notes on this page include a comical list of jobs for Marjorie (which include proofing and typing *Bound for Glory*), a sketch of Marjorie drawn from memory, a lyric about the U.S. Army, and a note about the "sentimental" music he hears coming from a saloon. Many of these notes were later fleshed out as songs or artworks.

APPOINTMENTS ★ MEMORANDA ★ REMINDERS ★ 1942
JANUARY 2 FRIDAY
Jobs for Marjorie
1. Type on book + Read
2. Write music for songs
3. Take good care of Pete
4. " " " " me
5. " " " " herself
6. " " " " everybody
7. " " " " Joseph
DRAWN FROM MEMORY — 10-15-1942
Woody
JANUARY 3 SATURDAY
This Is For The Army
This Is For The Navy
This is Hell on Hitler
And I don't mean maybe.
The number of this Book is One
Which is a whole lot Better than none.
Theres some awful sentimental music playing in one of the beer joints along the street. The saloons are the most sentimental places in town, so they fight a lot among themselves.
SUNDAY 4 JANUARY

A spontaneous song lyric written to Marjorie imagining their future. The artwork illustrates the lines "This book is just a hunting trip to see, If we can search the fathoms of the sea, And light the unfound bottom and the depths, Left undiscovered in both you and me."

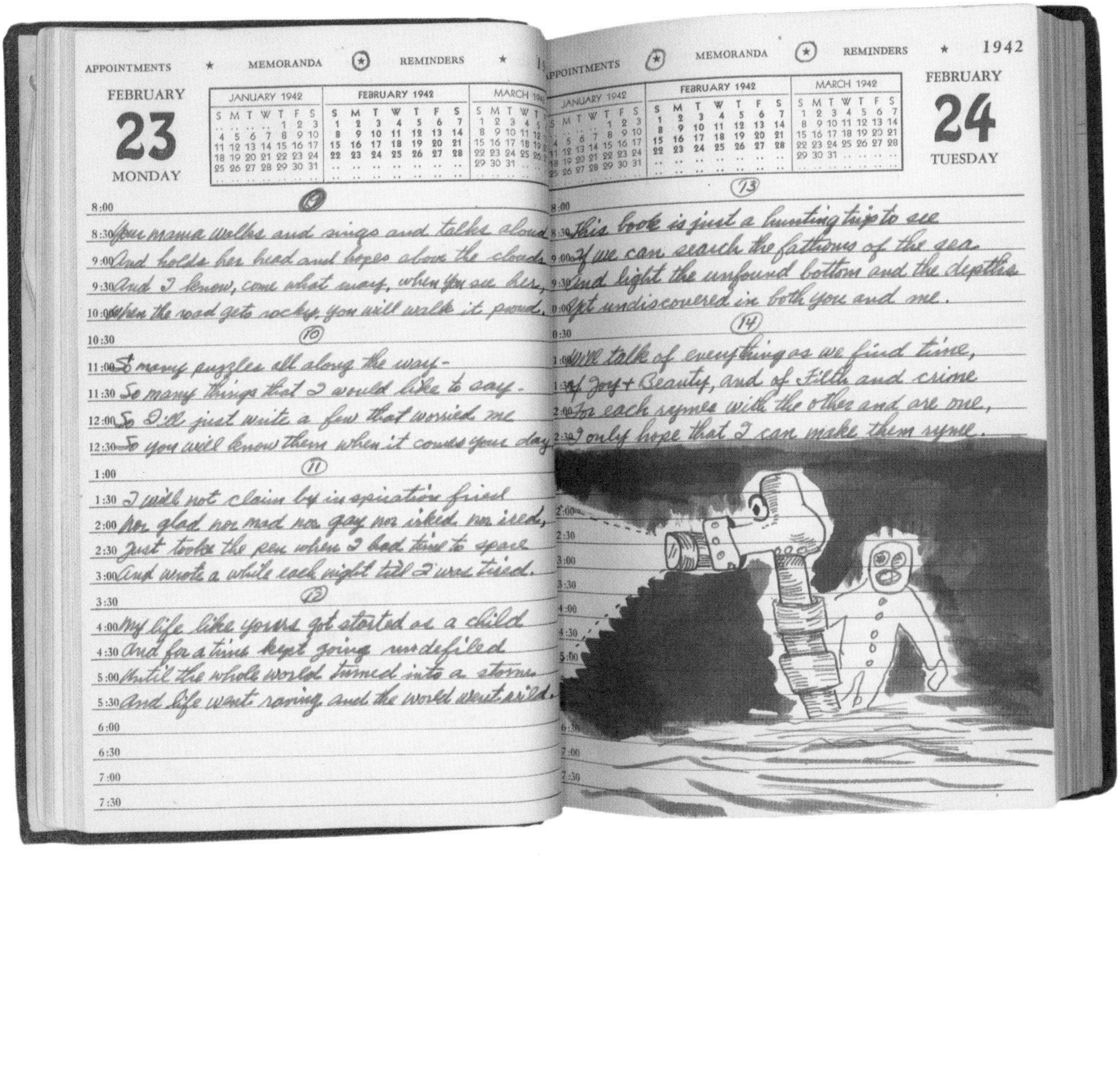

107

Woody sees himself as simply being "an Honest Man" in this diary entry written to his unborn child. He describes the process of writing *Bound for Glory* and Marjorie's role in helping to complete it.

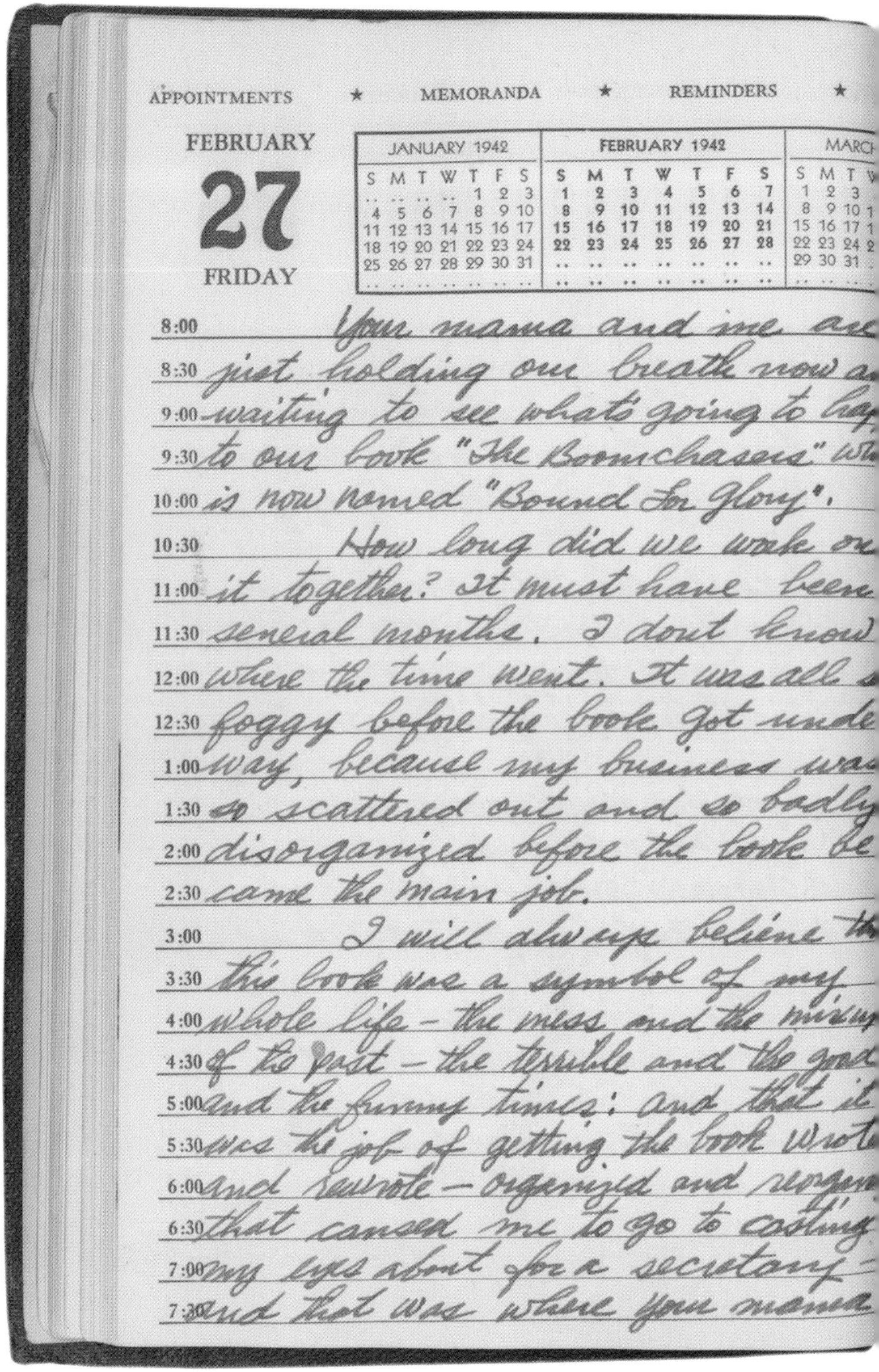

APPOINTMENTS ★ MEMORANDA ★ REMINDERS ★

FEBRUARY
27
FRIDAY

JANUARY 1942						
S	M	T	W	T	F	S
..	..	..	..	1	2	3
4	5	6	7	8	9	10
11	12	13	14	15	16	17
18	19	20	21	22	23	24
25	26	27	28	29	30	31

FEBRUARY 1942						
S	M	T	W	T	F	S
1	2	3	4	5	6	7
8	9	10	11	12	13	14
15	16	17	18	19	20	21
22	23	24	25	26	27	28

8:00 Your mama and me are
8:30 just holding our breath now a
9:00 waiting to see what's going to hap
9:30 to our book "The Boomchasers" wh
10:00 is now named "Bound For Glory".
10:30 How long did we work on
11:00 it together? It must have been
11:30 several months. I dont know
12:00 where the time went. It was all s
12:30 foggy before the book got unde
1:00 way, because my business was
1:30 so scattered out and so badly
2:00 disorganized before the book be-
2:30 came the main job.
3:00 I will always believe th
3:30 this book was a symbol of my
4:00 whole life — the mess and the mixup
4:30 of the past — the terrible and the good
5:00 and the funny times; and that it
5:30 was the job of getting the book wrote
6:00 and rewrote — organized and reorgan
6:30 that caused me to go to casting
7:00 my eyes about for a secretary —
7:30 and that was where your mama

OINTMENTS ★ MEMORANDA ★ REMINDERS ★ 1942

JANUARY 1942					
M	T	W	T	F	S
..	..	..	1	2	3
5	6	7	8	9	10
12	13	14	15	16	17
19	20	21	22	23	24
26	27	28	29	30	31

FEBRUARY 1942						
S	M	T	W	T	F	S
1	2	3	4	5	6	7
8	9	10	11	12	13	14
15	16	17	18	19	20	21
22	23	24	25	26	27	28
..	..	..	..	..	..	..

MARCH 1942						
S	M	T	W	T	F	S
1	2	3	4	5	6	7
8	9	10	11	12	13	14
15	16	17	18	19	20	21
22	23	24	25	26	27	28
29	30	31	..	..	..	..

FEBRUARY

28

SATURDAY

SUNDAY **1** MARCH

came in. She jumped in and took
about three or four flying leaps, and
ailed handfuls of loose papers all
ver fourteenth street – and when the
ir got clear again, I was surprised
o see all of the notes, and papers, and

110

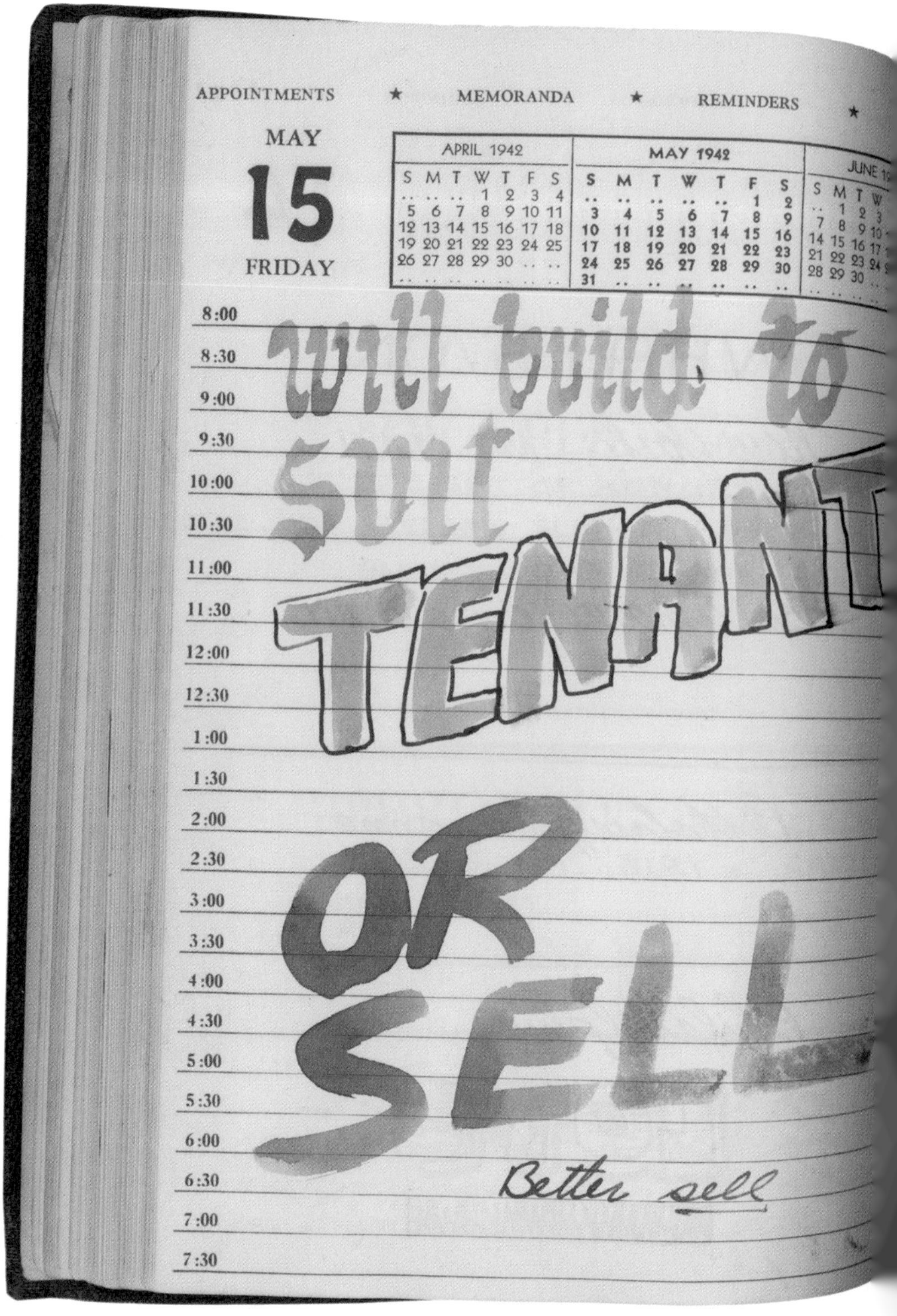
APPOINTMENTS ★ MEMORANDA ★ REMINDERS ★
MAY
15
FRIDAY
APRIL 1942
MAY 1942
8:00
8:30
9:00
9:30
10:00
10:30
11:00
11:30
12:00
12:30
1:00
1:30
2:00
2:30
3:00
3:30
4:00
4:30
5:00
5:30
6:00
6:30
7:00
7:30
will build to suit
TENANT
OR SELL
Better sell

MEMORANDA
REMINDERS
1942
MAY 1942
S M T W T F S
1 2
3 4 5 6 7 8 9
10 11 12 13 14 15 16
17 18 19 20 21 22 23
24 25 26 27 28 29 30
31
JUNE 1942
S M T W T F S
1 2 3 4 5 6
7 8 9 10 11 12 13
14 15 16 17 18 19 20
21 22 23 24 25 26 27
28 29 30
MAY
16
SATURDAY
SUNDAY
17
MAY
CLOSED
SUN.

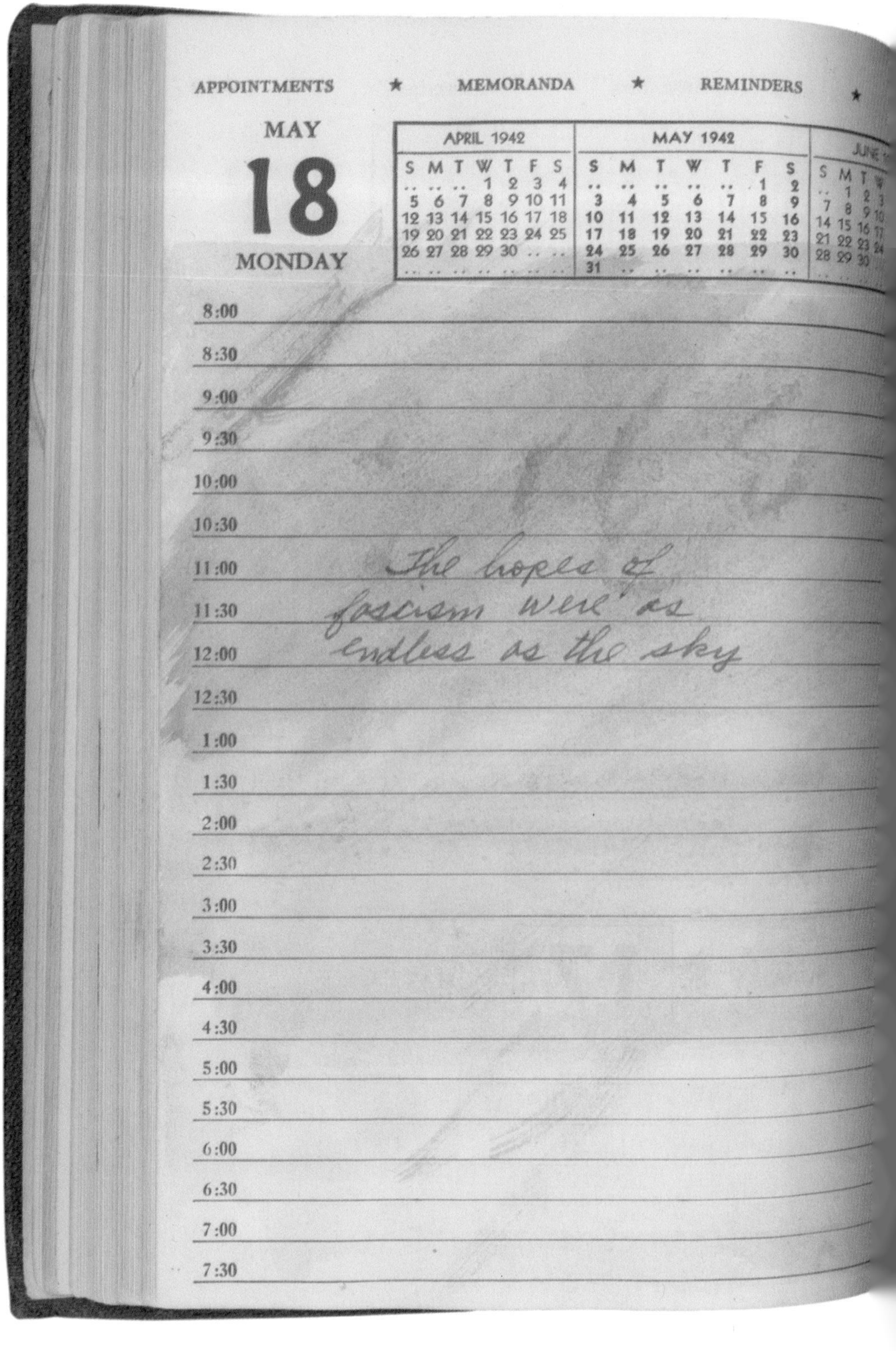
APPOINTMENTS ★ MEMORANDA ★ REMINDERS ★
MAY
18
MONDAY
APRIL 1942
MAY 1942
8:00
8:30
9:00
9:30
10:00
10:30
11:00
11:30
12:00
12:30
1:00
1:30
2:00
2:30
3:00
3:30
4:00
4:30
5:00
5:30
6:00
6:30
7:00
7:30
The hopes of
fascism were as
endless as the sky

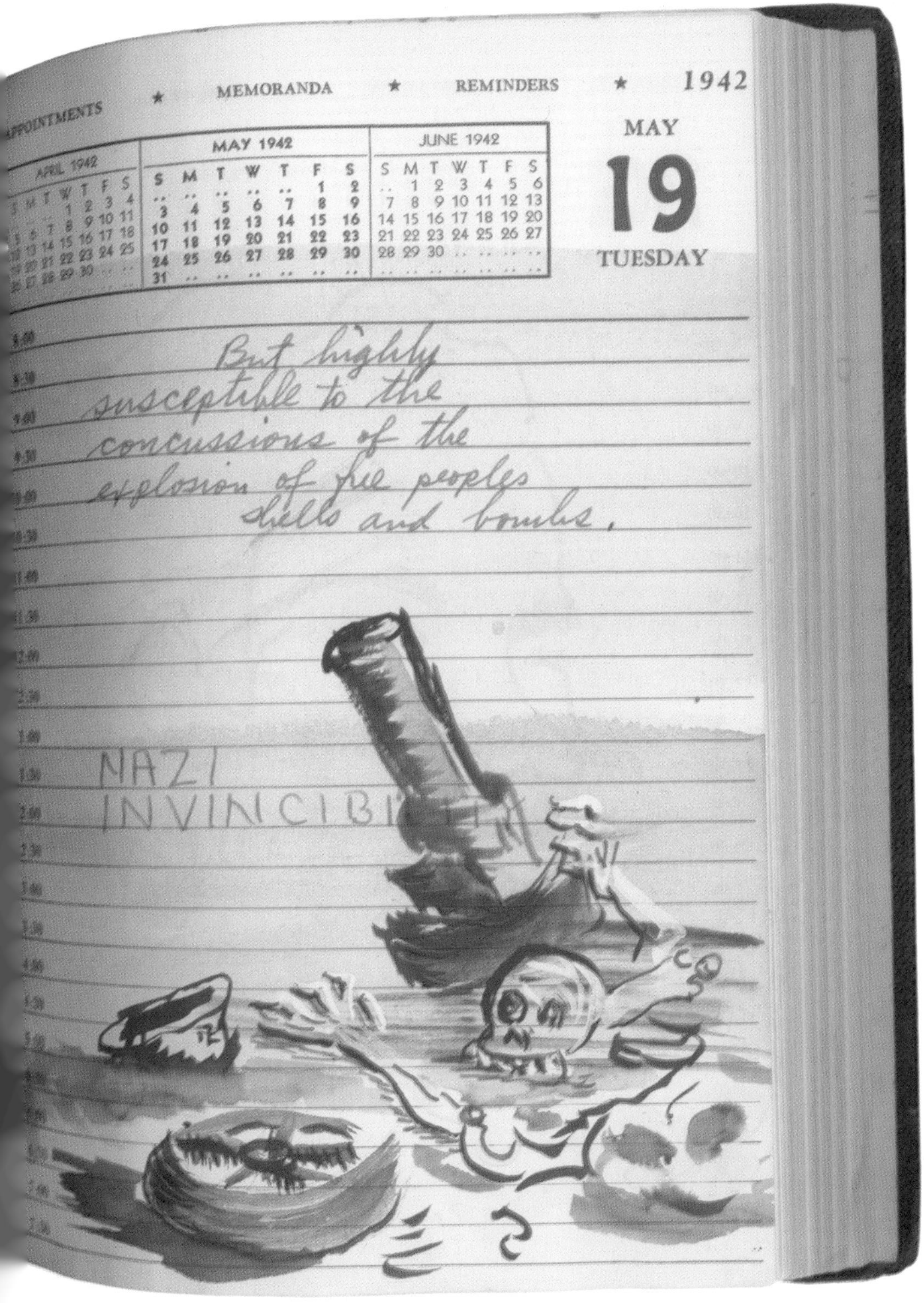
APPOINTMENTS ★ MEMORANDA ★ REMINDERS ★ 1942
MAY 1942
JUNE 1942
MAY
19
TUESDAY
But highly susceptible to the concussions of the explosion of free peoples shells and bombs.
NAZI
INVINCIBI

These pages introduce Woody's character "Rubberface John," who demonstrates some of the basic human emotions to "Railroad Pete," Woody's unborn child.

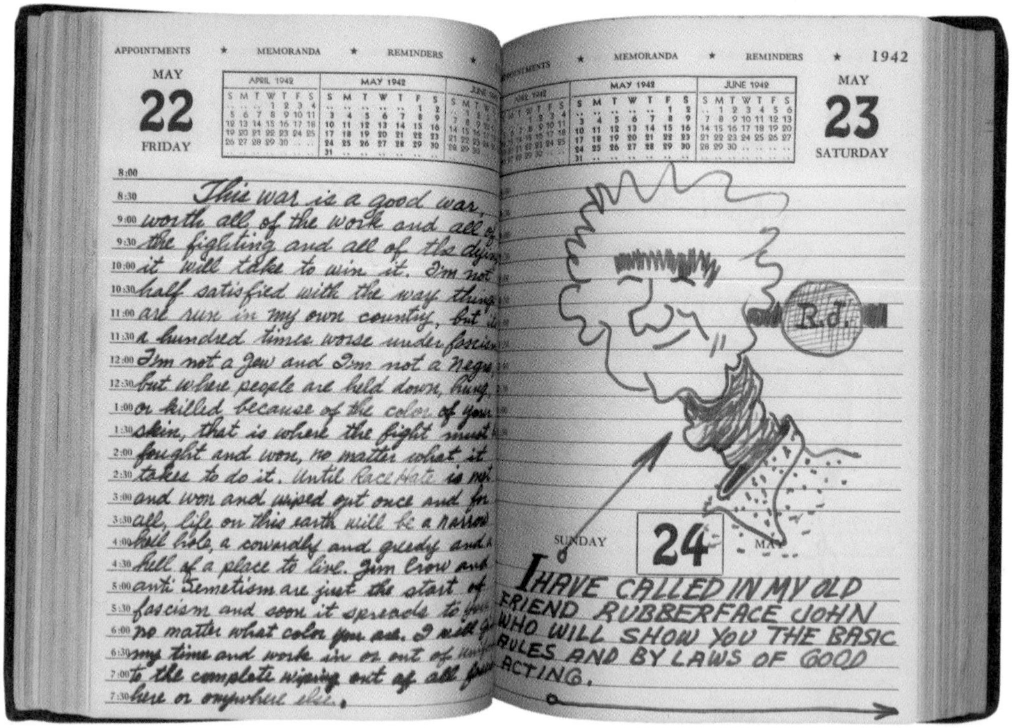

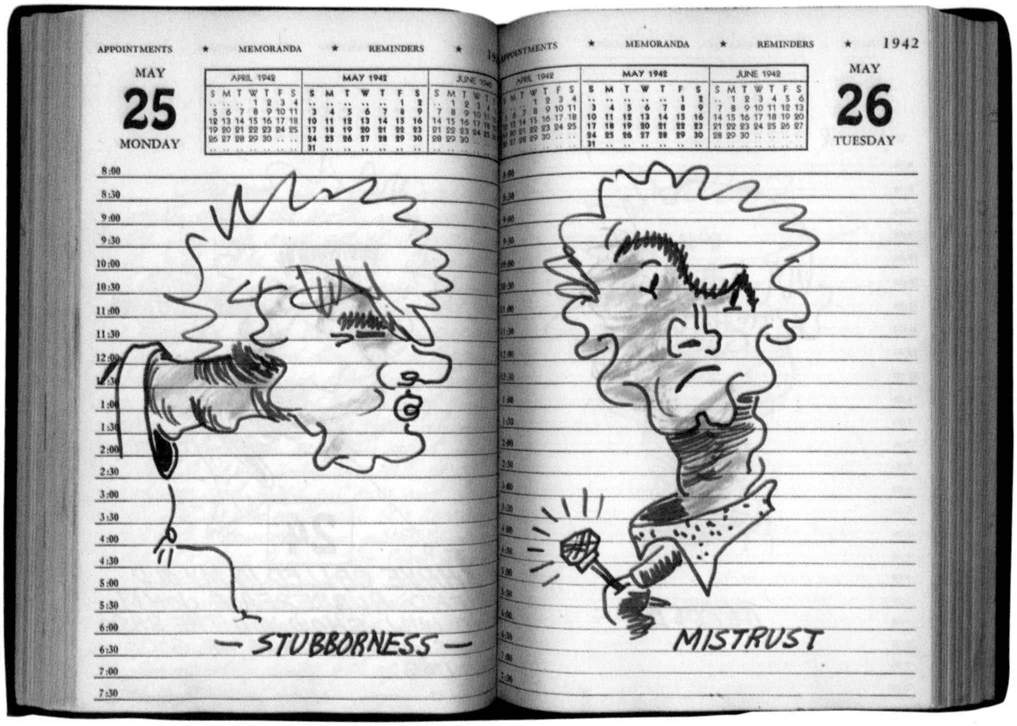

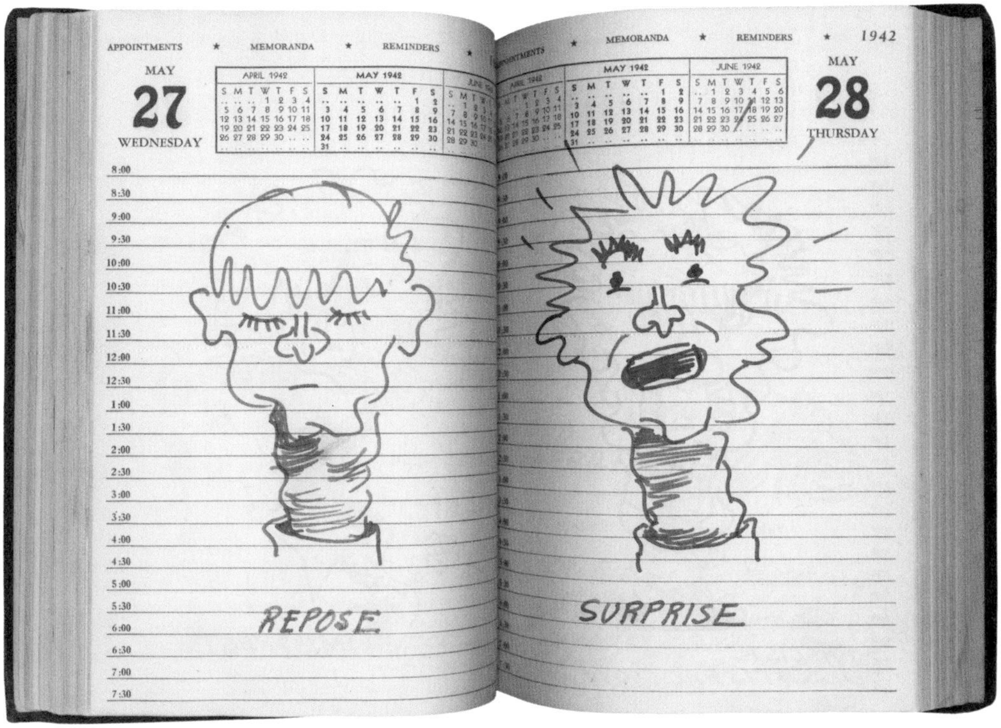
APPOINTMENTS ★ MEMORANDA ★ REMINDERS
MAY
27
WEDNESDAY
REPOSE
APPOINTMENTS ★ MEMORANDA ★ REMINDERS ★ 1942
MAY
28
THURSDAY
SURPRISE

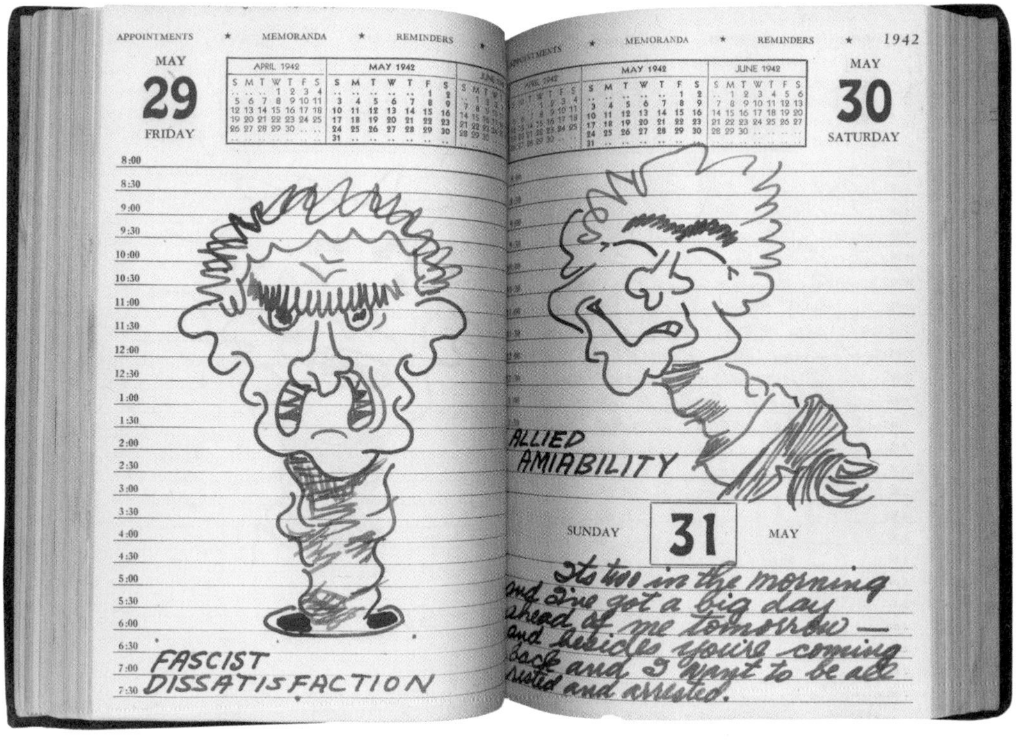
APPOINTMENTS ★ MEMORANDA ★ REMINDERS
MAY
29
FRIDAY
FASCIST
DISSATISFACTION
APPOINTMENTS ★ MEMORANDA ★ REMINDERS ★ 1942
MAY
30
SATURDAY
ALLIED
AMIABILITY
SUNDAY 31 MAY
Its two in the morning
and I've got a big day
ahead of me tomorrow—
and besides you're coming
back and I want to be all
rested and arrested.

Marjorie became pregnant with their first child, Cathy Ann, in the spring of 1942. Their unborn child was nicknamed "Railroad Pete," to whom Woody wrote letters and illustrated diaries filled with family memories, advice, and philosophy. Pete continued to reappear over the years in various writings, postcards, and notes, and became the persona for all of Marjorie and Woody's children to come. Pete was Woody's version of a superhero and was particularly known for his aerodynamic, antifascist, projectile spitting, which could take out even Hitler in one blow.

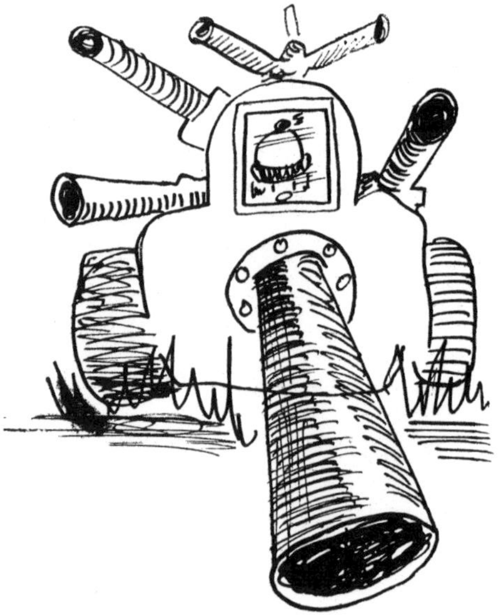

This is one way of getting across a page

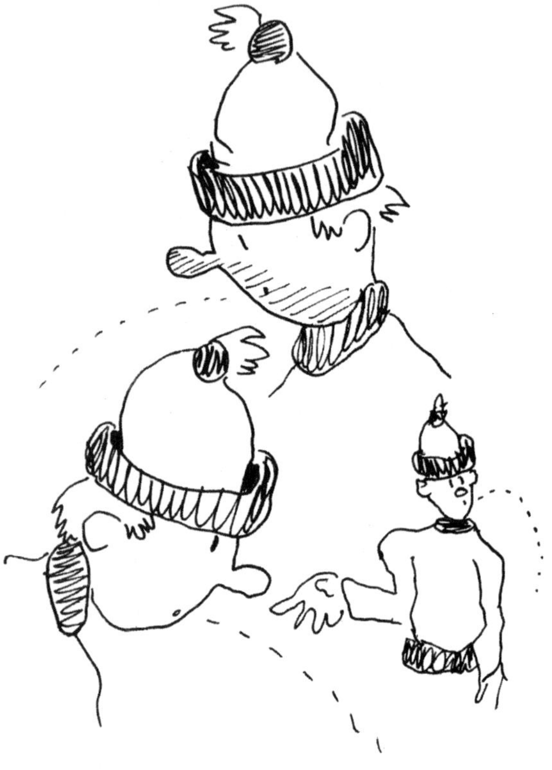

BONG

Cathy Rooney
Sep. 11, 1944
Coney Island

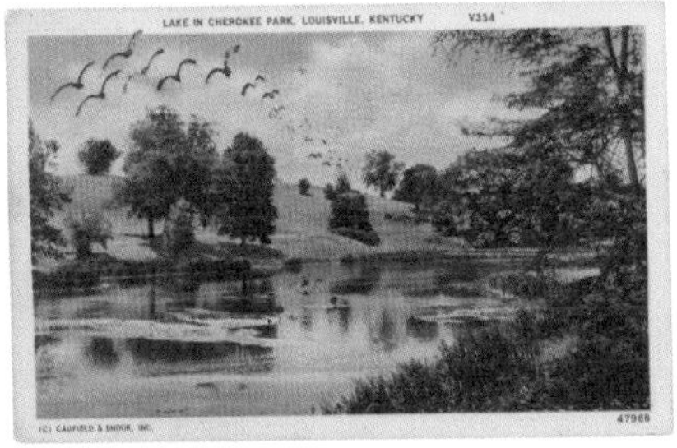

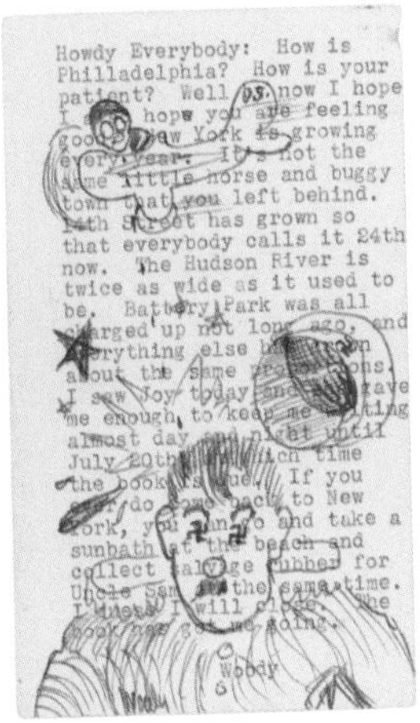
Howdy Everybody: How is Philadelphia? How is your patient? Well US now I hope I ... hope you are feeling good. New York is growing every year. It's not the same little horse and buggy town that you left behind. 14th Street has grown so that everybody calls it 24th now. The Hudson River is twice as wide as it used to be. Battery Park was all charged up not long ago, and everything else has grown about the same proportions. I saw Joy today and she gave me enough to keep me writing almost day and night until July 20th at which time the book is due. If you ever do come back to New York, you can go and take a sunbath at the beach and collect salvage rubber for Uncle Sam at the same time. I guess I will close. The book has got me going.

Woody

R. C. A. Building, a magnificent structure of 70 stories, is the tallest building in the Rockefeller Center. There are 27 radio studios in the building, among them the largest in the world. Its observatory roof is an expansive promenade of 200 feet long with an unobstructed view of 50 miles.

POST CARD
THIS SPACE FOR ADDRESS ONLY
PLACE STAMP HERE
MANHATTAN POST CARD PUBLISHING CO., INC.

marjorie mazia
148 W. 14 St.,
New york
N. Y.
Room 14

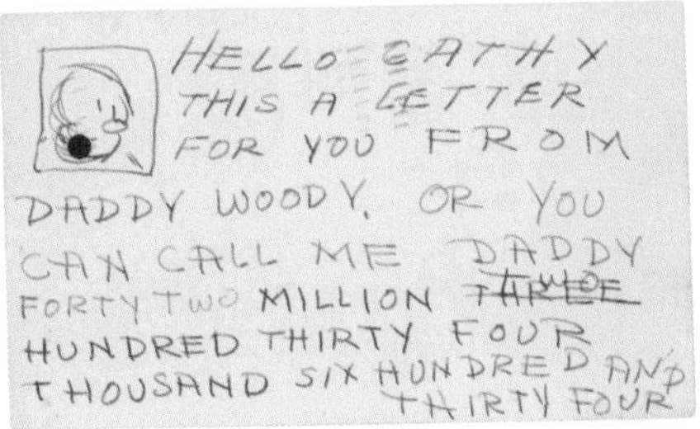
HELLO CATHY
THIS A LETTER
FOR YOU FROM
DADDY WOODY. OR YOU
CAN CALL ME DADDY
FORTY TWO MILLION ~~THREE~~
HUNDRED THIRTY FOUR
THOUSAND SIX HUNDRED AND
THIRTY FOUR

ABOVE: Postcards from 1941–44 written to Marjorie and Cathy Ann. Woody added a personal touch to the images, a reminder of his presence. ACROSS: Woody had many nicknames for all his children. Cathy Ann was "Cathy Rooney" or "Stackabones." He humorously commented that holding a newborn baby was like holding a "stack of bones."

A 1943–44 journal called "Cathy," which contains writings, essays, and songs for and about his baby daughter, Cathy Ann.

Upon discharge from the army, Woody designed his dream home for Marjorie in a notebook from 1942.

"Our house ought to be built and not bought. We have to think of so many working details that no outside person could ever have built it for his own use at the right location. No matter how we manage the rooms space you will need floor space for dancing. This same floor space ought to be at times a way to make money in the shape of parties to which we will invite all of the free talent that will help us. . . . A little house with two thousand dollars worth of walks and paths might be a good idea to think about."

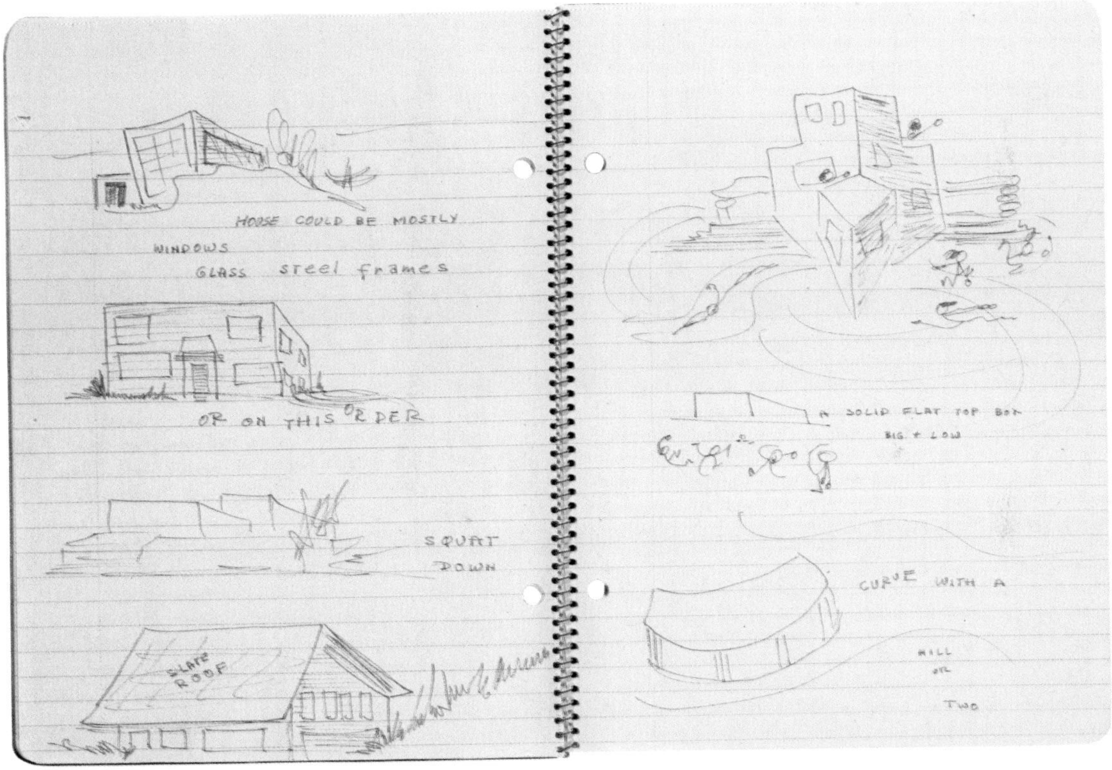

In 1944, Woody was traveling on Liberty ships for the merchant marines. He filled notebooks with sketches, stories, and songs that described his daily experiences onboard: the seamen, the troops, the war, fascism, unions. He continued to publish articles for the Communist Party's *Daily Worker* and the *Sunday Worker*, as well as the National Maritime Workers' publication, the *Pilot*. While on shore leave, Woody was anxious to get performance bookings. This notice advertises his limited availability.

123

Cisco Houston was Woody's close friend and singing partner. Throughout the war years they served on the merchant marine ships together. "Slim" was Cisco's brother.

DOLLAR LIMIT
WOODY GUTHRIE
3-21-44

126

Although blacklisted by Naval Intelligence for his Communist associations, Woody was inducted into the U.S. Army on May 8, 1945—VE Day. Stationed at various bases in New Jersey, Texas, and Illinois, he made efforts to complete his novel, *Sea Porpoise*. Although the novel was never finished, the manuscript and some of his sketches and illustrations for the book remain.

128

Pencil sketches from 1946. Woody depicted every aspect of Cathy Ann's daily life: her activities, friends, family, and neighbors, as well as the comments she made.

I'M MAKING A
BIGGER ONE
.... STACKADONES
Nov. 2, 1940

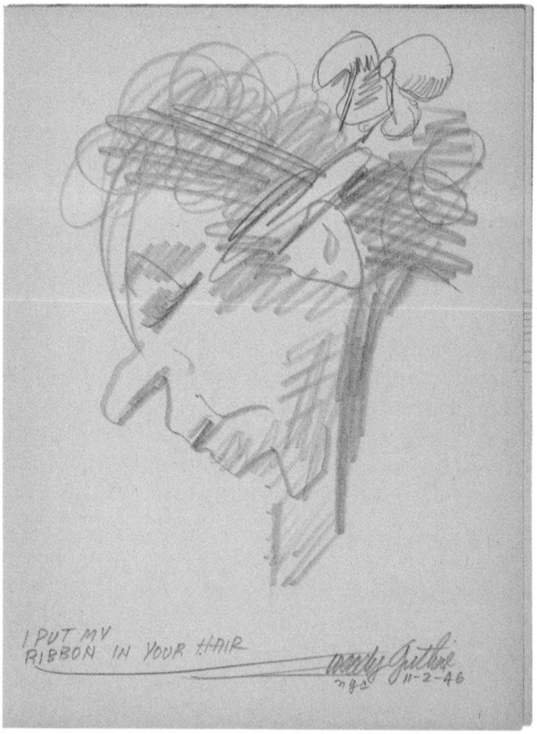

An apparent self-portrait, with Woody sporting Cathy's ribbon.

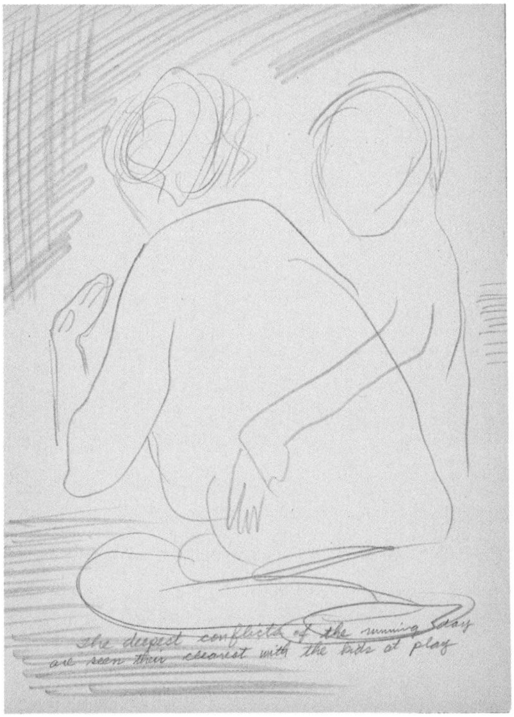

"The deepest conflict of the running day, as seen thru clearest with the kids at play." Woody expressed a child's vulnerability to the difficulties in relationships.

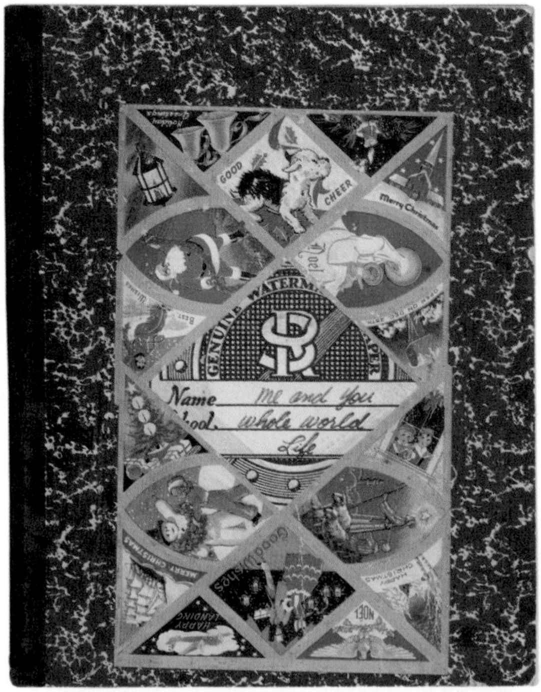
GOOD
CHEER
Merry Christmas
Name me and you
whole world
Life

my
Dusty
Road
woody guthrie

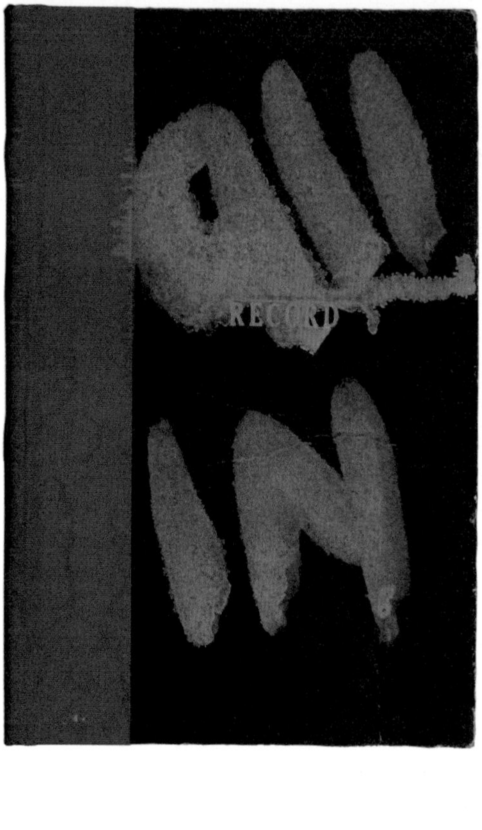
RECORD

COMPOSITIONS

Some hand-painted notebooks from the 1940s. Woody often painted or designed the covers of his notebooks, giving each one a unique personality or mood to represent its particular theme or content.

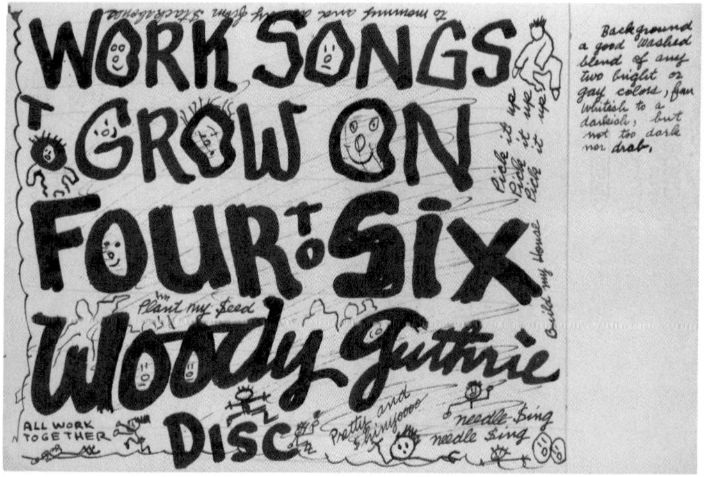

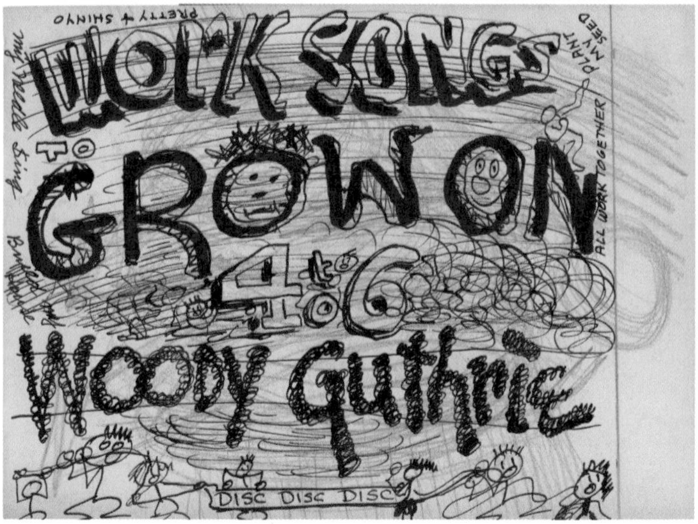

Drafts of album covers for *Work Songs to Grow On*. NEXT PAGE BOTTOM LEFT: A printed booklet insert for the album *Work Songs to Grow On* on the Disc Record label.

I WANTA
HUG!

BLEED ONE INCH
BACKGROUND: A GAY, LIGHT WASH OF PINK REDDISH, AND ORANGE OR ANY LIGHT, GAY TONE,
LETTERS WILL BE OF SAME WASH TONES AS THE BACKGROUND, A PART OF IT, WILL RAISE UP OUT OF BACKGROUND COLORING
A GOOD GREENISH WHITE AND YELLOWISH GREEN WOULD BE GOOD — TRY ALL TONES OF GREEN....
W.G.
BLEED OUT ONE INCH
WORK SONGS
TO
GROW ON
PLANT MY SEED
ALL WORK TOGETHER
PRETTY AND SHINYO
BUILD MY HOUSE
PICK IT UP
4 TO 6
WOODY GUTHRIE
4-29-'46
disc
disc
disc
disc
disc
disc

DISC YOUNG FOLKSAY SERIES Album 602
TO GROW ON
sung by WOODY GUTHRIE

WORK SONGS TO GROW ON
LET'S DO IT AGAIN
woody Guthrie
ENDPIECE

Portraits of Marjorie, 1944.

MY SWEET MAMA!

OVERLEAF: While on shore leave just before the end of the war, Woody tried to get his musical career back on track. Hoping to encourage new recordings of his songs, he created one hundred mimeographed songbooks to send out to various friends and musicians, and to sell while performing at rallies and picket lines. Each songbook cover was personalized with bright watercolors done in succession. His hopes for reigniting his career quickly ended when he was inducted into the army within the month. The songbooks were left with Marjorie in a box in their apartment in Coney Island, New York, and most remained unopened until the mid-1980s.

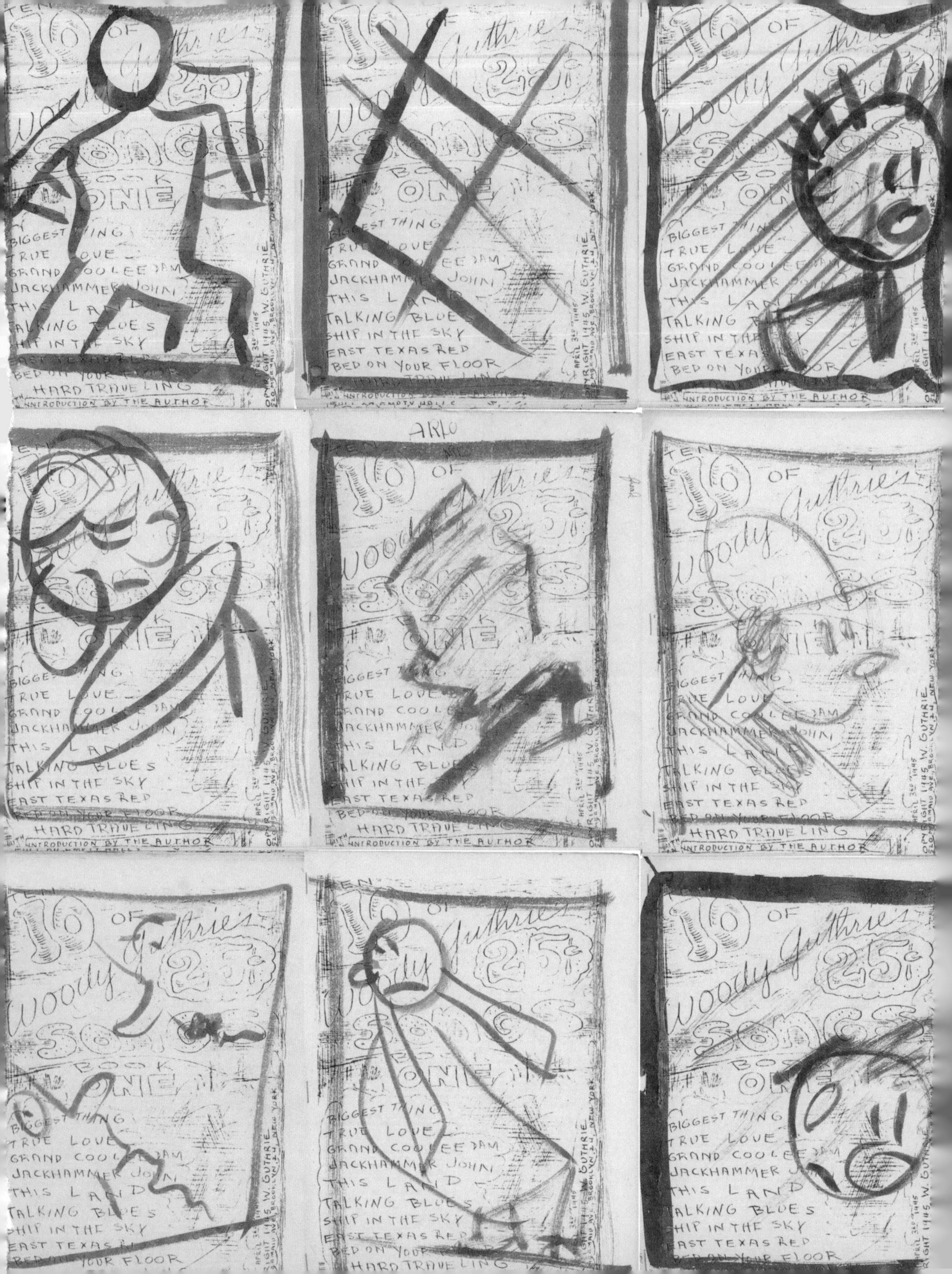
TEN
10 OF
Woody Guthrie's
25¢
SONGS
BOOK
ONE
BIGGEST THING
TRUE LOVE
GRAND COOLEE DAM
JACKHAMMER JOHN
THIS LAND
TALKING BLUES
SHIP IN THE SKY
EAST TEXAS RED
BED ON YOUR FLOOR
HARD TRAVELING
INTRODUCTION BY THE AUTHOR
APRIL 3RD 1945
COPYRIGHT 1945 W. GUTHRIE
BROOKLYN 24, NEW YORK
ARLO

TEN OF
Woody Guthrie's
25¢
SONGS
BOOK ONE
BIGGEST THING
TRUE LOVE
GRAND COOLEE DAM
JACKHAMMER JOHN
THIS LAND
TALKING BLUES
SHIP IN THE SKY
EAST TEXAS RED
BED ON YOUR FLOOR
HARD TRAVELING
INTRODUCTION BY THE AUTHOR
APRIL 3RD 1945
COPYRIGHT 1945 W. GUTHRIE
NEW YORK

OF
Woody Guthrie's
BIGGEST THING
TRUE LOVE
GRAND COOLEE DAM
JACKHAMMER JOHN
THIS LAND
TALKING BLUES
SHIP IN THE SKY
EAST TEXAS RED
BED ON YOUR FLOOR
HARD TRAVELING
WITH INTRODUCTION BY THE AUTHOR
APRIL 3RD 1945
COPYRIGHT 1945 W. GUTHRIE
3520 MERMAID AVE, BROOKLYN 24, NEW YORK

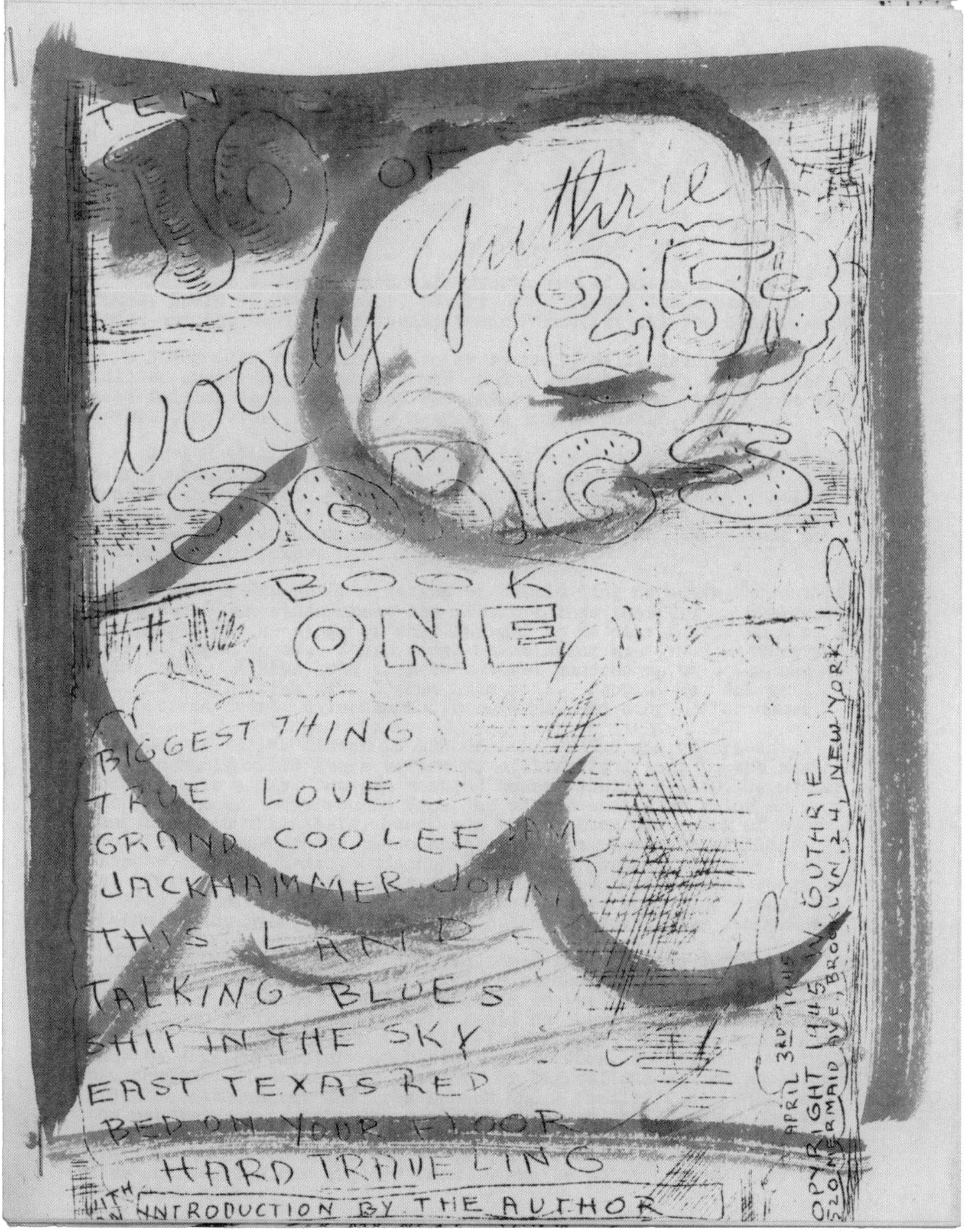
TEN 10 OF
Woody Guthrie
25¢
SONGS
BOOK
ONE
BIGGEST THING
TRUE LOVE
GRAND COOLEE DAM
JACKHAMMER JOHN
THIS LAND
TALKING BLUES
SHIP IN THE SKY
EAST TEXAS RED
BED ON YOUR FLOOR
HARD TRAVELING
WITH AN INTRODUCTION BY THE AUTHOR
APRIL 3RD 1945
COPYRIGHT 1945 W. GUTHRIE
5420 MERMAID AVE, BROOKLYN, 24, NEW YORK

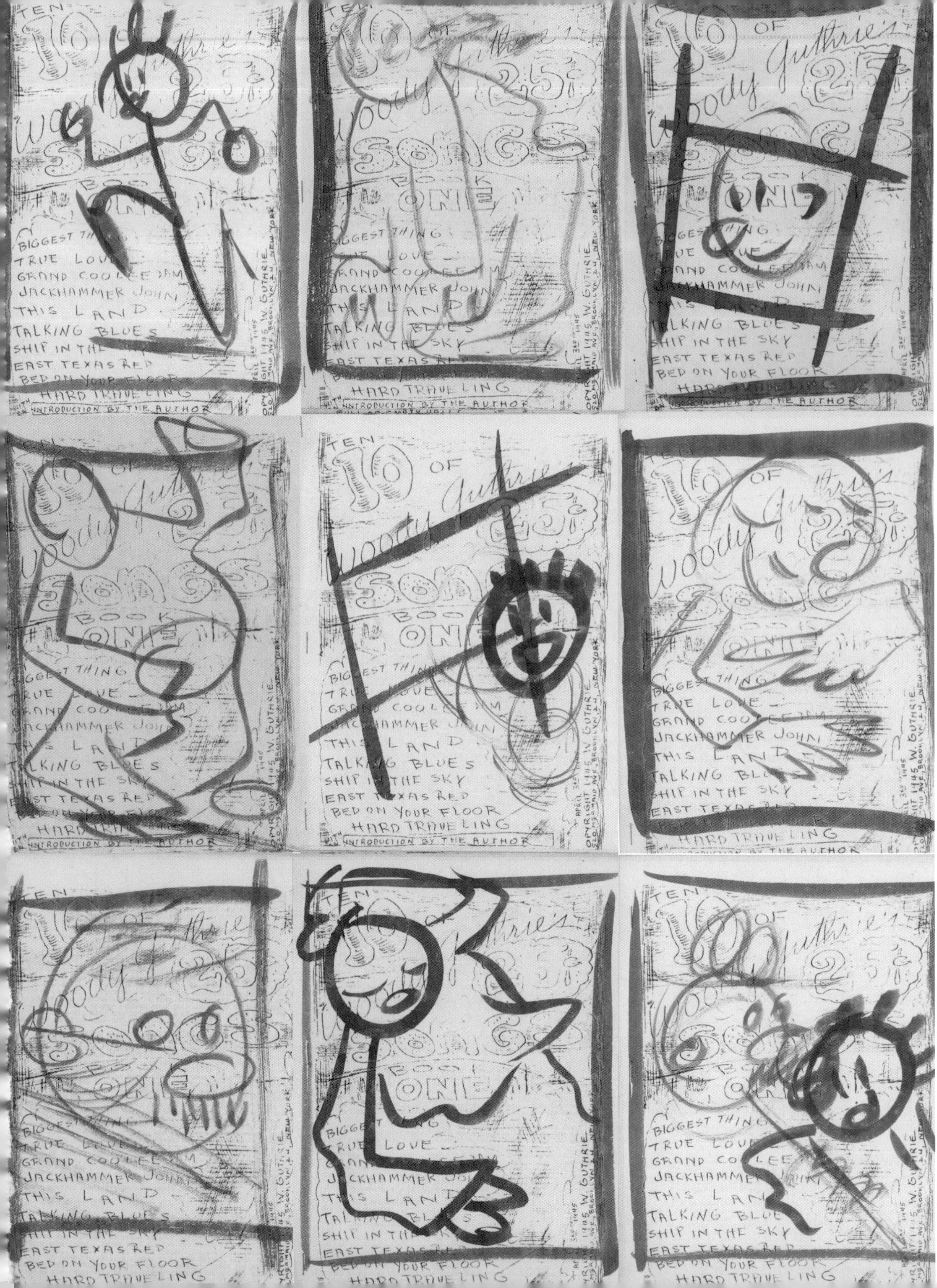
TEN
10 OF
Woody Guthrie's
25¢
SONGS
BOOK
ONE
BIGGEST THING
TRUE LOVE
GRAND COULEE DAM
JACKHAMMER JOHN
THIS LAND
TALKING BLUES
SHIP IN THE SKY
EAST TEXAS RED
BED ON YOUR FLOOR
HARD TRAVELING
INTRODUCTION BY THE AUTHOR
APRIL 3RD 1945
COPYRIGHT 1945 W. GUTHRIE
3520 MERMAID AVE, BROOKLYN 24, NEW YORK

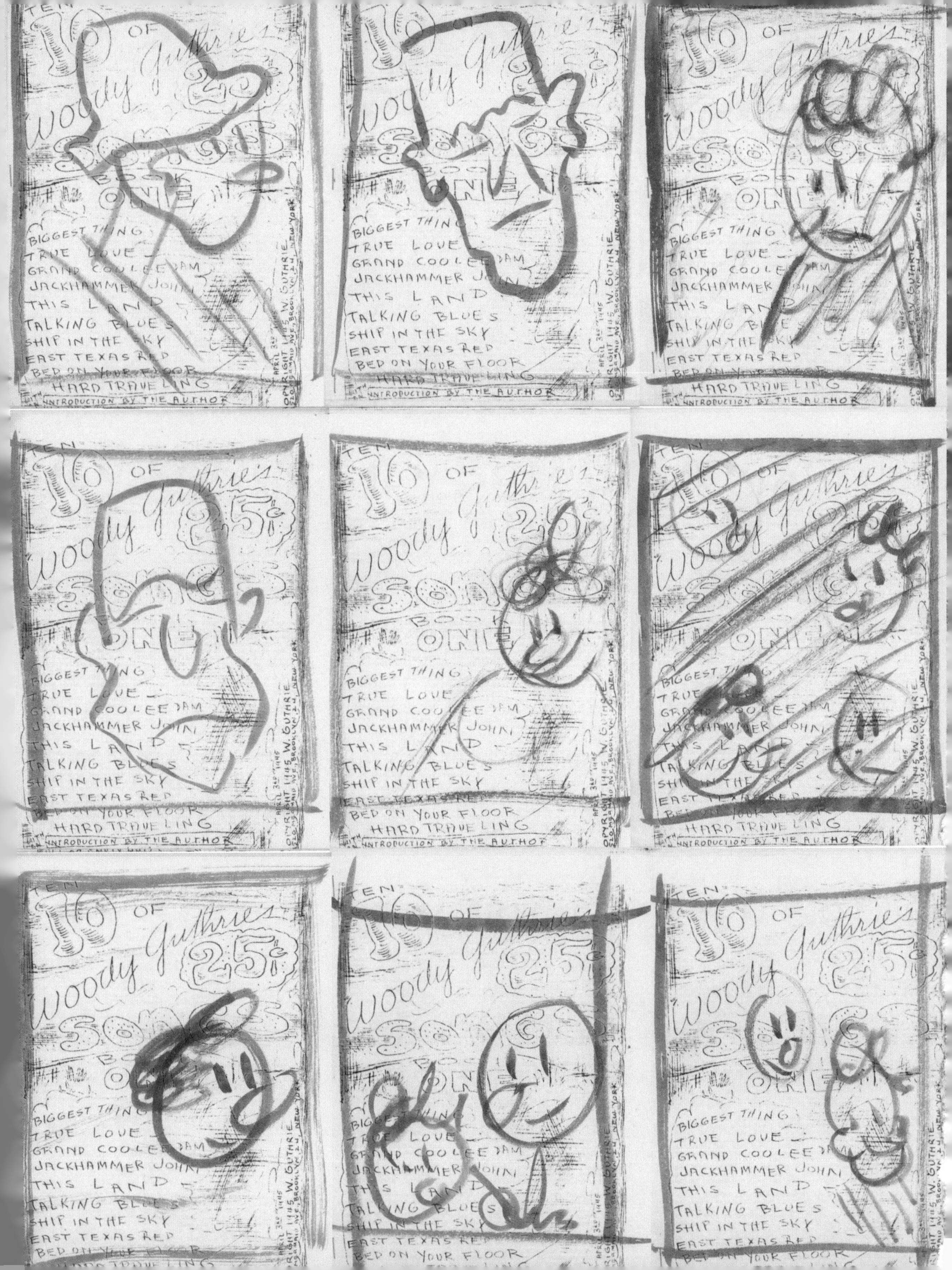
TEN
10 OF
Woody Guthrie's
25¢
SONGS
BOOK
ONE
#1
BIGGEST THING
TRUE LOVE
GRAND COOLEE DAM
JACKHAMMER JOHN
THIS LAND
TALKING BLUES
SHIP IN THE SKY
EAST TEXAS RED
BED ON YOUR FLOOR
HARD TRAVELING
INTRODUCTION BY THE AUTHOR
COPYRIGHT 1945 W. GUTHRIE
BROOKLYN 24, NEW YORK
APRIL 3rd 1945

Drawings from Woody's army days, signed Pvt. W.W. Guthrie. His serial number was 42234634.

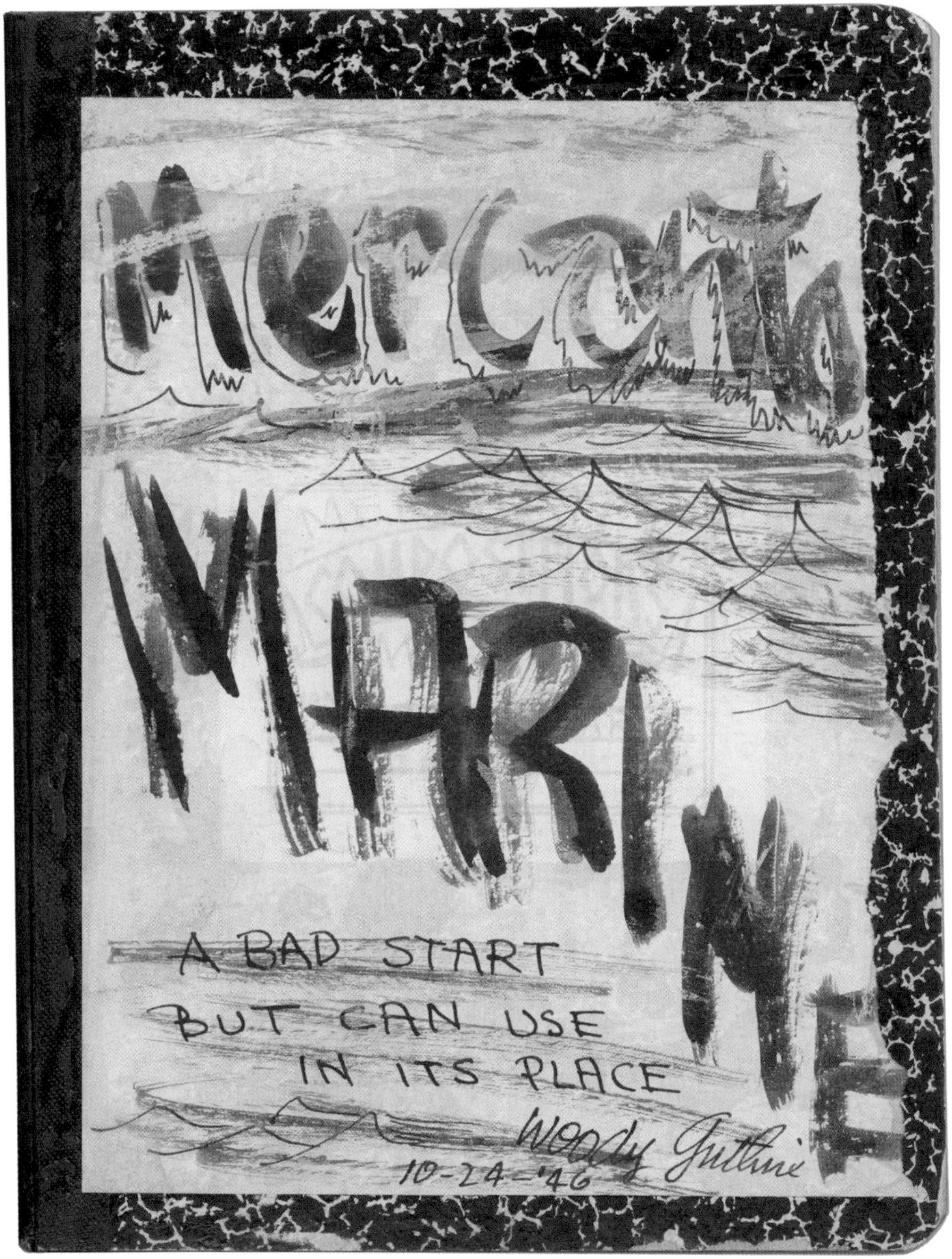

The cover of a notebook in which Woody recalls his time in the merchant marines.

Selected untitled drawings from the notebook titled "Sterling," a 1946 journal dealing with eroticism and censorship. The notebook is filled with sensuous drawings of lovers, which contrast the more linear depictions of the censors, or "judges." Woody's ideas of sexuality, creation, union, and freedom converge and have to be defended against shame, death, division, and censorship.

13

14

Woody often filled entire notebooks with a single letter. This 1946 marble notebook was sent to friend, writer, radio host, and satirist John Henry Faulk. Faulk, a native of Austin, Texas, was known for his outspoken stance on preserving freedom of speech and the First Amendment. He actively fought the McCarthy blacklist in the courts and won. Excerpts from this lengthy correspondence delve into both profound and unconventional ideas on love and marriage. Though serious and thoughtful, it also comically applies Darwin's theory for comparison, illustrating Woody's own style and advice on "survival of the fittest" relationships. Handwriting changes suggest he was riding a bus or train at the time of writing.

a kiss they say is worth a dozen wise cracks. a hug is worth a catalog of jokes. a word in a low whisper moves more dirt than words that run like a farm tractor. and when the marriage bed is operated like a coal mine or a gold dredge, or like the mean broncs and brahma steers at the rodeo, then, as soon as your tank of first energy runs dry, the love and love spark dies. These are the times when you've got to have the reserve tank quick and handy and filled with nothing but the drops that you whispered or nearly whispered all of your season.

I am not taking the position of an advisor, telling you who to love, kiss, hug, rub, work with nor sleep with. I'm not saying to stay apart, to stay together, nor to stay anywhere.

but it is more of an electric time and a magnetic season when, instead of wearing our most repulsing feelings for a worn mate every day, we wear our most positive and our most attractive feelings for everybody around us.

Because of this, I, for one, do not hate to see separations come about. an early separation would have kept my own mother from a lifetime of nervous breakdows and a death in the cells of the State Insane Asylum at Norman, Oklahoma. I don't know if I am ancient or modern, or neither, or both, but, I still say that where my sex organs lead me I will follow, and that the people who live the life of highest passion are the ones who do not pass much money over to the desk of the mental doctor.

Perhaps Woody's take on Darwinism?

59

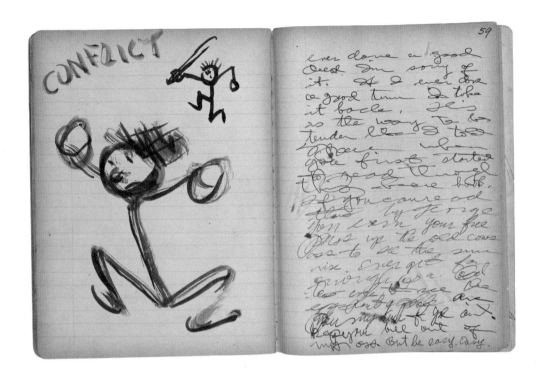

ever done a good
deed I'm sorry of
it. If I ever done
a good turn I take
it back. This
is the way to be
tender like I told
[illegible] when
you first started
to read through
this [illegible] book.
If you can read
this by George
you learn your free
[illegible] up the old cows
[illegible] to see the sun
rise. Every [illegible]
[illegible]
[illegible] to see the
[illegible] are
[illegible] out.
[illegible] bell out of
[illegible] But be easy. Easy.

60

And for the reasons I've
already made plain, I say
unto you practice easy care,
practice tenderness, practice the
long, the deep, the deeper, the
waiting and low whispering that
goes with it. You have missed
out on 3/4 of living if you've
not already learned how, why,
when, where and which about
all of this. And I know it
pains you. I know it hurts you.
Dont let new yorkee fast nervous
speed run away nor run over
nor run over your love life.
The reason why it hurts you like
it does is because your soul
is alive to what is missing.
It dont hurt most folks because they are not even
passionate nor hot enough
to look for their best part
missing.

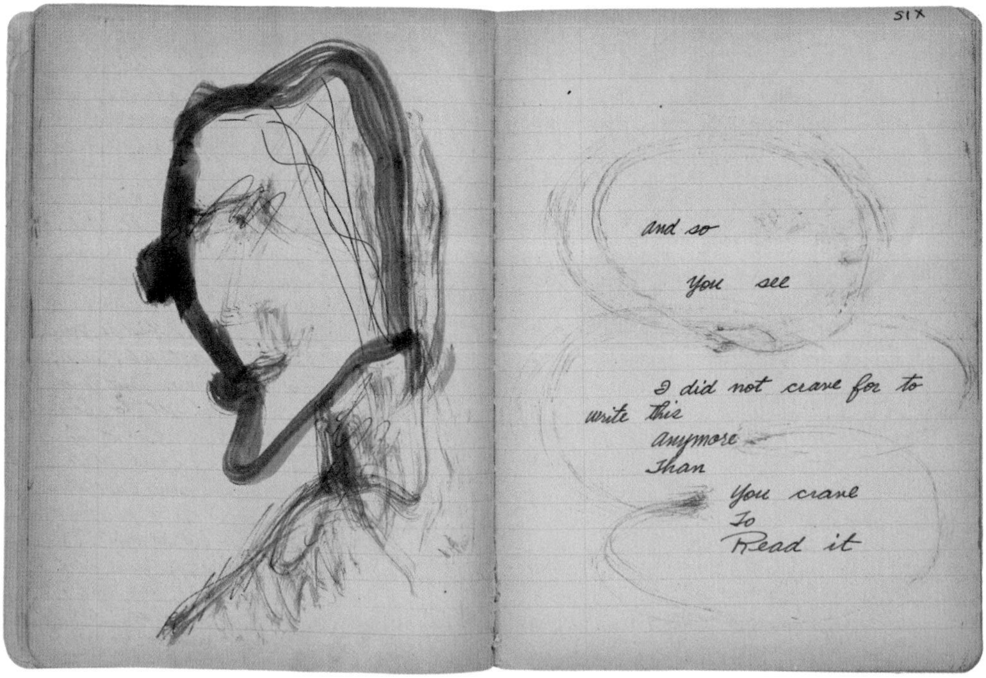
SIX
and so
You see
I did not crave for to
write this
anymore
Than
You crave
To
Read it

NINE
only the ones that walk
here where I walk, that see my
same tangle and whirl, my same
thought and vision, my same
feeling of lostness, foundness,
and hope, well, only these ones,
or only this single and solitary
one, will catch the one word
that is missing.
I can preach here about
my great ignorance. I can
say that my sourest enemy
hasn't got the sum and total
of my ignorance spoken, said,
sung nor written down. I aim
to write my thickest books on
the subject of my own personal
ignorance.
I only know a very few
words and these not very plain,
and it is to teach myself one
more word that I let all of these
run to your mail box there.

aint no use
me working
so hard
Woody Guthrie
4-23-'46

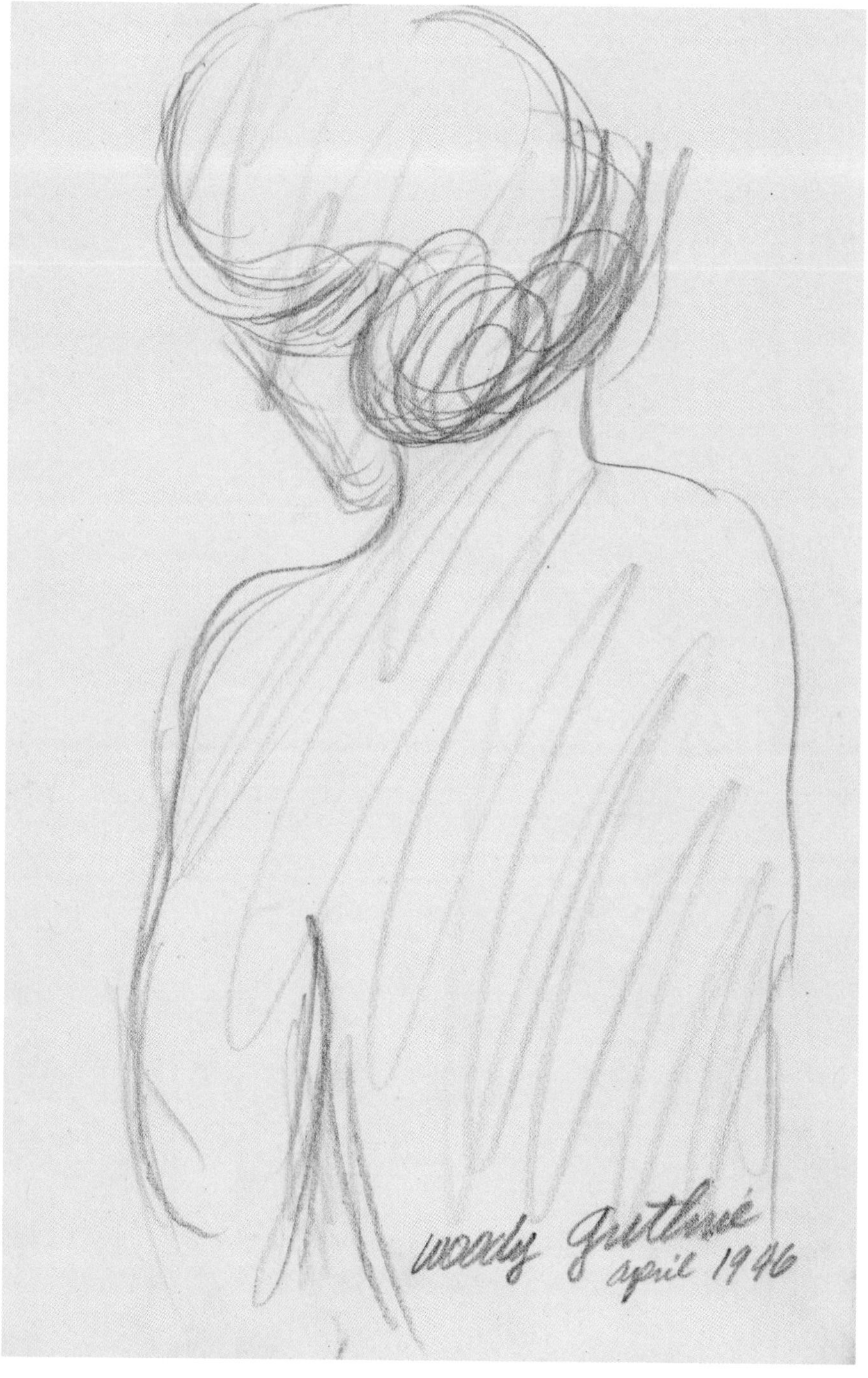
woody guthrie
april 1946

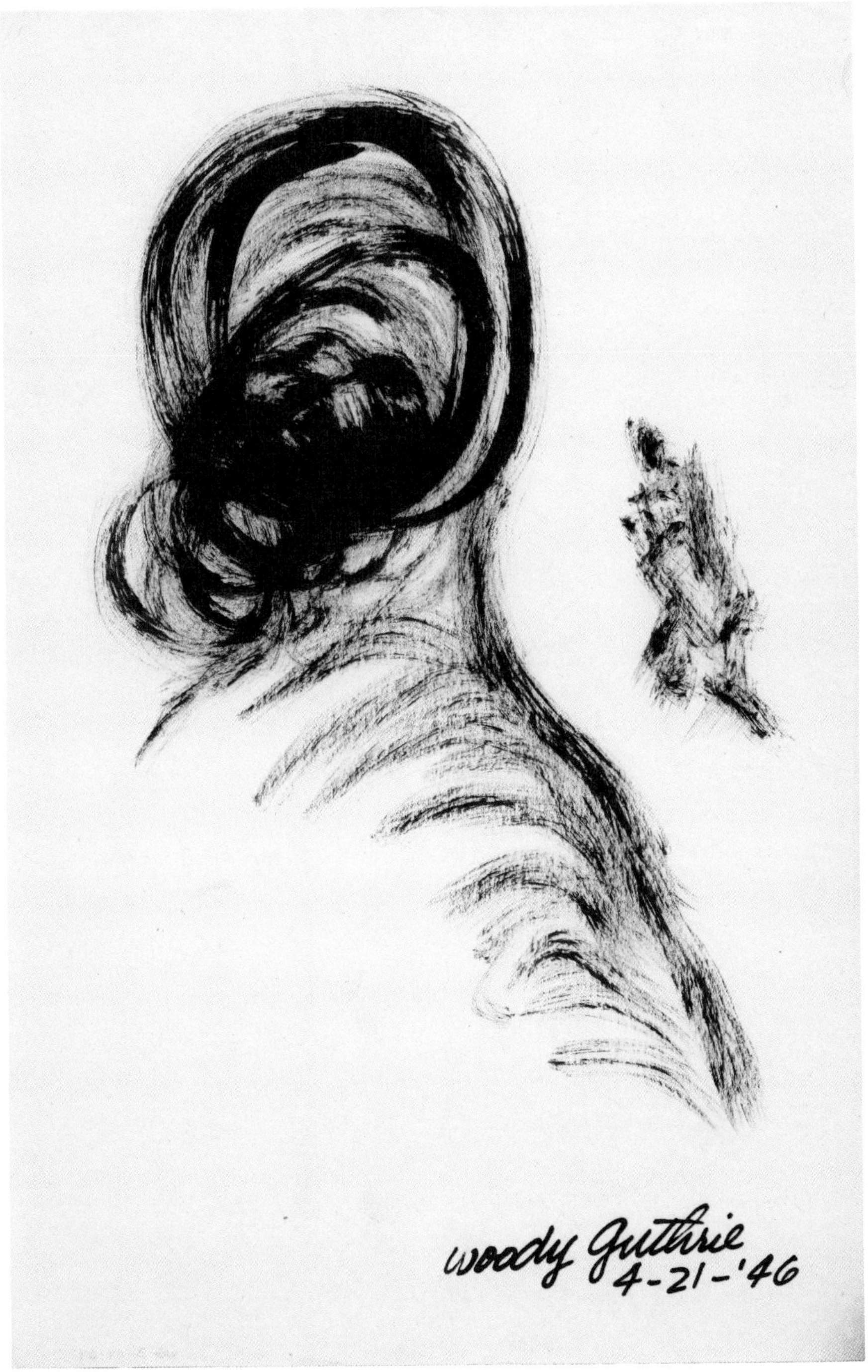

Over the course of a few days in April 1946, Woody created dozens of lively drawings, one right after the other. The energy he put into them reflects back from these pages. The result is a visual diary of what he was seeing, experiencing, and imagining.

Woody depicts a woman performing household chores and activities. Interestingly, we only see the woman from behind. Prior to 1940, Woody's impressions of women were steeped in traditional, and often sad and desperate, roles. His own mother, Nora Belle, reared five children in dire circumstances. When Woody was nine years old, Nora Belle was misdiagnosed and sent to live out her days in an insane asylum, where she died from Huntington's Disease.

Upon arriving in New York in 1940, Woody was surprised to discover women who were active—politically, artistically, and sexually. His personal relationships with women like Martha Graham, Mother Bloor, Aunt Molly Jackson, and others educated him to a broader outlook on women. Or maybe he was just listening to the Carter Family's hit song "Single Girl." Woody often drew inspiration from song lyrics.

Woody recorded most of his songs for Folkways Records, a small recording studio founded by Moses Asch, a progressive thinker and son of the controversial Yiddish writer Sholom Asch. They often brainstormed together, looking for interesting new projects for Woody to work on, with Asch suggesting various topics to explore. Asch equally appreciated Woody as a visual artist and often asked him to create illustrations for his various projects. Woody created dozens of paintings and drawings that he sent to Asch. They highlight the wide range of topics that Woody explored: women's roles, musical instruments, sexual and romantic passions, the body, parenthood, workers, reefer, kids, the blues, racism, and history. The energy he put into them reflects back from these pages.

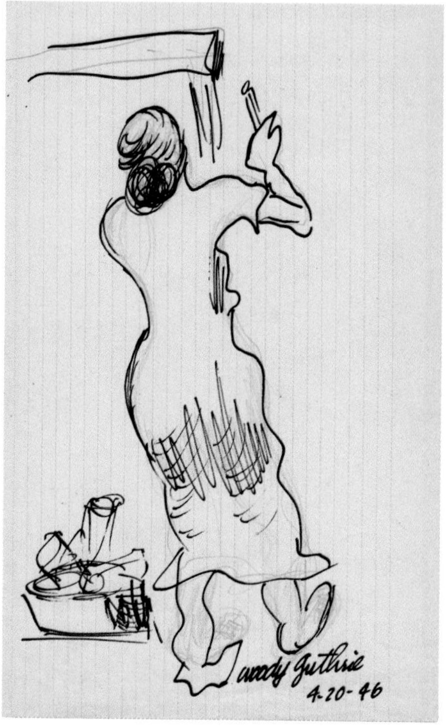

Woody Guthrie
4-20-46 NYC

Woody Guthrie
4-23-'46

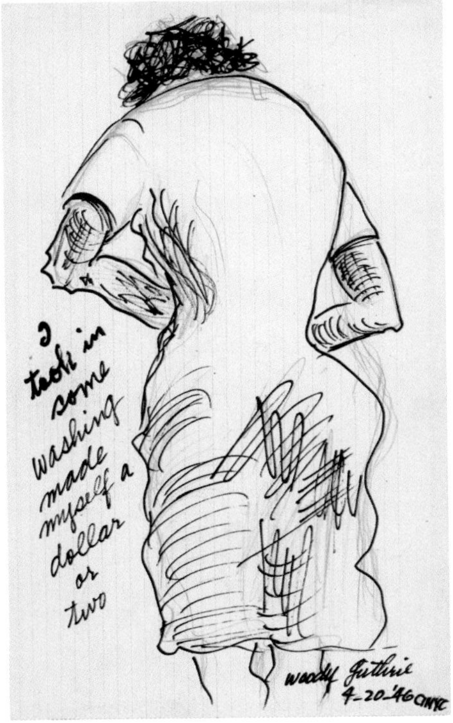
I took in some washing made myself a dollar or two
Woody Guthrie
4-20-'46 NYC

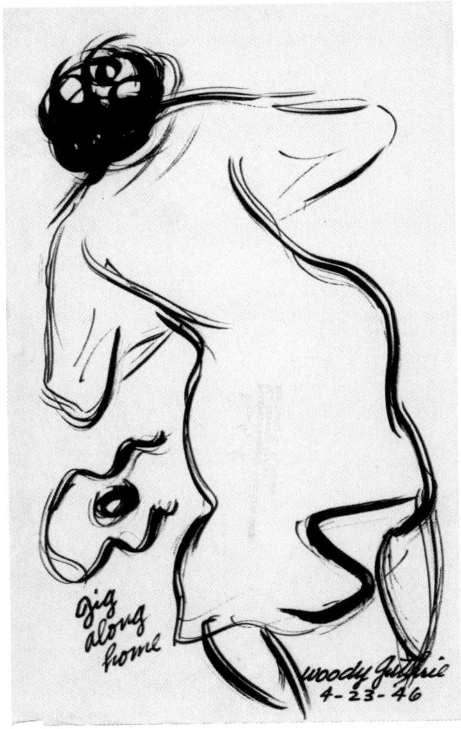
Jig along home
Woody Guthrie
4-23-46

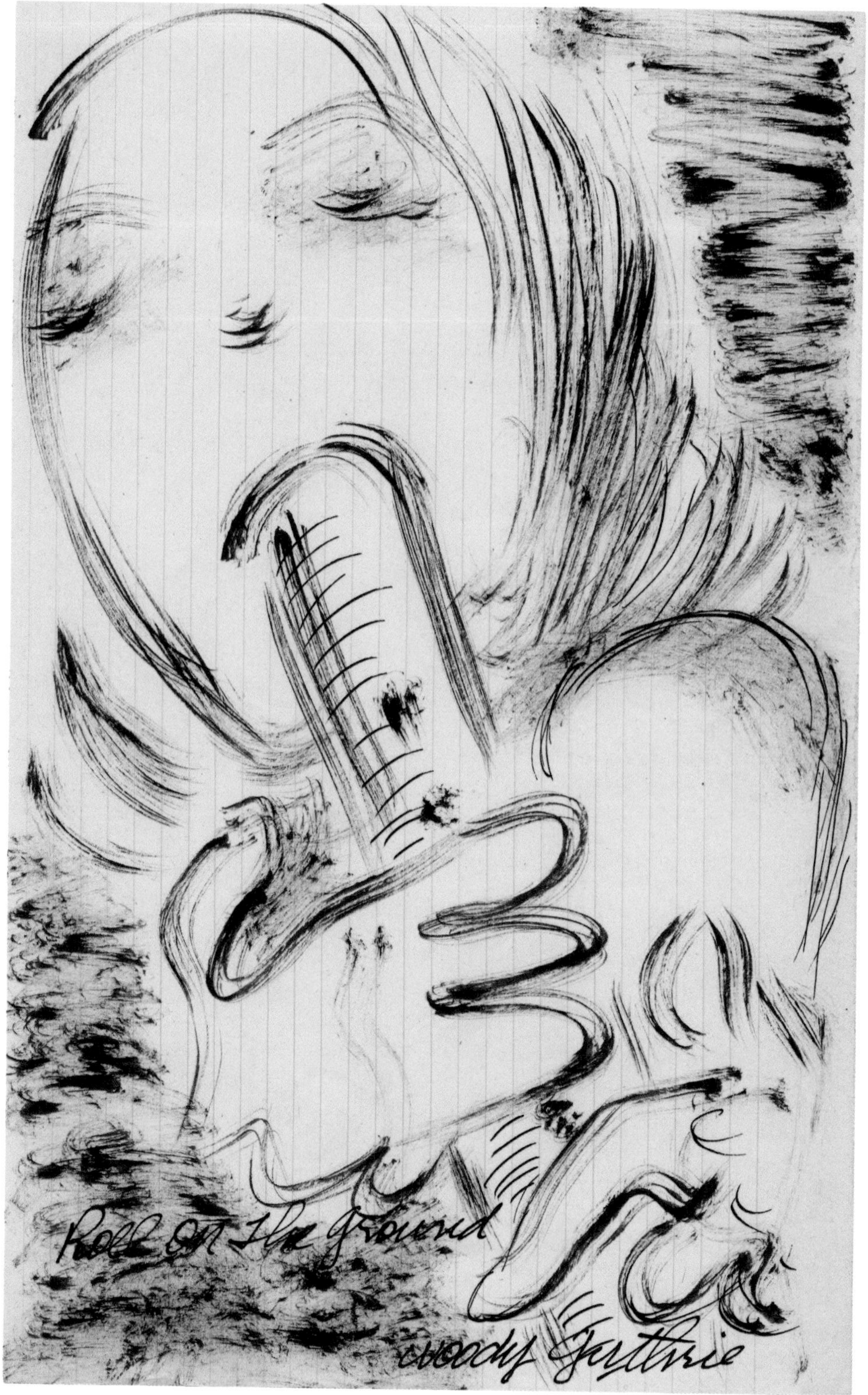
Roll on the Ground
Woody Guthrie

A series of drawings of musical instruments. Woody loved and played many: guitar, mandolin, fiddle, harmonica, recorder, piano, drums, spoons, and more. He also jig danced. A natural understanding of both music and movement is clearly expressed in these pieces.

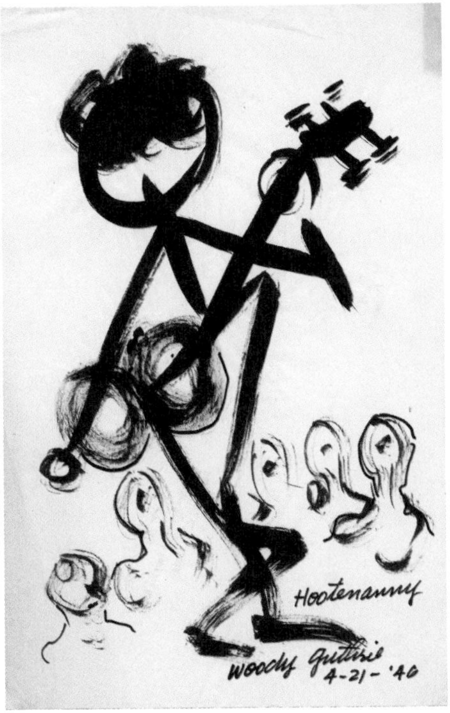

In contrast to his earlier works, Woody began to depict woman as strong, emotive, confident, mature, and often erotic figures that actively create their own image and participate on their own terms.

Woody Guthrie
4-22-46

NEW MORNING SUN
Woody Guthrie
4-23-'46

Woody Guthrie

Woody Guthrie
4-23-'46

these
woody guthrie
4-22-'46

and I know I'm
getting home
woody guthrie
4-22-46

your clothes dont
fit you right
woody guthrie
4-22 '46

new morning
Woody Guthrie
4-23-'46

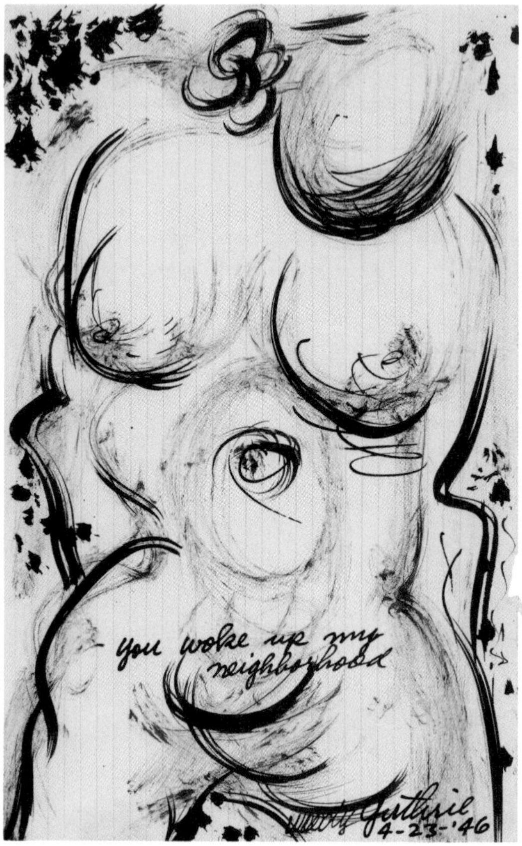
You woke up my
neighborhood
Woody Guthrie
4-23-'46

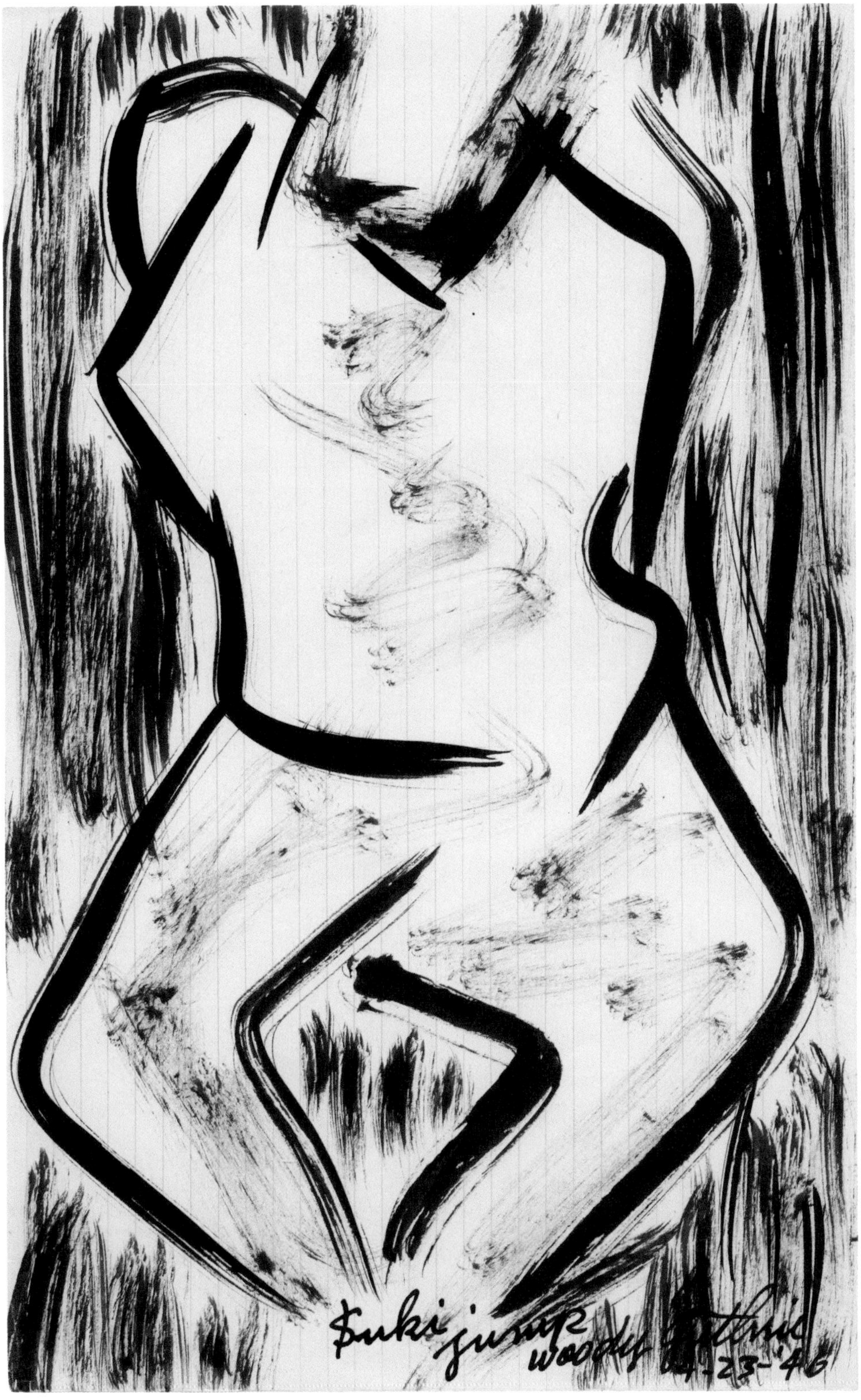
$uki jump
woody

late
last
night
Woody Guthrie
4-20-'46

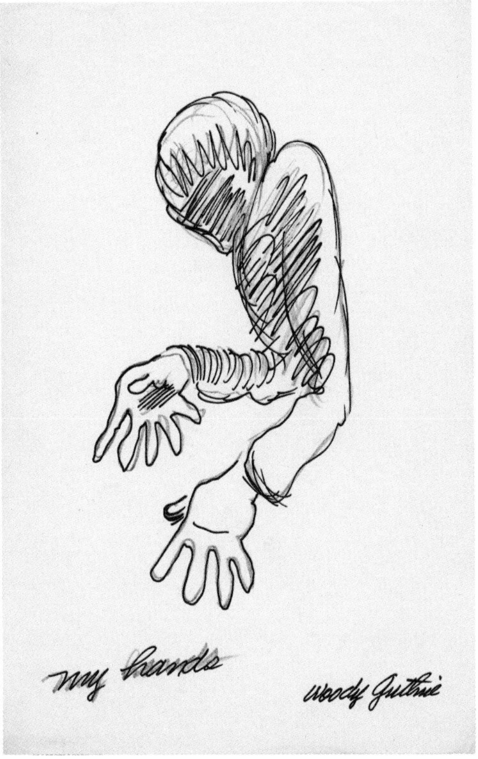
my hands
woody guthrie

woody guthrie

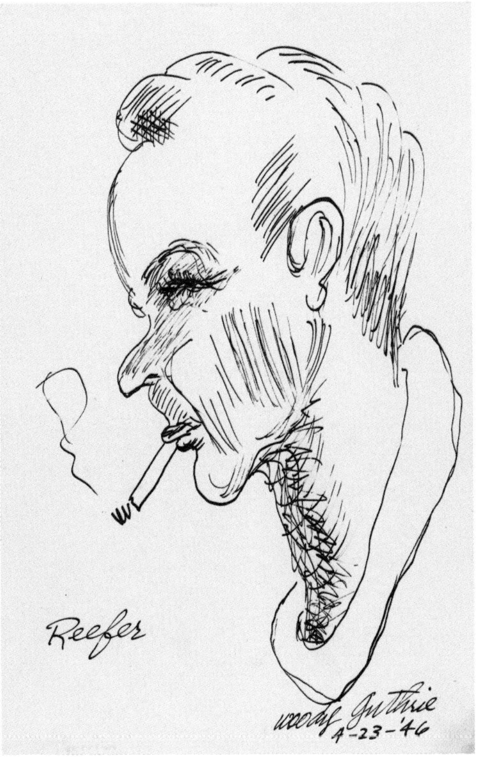
Reefer
woody guthrie
4-23-'46

Woody Guthrie
Pretty and Things

But I'll
sing
again

of the
people
I met

and the
places I've
been

SOME
of the
troubles

I've sung the song

Rope dance
Woody Guthrie

SO LONG

that
bothERED
MY MIND

and a lot
of good
PEOPLE

that
I LEFT
BEhind

singing

Woody Guthrie
all work together

Woody Guthrie

The blues is made
out of trouble
Woody Guthrie
4-23-'46

DLE
F
OK

Looking for
a woman
that's hard
to find
Woody Guthrie
4-23-'46

An illustration for his song "Slipknot" illustrates a lynching with a harsh honesty of its existence. As with his perception of women, Woody's learned attitudes toward racism and segregation evolved in New York. Black musicians Leadbelly, Sonny Terry, and Brownie McGee became his closest friends, with whom he often toured. Woody's growing understanding of and anger toward segregation policies often erupted in violent, confrontational outbursts.

People are often seen fading in Woody's portraits. Perhaps this was an expression of Woody's experience of being poor, therefore expendable and "irrelevant."

Catching a moment in the day, a pencil sketch of a lady on a train, 1946. BELOW: A phrase and mood possibly from Cathy Ann. Woody often noted children's quotes, thinking them both original and insightful. "*Twice I Fell Down Once*" might be used later in a song.

I couldnt say
I changed my mind
I saw
I didnt think
I seek
I'm pretty sure
THAT IS
IT IS CONSISTENT

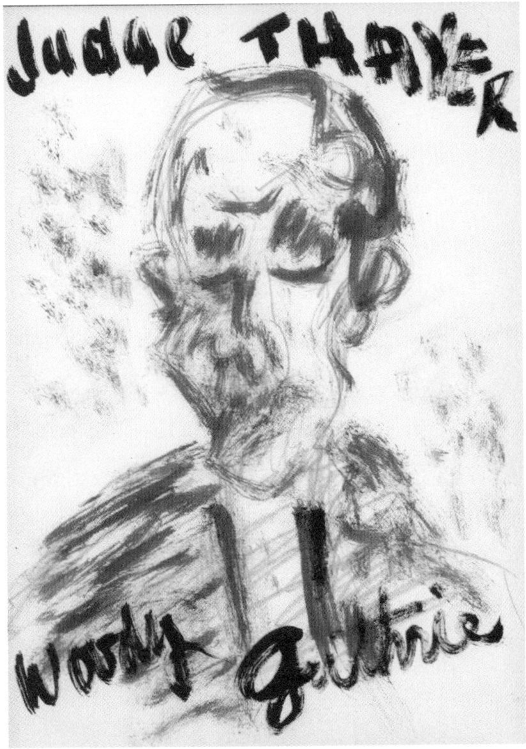

In 1946, Moses Asch sent Woody and Cisco Houston to Boston to investigate the history of the Sacco and Vanzetti trial of 1927. Italian immigrants involved in radical politics, they were falsely charged with a murder and executed. Asch wanted Woody to compose a collection of songs based on the story, much like he did with his *Dust Bowl Ballads* album and his "Columbia River" series of songs. Woody often worked this way, creating anthologies on a single topic, which he would then view from social, political, personal, and historic perspectives. Woody created many illustrations for the *Ballads of Sacco & Vanzetti* album, which wasn't released until 1960. In the final published booklet insert, only four were ultimately included.

ACROSS: A portrait of the witness at the Sacco and Vanzetti trial.

Words and imagery assume equal weight, one sometimes obscuring the other, in this personal journal.

Sunday, Jan. 20, 1946

20th day — 345 days follow

I will say this, though, then you can dance on past me. And that is this.

Your own people will sing loud yells about Woody Guthrie being two sex maniacs. But if I took the other road these same several yellers would scream that I'm a queer. I fully aim at this time, dear lay man and lay woman, to walk up and to run bare back down both of these trails and to get my soul known again as the two, both, the sexual maniac, the saint, the sinner, the drinker, the thinker, the queer. The works.

the whole WORKS

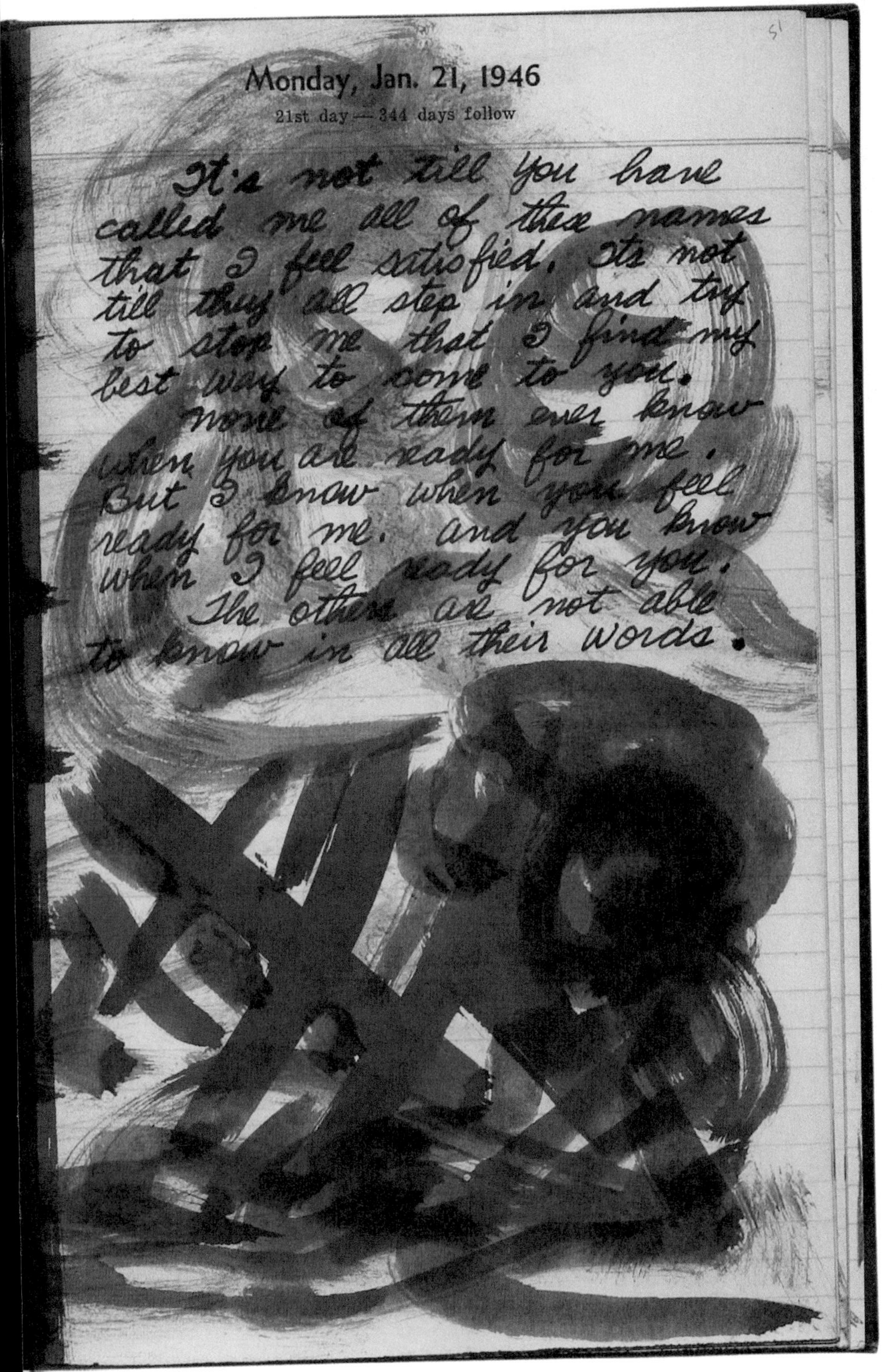

51

Monday, Jan. 21, 1946

21st day — 344 days follow

It's not till you have called me all of these names that I feel satisfied. Its not till they all step in and try to stop me that I find my best way to come to you.

None of them ever know when you are ready for me. But I know when you feel ready for me. and you know when I feel ready for you.

The others are not able to know in all their words.

196

Thursday, Jan. 24, 1946

24th day — 341 days follow

You danced out of two people fighting againt the Nazis and fighting against the fascists, yes, to give the Jews back their own land in the Holy Land. You dance as pretty as a scrubby olive bush on a rock hill in the Holy Land. And this is the mainest reason I guess why it is that Natanya always looks so nice and so

Friday, Jan. 25, 1946

25th day — 340 days follow

pretty to me. To me as a man. I see you as your man sees you. I know that you move your body for good reasons, I mean, as a part of this big fight that all of us are dancing through. I do wish that I was 10 years younger. I'd tear into you like a horse eats his corn. Your legs and your feet are all in my same fight to kill out fascism.

Artwork sans words, a single page per spread, appears throughout this sketchbook.

25/9

Woody

25/12

SMACK

Woody Guthrie

EAT
DRINK
2.9.47
CUT RATE
WOODY GUTHRIE
RENT
LB 68¢
79¢
57¢
74¢
FOWL
BEST
83¢

Woody's wife Marjorie was the daughter of Yiddish poet and songwriter Aliza Greenblatt. "Bubbie," as she was called, lived a few blocks from the Guthries' apartment in Coney Island and introduced Woody to Jewish religion, history, holidays, culture, and food. Woody created many artworks to illustrate her poetry and lyrics that were published in Yiddish.

This series, from an artist's notepad titled *What a Beautiful World*, includes illustrations for some of the songs in Greenblatt's book *Ich Zing*, published in 1947. ACROSS: "Ten Hens and a Duck." BELOW LEFT: "Passover Night." BELOW RIGHT: "The Blintze Tree."

LEFT: *Snow.* BOTTOM: *Kids Band.* NEXT PAGE: TOP: *Pot and Skillet.* BOTTOM: *Girl on Beach.* OVERLEAF: *Jewish Madula and Jewish School.*

Woody Guthrie

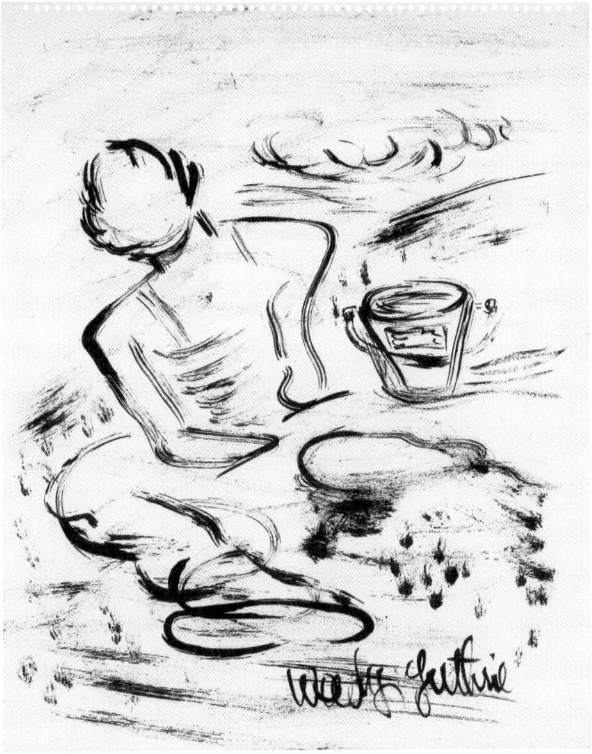
Woody Guthrie

Woody Guthrie

Woody Guthrie

Woody Guthrie

ACROSS TOP: *Easter, all dressed up.* ACROSS BOTTOM: *Three Trees.* THIS PAGE: *Kat and Kitten.* OVERLEAF: *When I grow big.*

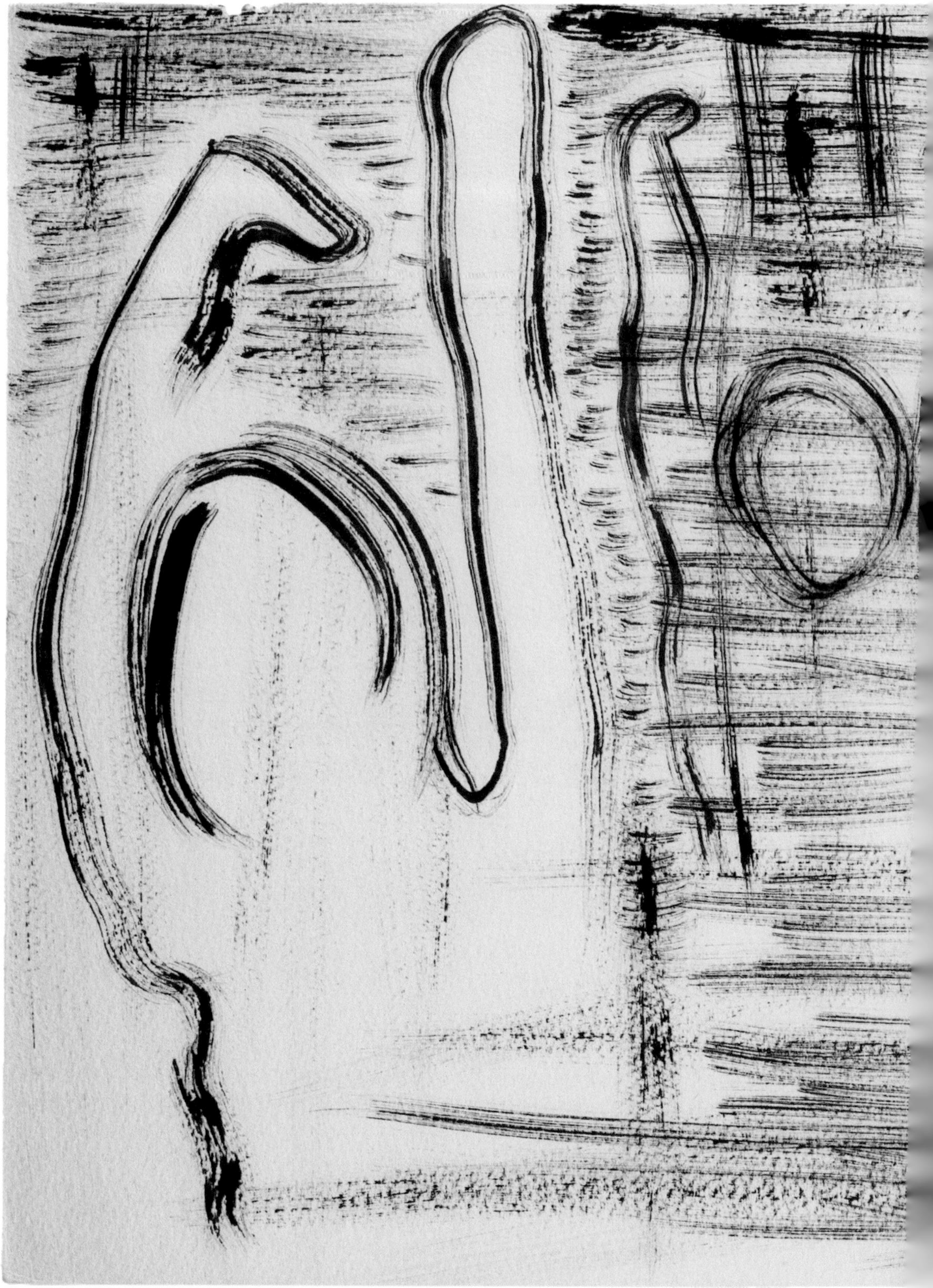

I HOPE YOU'RE

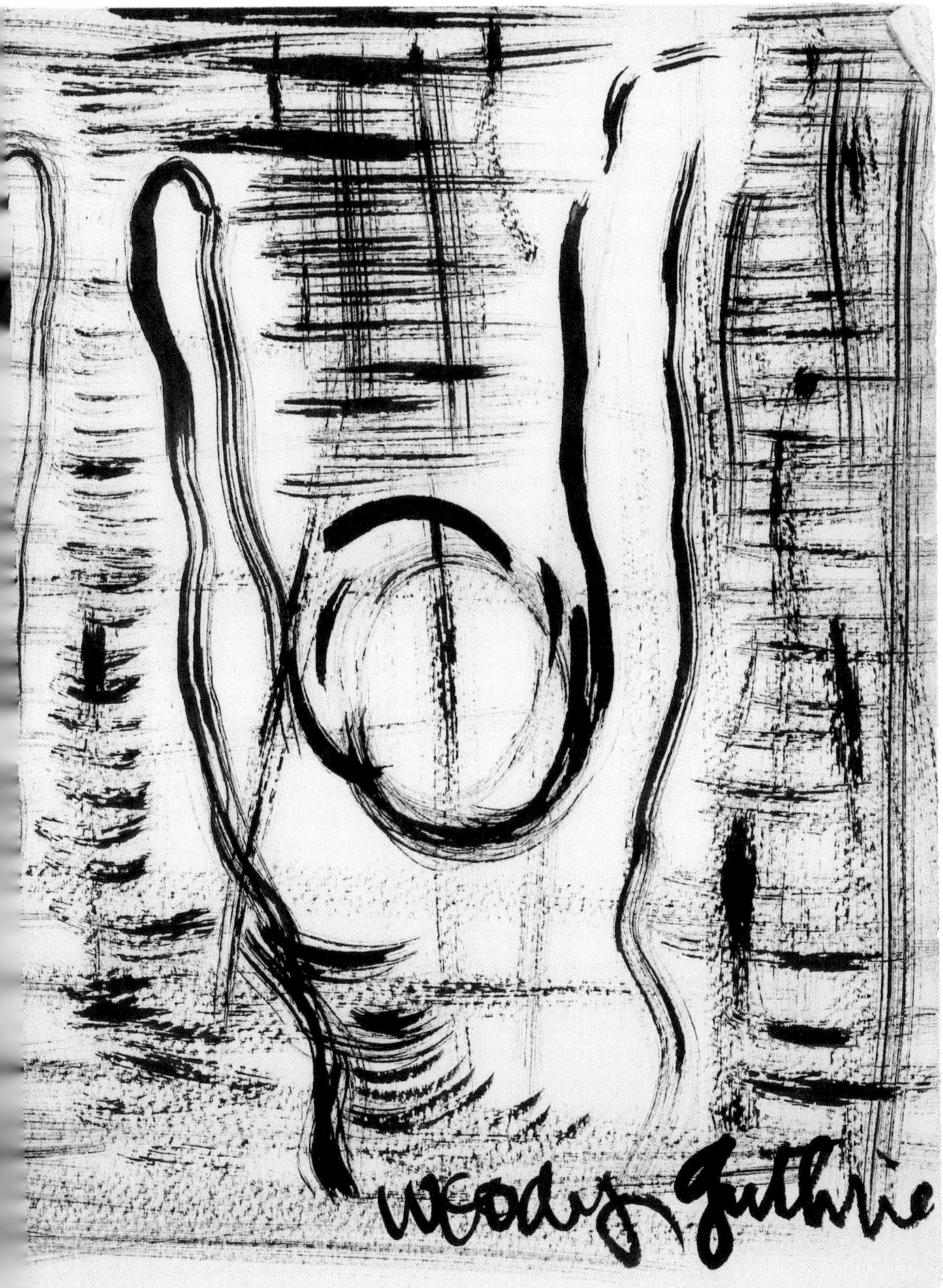
Woody Guthrie

Woody's boldly personal and political musings are in contrast to his decorative approach, in a notebook entitled *Short Hauls*.

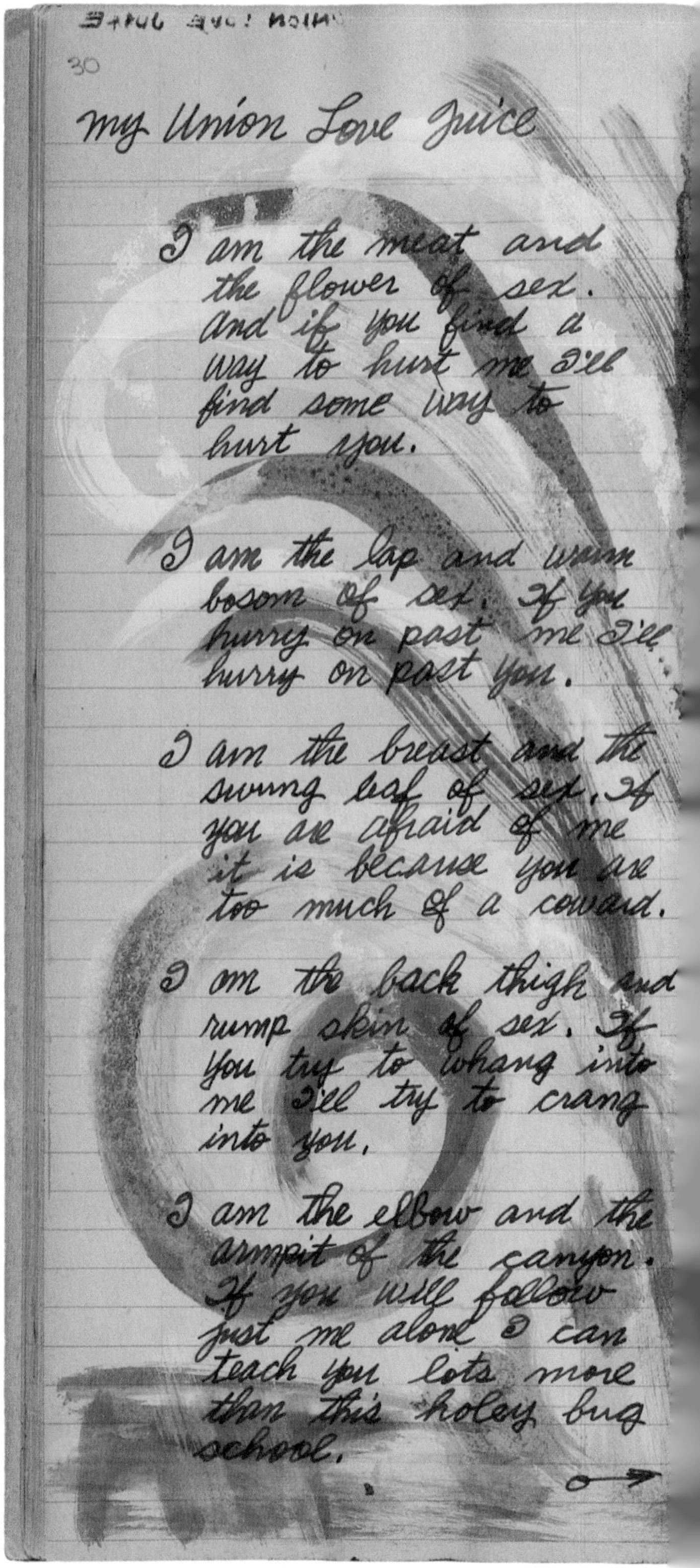
30

my Union Love Juice

I am the meat and
the flower of sex.
And if you find a
way to hurt me I'll
find some way to
hurt you.

I am the lap and warm
bosom of sex. If you
hurry on past me I'll
hurry on past you.

I am the breast and the
swing leaf of sex. If
you are afraid of me
it is because you are
too much of a coward.

I am the back thigh and
rump skin of sex. If
you try to whang into
me I'll try to crang
into you.

I am the elbow and the
armpit of the canyon.
If you will follow
just me alone I can
teach you lots more
than this holey bug
school.

UNION LOVE JUICE

81

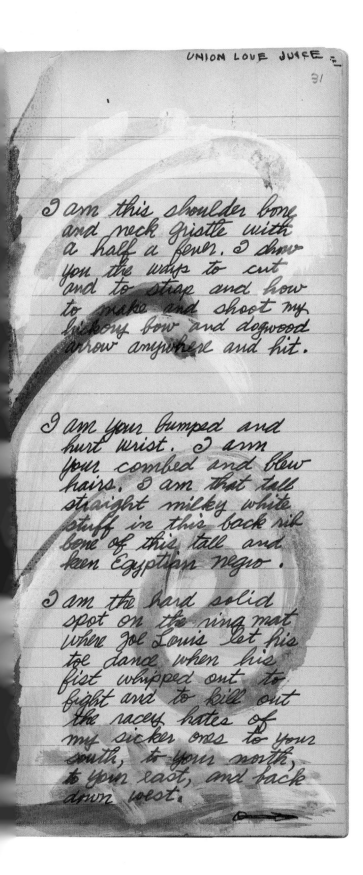

I am this shoulder bone
and neck gristle with
a half a fever. I show
you the ways to cut
and to strap and how
to make and shoot my
hickory bow and dogwood
arrow anywhere and hit.

I am your bumped and
hurt wrist. I am
your combed and blew
hairs. I am that tall
straight milky white
stuff in this back rib
bone of this tall and
keen Egyptian negro.

I am the hard solid
spot on the ring mat
where Joe Louis let his
toe land when his
fist whipped out to
fight and to kill out
the racey hates of
my sicker ones to your
south, to your north,
to your east, and back
down west.

→

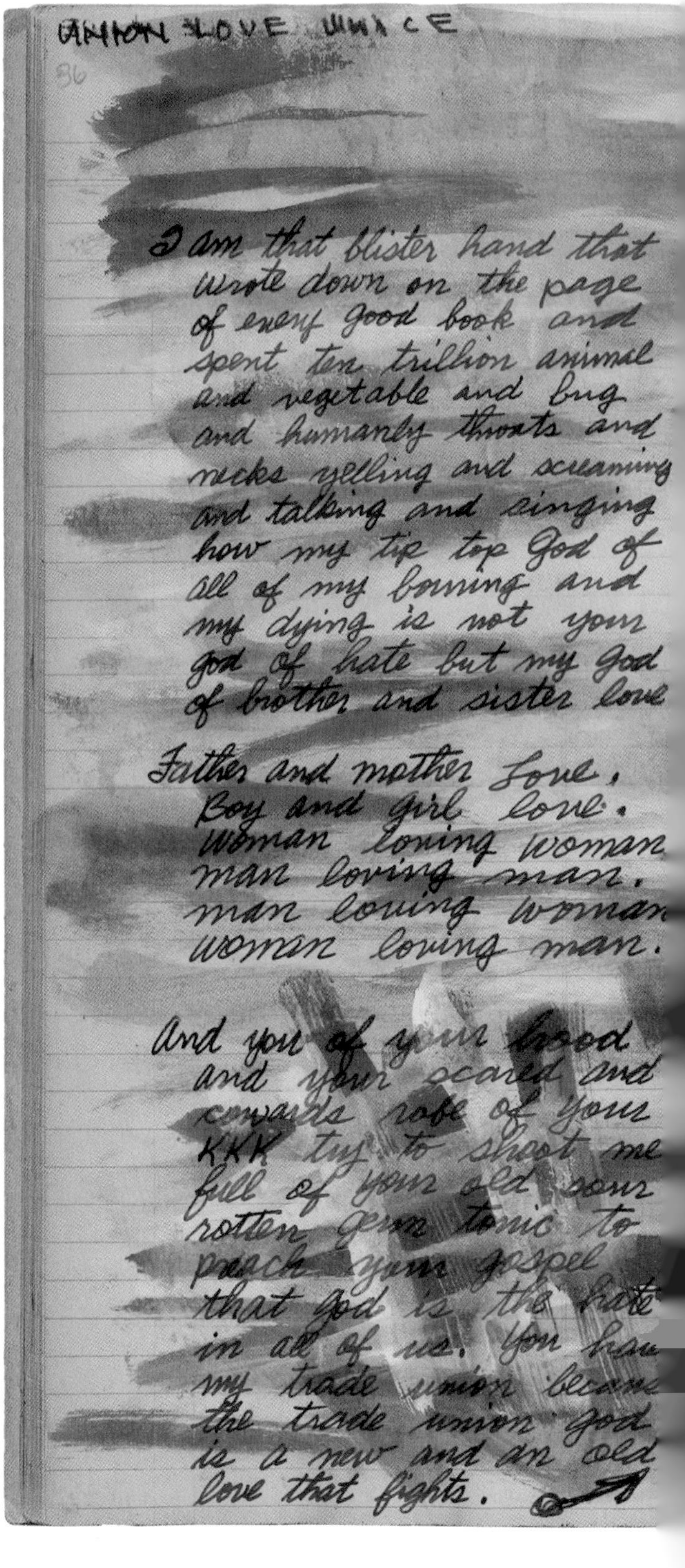

UNION LOVE [illegible]

86

I am that blister hand that
wrote down on the page
of every good book and
spent ten trillion animal
and vegetable and bug
and humanly throats and
necks yelling and screaming
and talking and singing
how my tip top God of
all of my borning and
my dying is not your
god of hate but my God
of brother and sister love

Father and mother Love.
Boy and girl love.
Woman loving woman
man loving man.
man loving woman
woman loving man.

And you of your hood
and your scared and
cowards robe of your
KKK try to shoot me
full of your old sour
rotten germ tonic to
preach your gospel
that god is the hate
in all of us. You hate
my trade union because
the trade union god
is a new and an old
love that fights.

UNION LOVE JUICE

37

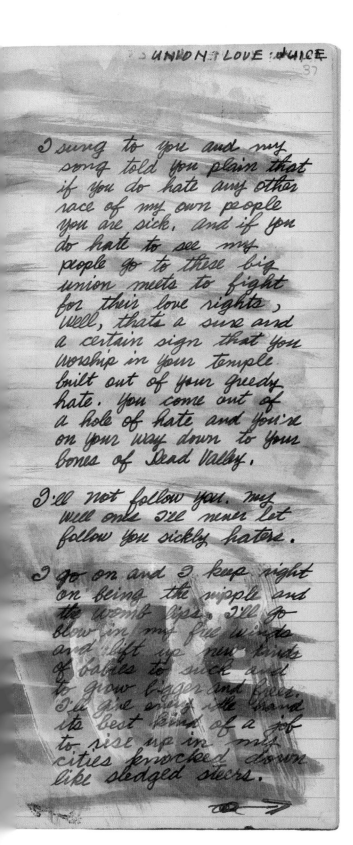

I sung to you and my song told you plain that if you do hate any other race of my own people you are sick. and if you do hate to see my people go to these big union meets to fight for their love rights, well, thats a sure and a certain sign that you worship in your temple built out of your greedy hate. You come out of a hole of hate and you're on your way down to your bones of Dead Valley.

I'll not follow you. my well ones I'll never let follow you sickly haters.

I go on and I keep right on being the nipple and the womb lips. I'll go blow in my free winds and lift up new kinds of babies to suck and to grow bigger and freer. I'll give every idle hand its best kind of a job to rise up in my cities knocked down like sledged steers.

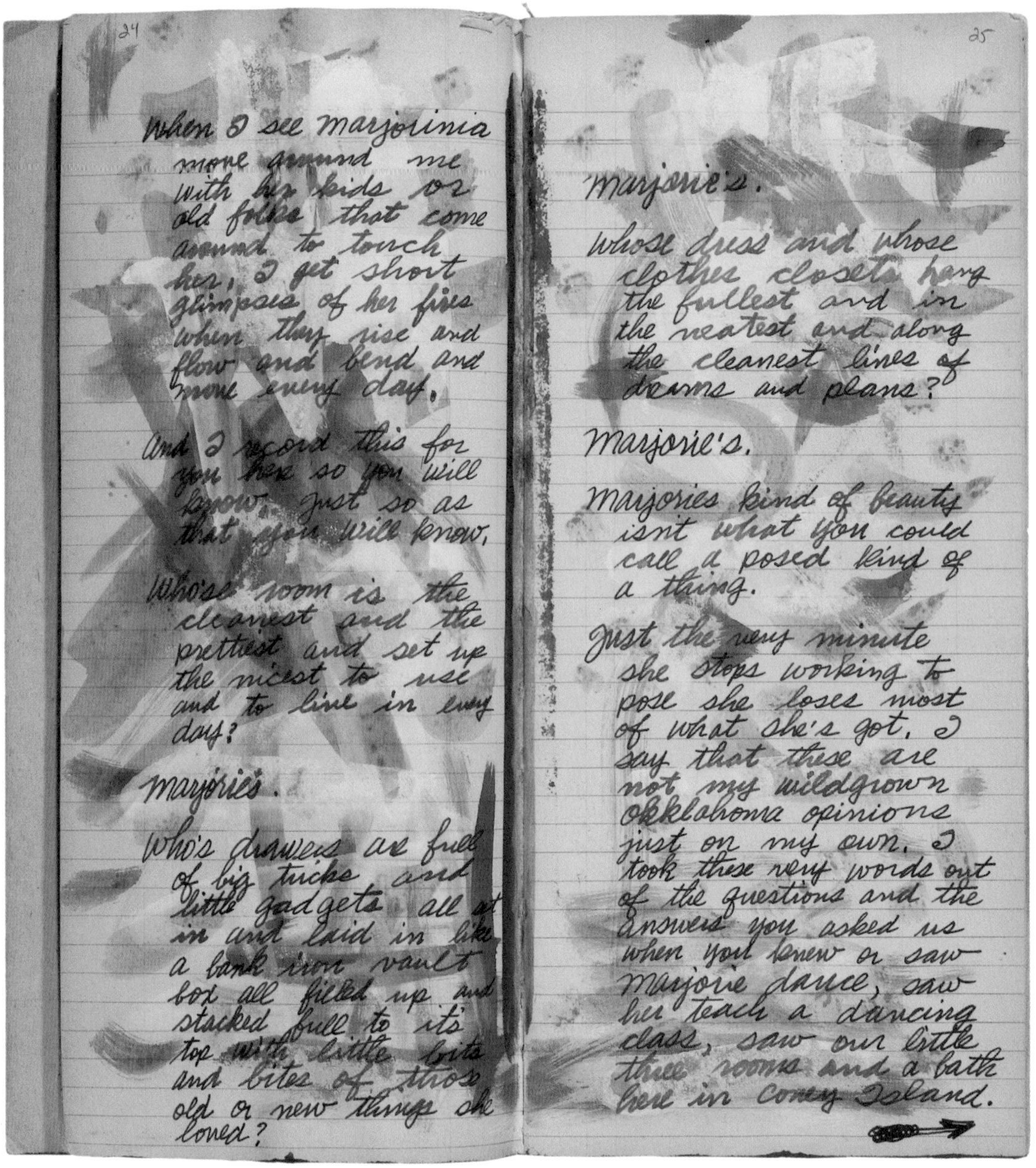
24

When I see Marjorinia
move around me
with her kids or
old folks that come
around to touch
her, I get short
glimpses of her fires
when they rise and
flow and bend and
move every day.

And I record this for
you here so you will
know. Just so as
that you will know.

Who'se room is the
cleanest and the
prettiest and set up
the nicest to use
and to live in every
day?

Marjorie's.

Who's drawers are full
of big tricks and
little gadgets all at
in and laid in like
a bank iron vault
box all filled up and
stacked full to it's
top with little bits
and bites of those
old or new things she
loved?

25

Marjorie's.

Whose dress and whose
clothes closets hang
the fullest and in
the neatest and along
the cleanest lines of
dreams and plans?

Marjorie's.

Marjories kind of beauty
isn't what you could
call a posed kind of
a thing.

Just the very minute
she stops working to
pose she loses most
of what she's got. I
say that these are
not my wildgrown
Okklahoma opinions
just on my own. I
took these very words out
of the questions and the
answers you asked us
when you knew or saw
Marjorie dance, saw
her teach a dancing
class, saw our little
three rooms and a bath
here in Coney Island.

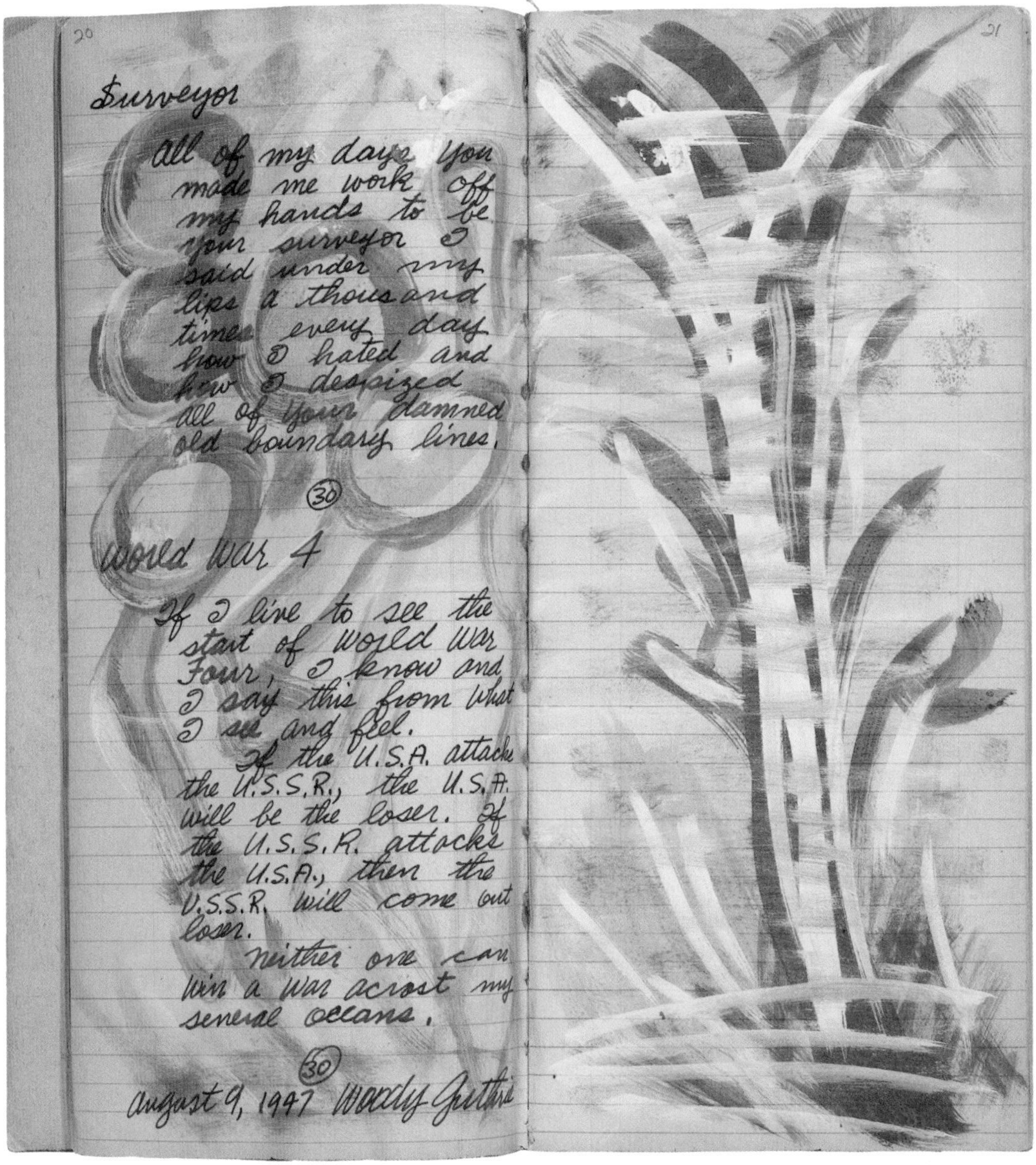
20
21
Surveyor
All of my days you made me work off my hands to be your surveyor I said under my lips a thousand times every day how I hated and how I despized all of your damned old boundary lines.
30
World War 4
If I live to see the start of World War Four, I know and I say this from what I see and feel.
If the U.S.A. attacks the U.S.S.R., the U.S.A. will be the loser. If the U.S.S.R. attacks the U.S.A., then the U.S.S.R. will come out loser.
Neither one can win a war acrost my several oceans.
30
August 9, 1947 Woody Guthrie

Woody utilized a vivid color palette in this watercolor series. An entire unlined notebook titled *A Book For Cathy*, 1947, it was created in a single day. It is filled with spreads of dramatic and often mysterious abstract forms.

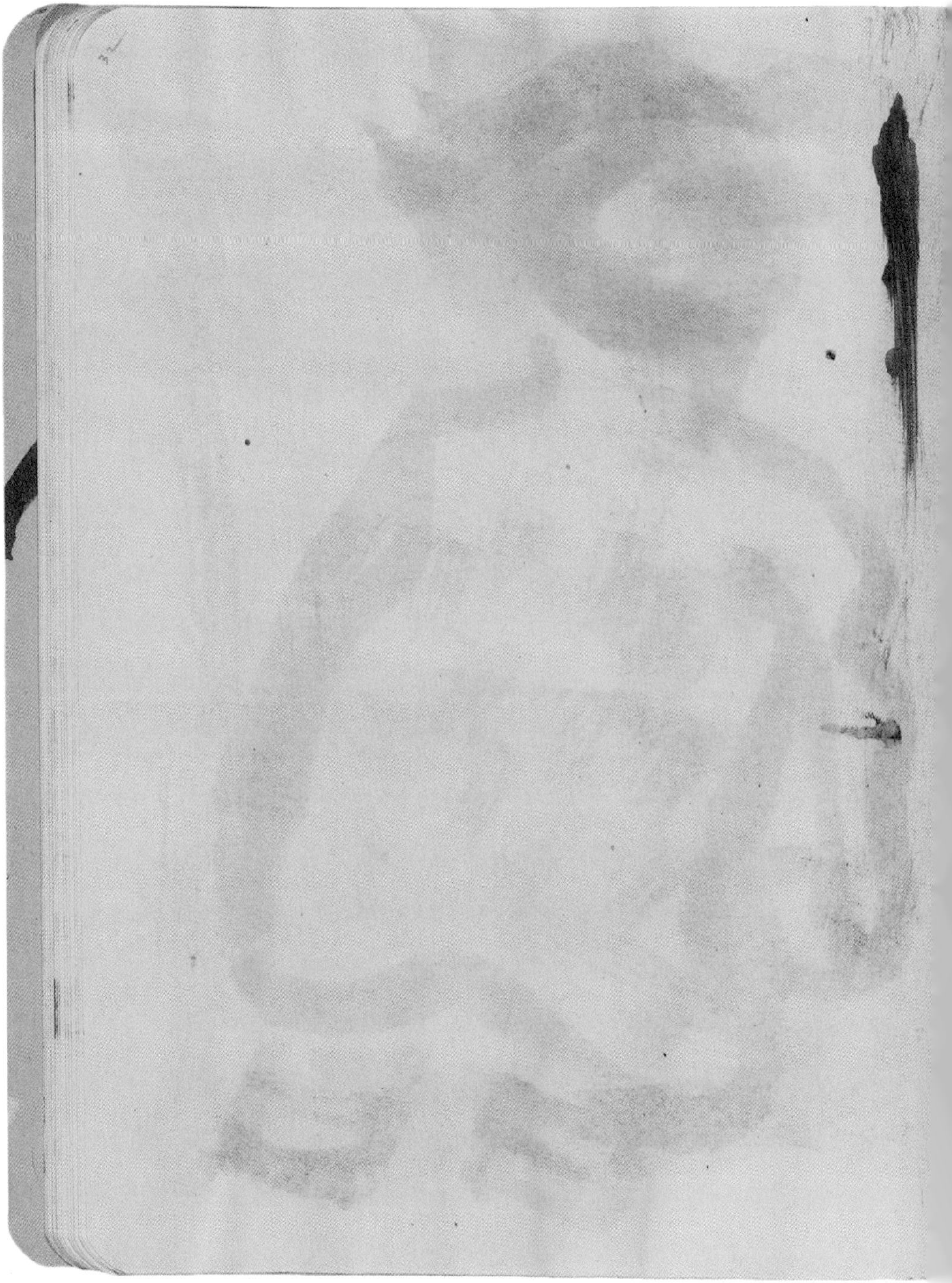

226

A continuous outpouring of highly charged watercolor images and prose fill an entire unlined marble notebook, created as a single letter to Marjorie in November 1947. The previous February, Cathy Ann had died in a fire. Woody and Marjorie's individual ways of dealing with the grief and devastation in their mutual loss created a strained tension between them, tainted with guilt and anger. Images of confusion, separation, and closed walls abound.

woody Guthrie
In the exact proportion
to your most
I craved to come
into you as your warmest kind
of thoughts would let me. I know
my warmest thoughts will sound
sadly out of place in your
court room. But didnt find
court room.

dear Max

I don't want to work the deal
woody
11-9
I begin
at four

EVERY
LINE
RUNS
TOGETHER

I just don't guess I know
I just couldn't say
you was the one
woody Guthrie
november 4th 1947
at home again

233

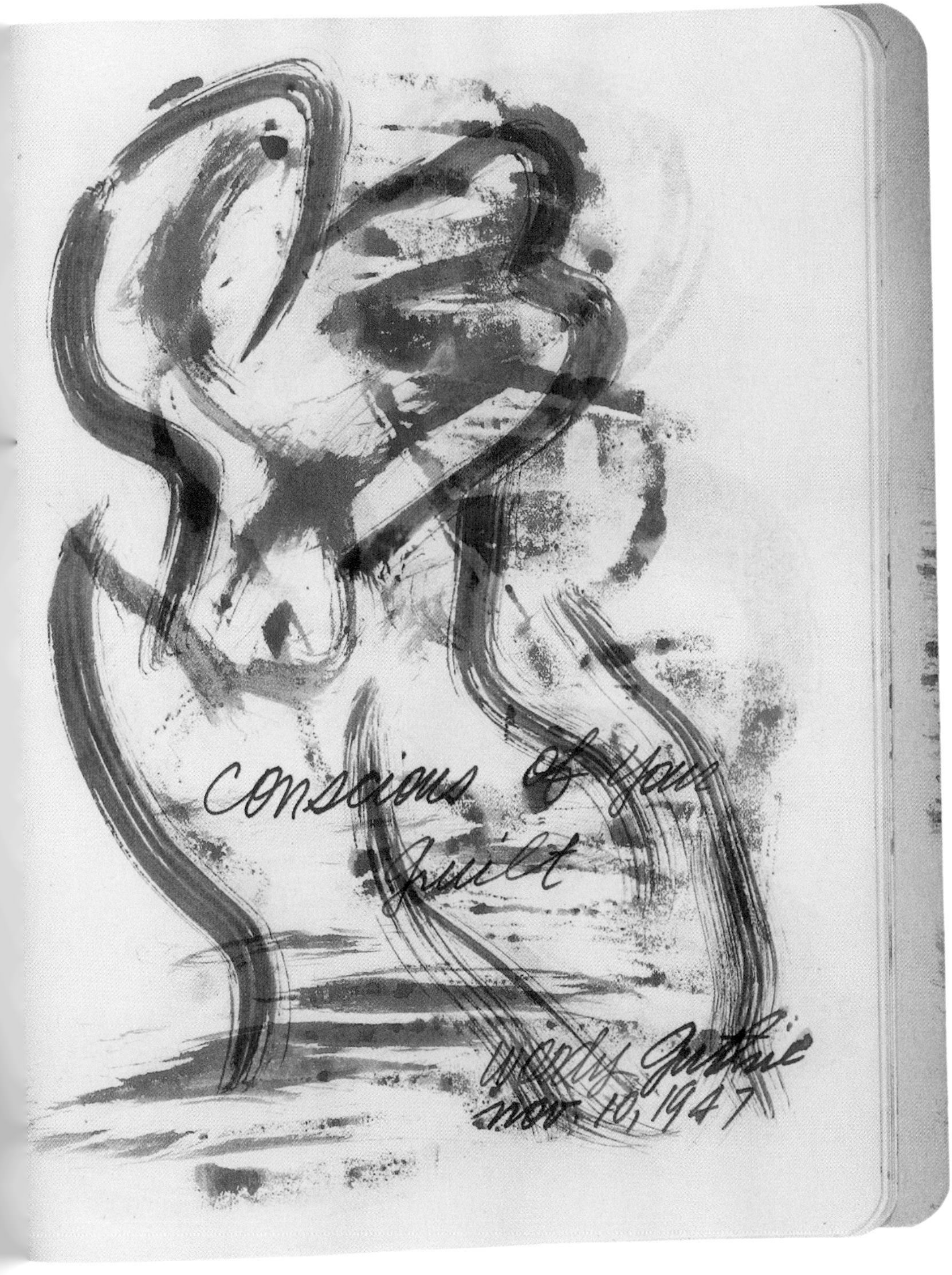
conscious of your
guilt
Woody Guthrie
nov. 10, 1947

The guilt of this high price
system is so
that we go out a thousand
times a day and commit
all careless suicide

238

Mineral waters
Natural gas
Natural gas gasoline
Petroleum
Potash (K20)
Quicksilver
Slate
Sulphur
Talc and soapstone
Tin
Tungsten
Uranium, vanadium
Elevation (Feet)
Below Sea Level
Mount McKinley, Alaska
Mount Aconcagua, Chile-Argentina
Mount Elbrus, Caucasus
Mount Everest, India-China
Kibo (Kilimanjaro), Tanganyika Terr.
Mount Kosciusko, New South Wales
20,300
22,834
18,465
29,141
19,710
7,328
Death Valley, California
Sea Level
Caspian Sea, Russia
Dead Sea, Palestine
Libyan Desert
Lake Eyre, So. Australia
276
86
1,200
440
38

241

242

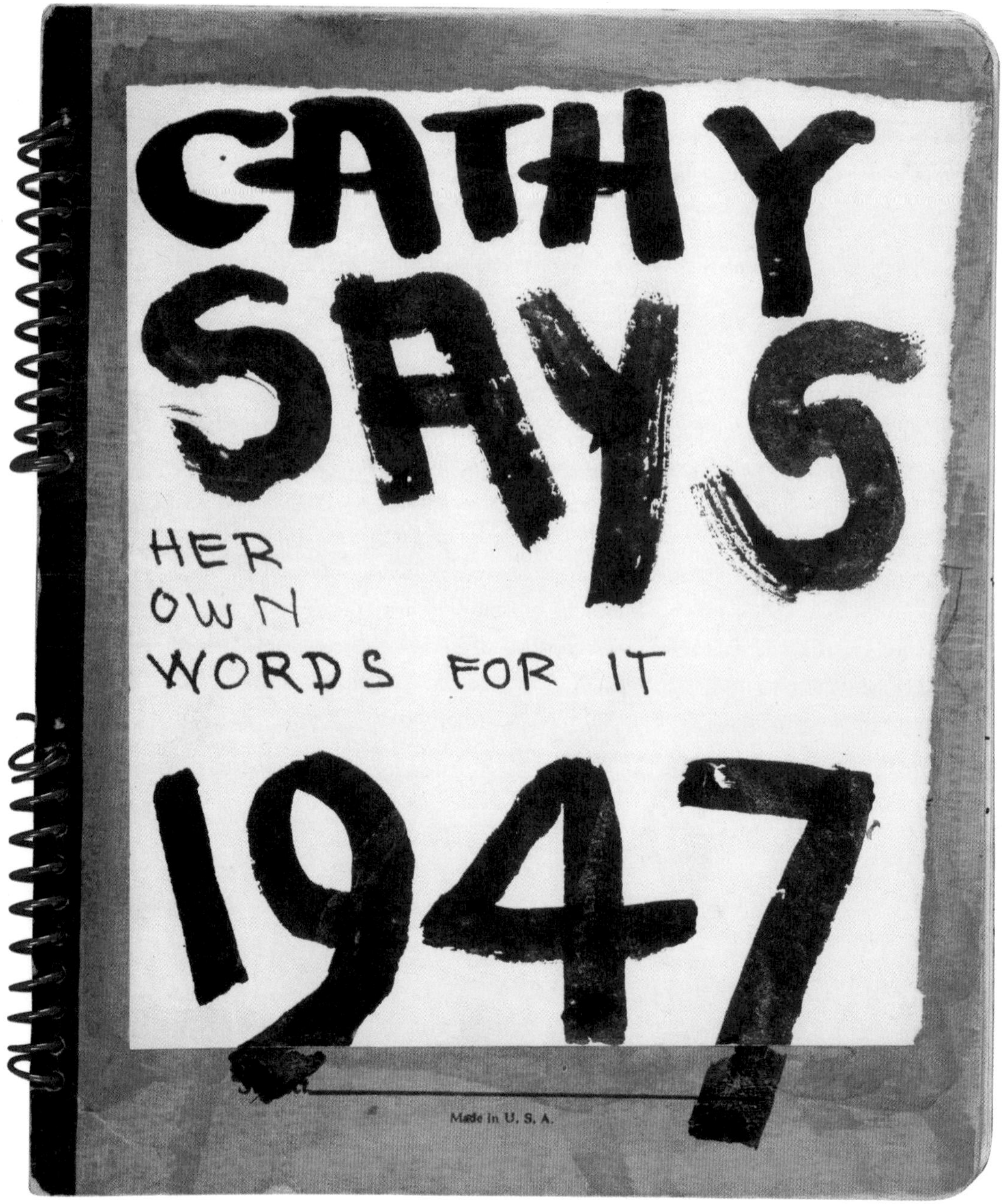

AND I'VE GOT TO BE DRIFTING ALONG

One day we'll all find out that all of our songs were just little notes in a great big song.

After the birth of son Arlo Davy in 1947, Marjorie and Woody had two more children, son Joady Ben, born in 1948, and daughter Nora Lee in 1950. Left with the children in his charge as Marjorie went off to work at her dance studio, Woody assumed the role of househusband. He would amuse himself and the children through art, creating comical figures and colorful flights of fancy in ledger books he brought home from his stint in the U.S. Army. Sometimes enigmatic, these seemingly abstract series would in due course reveal themselves to be depictions of routine household chores: a series of exuberant circles and swirls denotes a trip to the laundromat. He would create three-dimensional "Hoodis" out of discarded trash, washed-up wood from the beach, and items purchased at the five-and-dime. He enrolled in a ceramics class, creating hot plates and vases for family and friends. The wooden block that helped the toddlers reach the sink was covered with funny faces to delight the children. Their home environment became Woody's canvas.

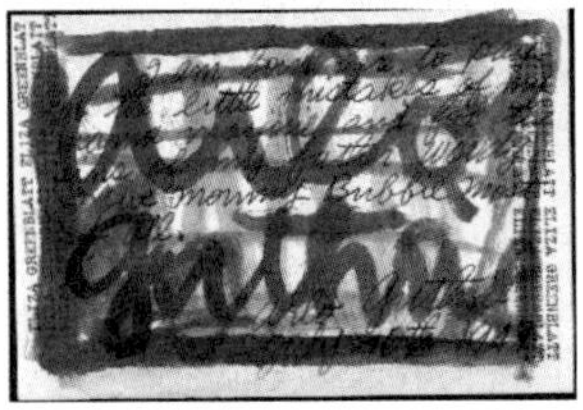

Both sides of Arlo Davy's birth announcement.

Guthrie continued to combine words and imagery, draw pictures of common folk ("Cripple Annie"), and create self-portraits. Through the self-portraits one can see an evolution that records and defines his journey. No longer the amusing yet confident figure of *Bound for Glory*, nor the bold Duchamp-like silhouette of only four years earlier, his visage now comprised random pencil squiggles that converged to form his likeness. In other work there is an intensified color palette, and a continued experimentation with media, including pastels and dyes. His sense of play remained intact, yet the work shifted widely between more adult subject matter and pieces for children, many based on *Woody's 20 Grow Big Songs*. In other books he would create an image on one side and close the book, then go back and embellish the ghost image. There was an increase of decorative work and graffiti-like scrawl during this time.

Woody on the back stoop in the "Jungle" at Mermaid Avenue.

Guthrie's illness was becoming more pronounced, resulting in loss of coordination and erratic behavior. He drank to cover up his symptoms, and as a result, Marjorie and he separated. He suffered from dizzy spells and blackouts, and his condition was misdiagnosed as alcoholism. No longer able to record, as he had great difficulty playing guitar and remembering lyrics, he once again began to travel. Back in California, he met Anneke Van Kirk Marshall, a kindred spirit.

Collaborative art by Woody and Anneke Van Kirk. The letter is from Woody.

Though she was twenty years his junior, they were bound together through song and art, and Anneke became Woody's third wife, albeit briefly. Anneke took to drawing in his ledger books, her pen-and-ink renderings of faces and horses displaying a sensuous line, in contrast to Guthrie's looser and broader strokes. Occasionally they would collaborate. While in California he continued to pot and set up still-life objects to photograph. Together they traveled to Florida, where they lived on the property of Guthrie's friend Stetson Kennedy, who was in Europe at the time. While there, Guthrie accidentally burned his arm over a campfire, and his condition worsened. He continued his downward spiral, and the marriage ended in spring 1954. On September 16, 1954, he checked himself into Brooklyn State Hospital. Correctly diagnosed with Huntington's Disease, a hereditary disorder of the nervous system for which there is no cure, he was transferred to New Jersey State Hospital at Greystone Park. Marjorie resumed his care. Still, he continued to create: "Paper and pencil is my only little dose of relief for me." He considered the possibility of returning to sign painting once more for a living.

Despite his illness he maintained his uniqueness and connection to his art. As he lost fine motor coordination, his line assumed a heavier stroke and keyed-up color palette. Yet his singular voice is unmistakable: lively, powerful, vibrant, filled with movement and childlike wonder. This art was not the result of Huntington's, but rather in spite of the disease. His speech was beginning to slur, and writing was increasingly difficult, yet he still expressed himself through art when his other abilities had failed him. Through sheer force of will, he created through whatever means possible. And in typical fashion he persisted in his optimistic outlook with messages of peace and love. His belief in the dignity of common men and women, and the importance of thinking positively, was unflappable, even as he faced his greatest challenge.

Love is all force.
Love is all power.
Love is all energy.
Love is all strength.
Love is all health.
Love is all beauty.
Love is all good work, well done.

And:

Gonna tell y' what t'do if y' wanta win some peace;
Pray for it in your home; sing peace along y'r street;
Dance in Peace around your block;
dance it alla 'round y'r town;
Bark it up tow'rds th' moon; laff it all this world around.
Stir it up! Git in that old groove: Keep it comin'.

Woody working on artwork in Florida, 1953.

Referring to himself as "Woody Adversity Guthrie," his persevered:

This world it's hit me in my face
It's hit me over my head.
It's beat me black and blue and green
But still tho' I ain't dead

Woody Wilson Guthrie died on October 3, 1967, at age fifty-five. He had been hospitalized for thirteen years. We are left to wonder what his artistic output would have been if he had not taken ill at such an early age.

He left behind an outpouring of creativity that took various forms, twists and turns, raucous and spirited. He followed his own muse and ignored conventions. Underlying it all was a belief in the potential of humanity and the wonder of life. He created art for the masses, for his loved ones, and for himself, and his faith in all of us never wavered:

Worth Quoting:
The worst thing that can happen to you is to cut yourself loose from people. And the best thing is to sort of vaccinate yourself right into the . . . big streams and blood of the people.

To feel like you know the best and the worst of folks that you see everywhere and never to feel weak, or lost, or even lonesome anywhere.

There is just one thing that can cut you to drifting from the people, and that's any brand or style of greed.

There is just one way to save yourself, and that's to get together and work and fight for everyone.

— Woody Guthrie

In 1948, Woody and Marjorie created a songbook of Woody's children's songs. Cathy Ann had died the previous year in a fire in their Coney Island apartment. Arlo Guthrie was born seven months later, in July 1948. Dedicating the songbook to Cathy Ann and to Woody's children from his first marriage, Gwendolyn, Sue, and Bill, as well as to Arlo, they struggled to keep Cathy Ann's spirit alive and their future hopeful. Woody wrote and illustrated all the songs. Marjorie organized the book and wrote the musical notations.

The original manuscript for *Woody's 20 Grow Big Songs* was lost for more than forty years, later to be discovered on a shelf by a librarian at Sarah Lawrence College in New York. In 1992, a replication of the songbook was published by HarperCollins, along with an accompanying album recorded by the Guthrie children, Arlo, Joady, and Nora, and their children.

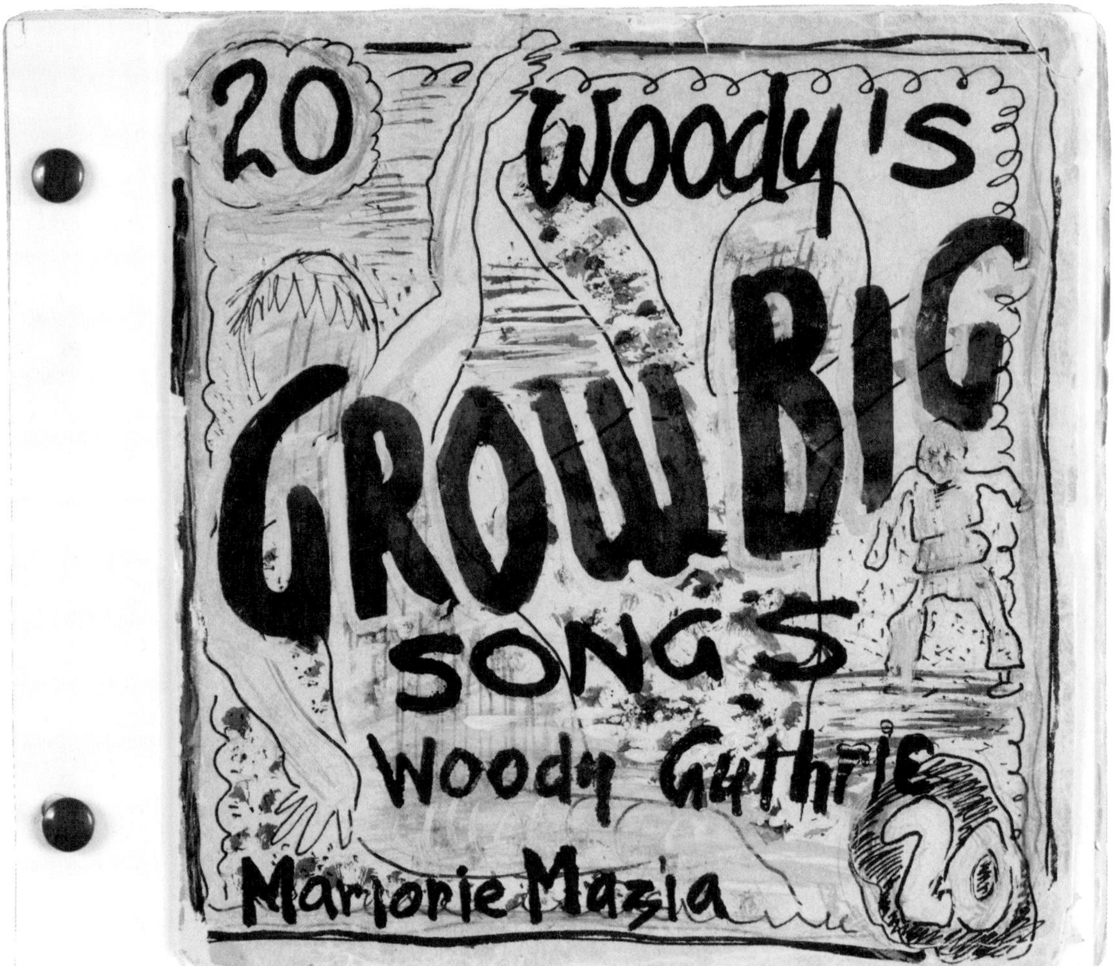

Song number
1. Wake up
2. Cleano
3. mailman
4. Put your Finger
5. Dance Around
6. Jigalong Home
7. MerryGoRound
8. Bling Blang
9. Howdy Doo
10. allWork Together
11. Build a House
12. Needle Sing
13. Pick it up
14. Riding In my Car
15. Race you Down the mountain
16. my Dolly
17. Little Seed
18. Little Bird
19. Pretty and Shinyo
20. Sleep Eye

No. 3

MAIL

I SEE THE MAIL MAN,
MAILY MAN, MAILER MAN,
I SEE MISTER MAIL MAN
WALKING DOWN MY STREET.

RUN, RUN, RUNNY RUN,
RUNNY RUNNY, RUN, RUN,
RUN, RUN, RUN, AND, RUN, RUN, RUN,
I RUNNY DOWN THE STREET.

HOWDY, MISTER MAIL MAN,
HOWDY, MISTER MAILY MAN,
HOWDY, MISTER MAILER MAN,
HAVE YOU A LETTER FOR ME?

I WILL LOOK AND SEE, SEE,
I WILL LOOK AND SEE, SEE,
I WILL LOOKY LOOK, SEE, S
IF I'VE A LETTER FOR YOU.

FLIPPITY, FLIPPITY, FLIP FLAP,
FLIP FLIP, FLIPPERTY, FLIP FLAP,
ZIPPERTY, ZIPPY, ZIP, ZOOP ZOOP,
I'M LOOKING IN TO SEE.

MAN

NO, NO, NOZIE, NO, NO,
NO, NO, NOZZELDY, NO, NO,
BIFFERTY, BOFFERTY, BOE, BOE,
I HAVE NO LETTER FOR YOU.

LOOK, LOOK, LOOK AGAIN, PLEASE,
LOOK, LOOK, LOOK AGAIN, PLEASE,
PLEAZEE, WEAZLEDY, CHEEZELDY, SQUEEZE,
LOOK ONCE MORE AND SEE.

O, NO, NISIR, NO, NO,
OPE SIR, NOPE SIR, DEAR SIR,
NIPPERS AND SNAPPERS AND RAINBOW CLAPPERS,
SEE NO LETTER FOR YOU.

WW, GOSH, AWW, GOLLY WHILLIKINZ,
ECK FIRE, GEE, MISTER MAILER MAN,
WW, SHUCKERS, JEEPERZ, CREEPLERZ,
NIFF. SNIFF. SNIFF, SNIFF. SNIFF.

GOODBYE, MISTER MAILY MAN,
I GUESS I'LL WALK BACK HOME AGAIN,
I'LL MEET YOU HERE TOMORROW,
AND ASKYOU ONCE AGAIN.

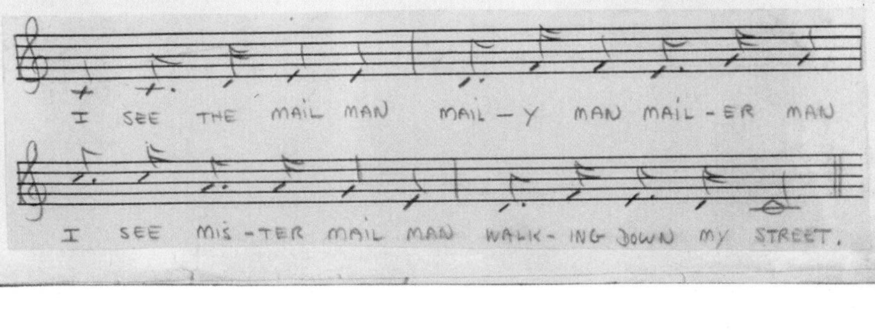
I SEE THE MAIL MAN MAIL — Y MAN MAIL - ER MAN
I SEE MIS - TER MAIL MAN WALK - ING DOWN MY STREET.

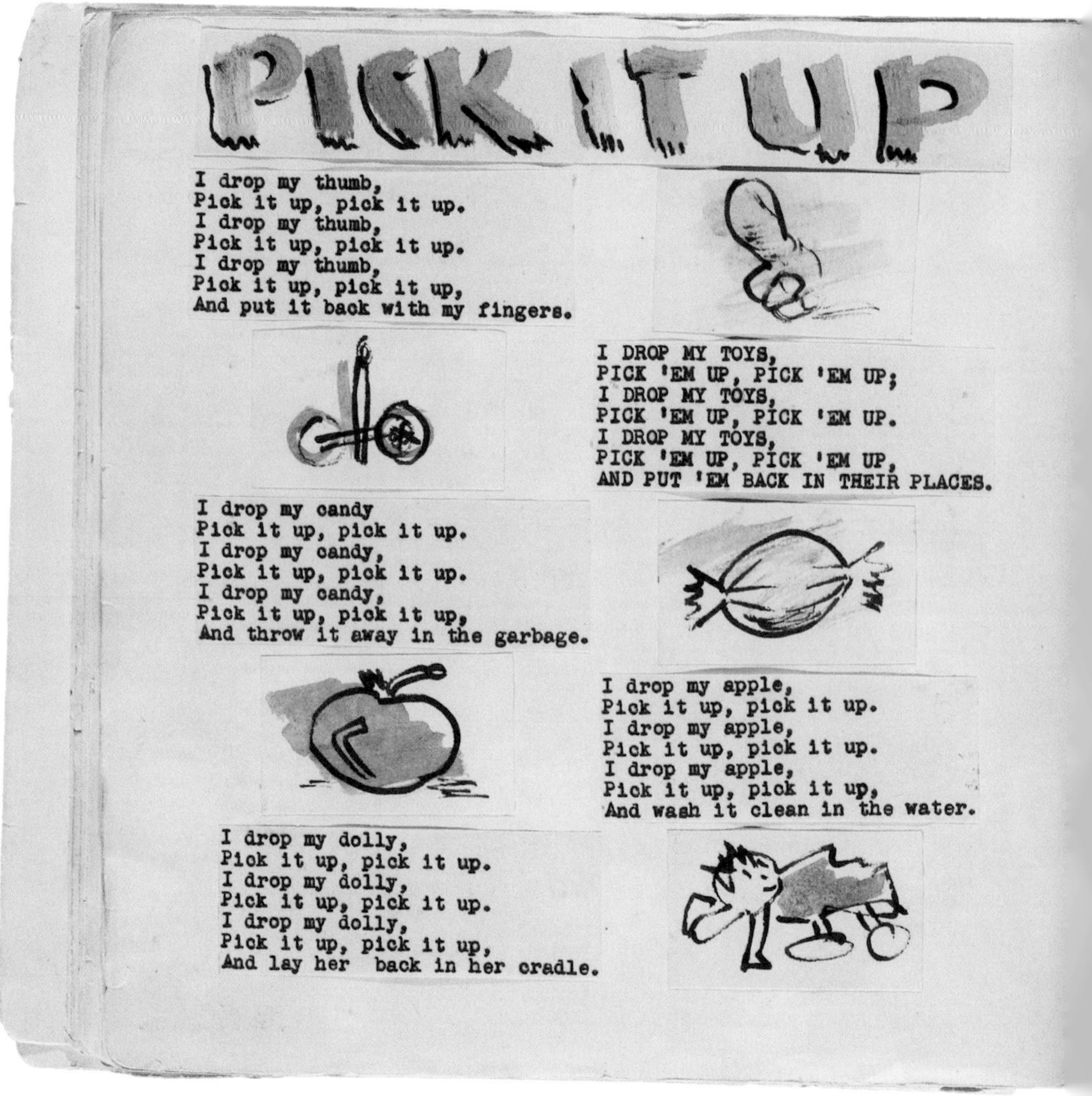

PICK IT UP

I drop my thumb,
Pick it up, pick it up.
I drop my thumb,
Pick it up, pick it up.
I drop my thumb,
Pick it up, pick it up,
And put it back with my fingers.

I DROP MY TOYS,
PICK 'EM UP, PICK 'EM UP;
I DROP MY TOYS,
PICK 'EM UP, PICK 'EM UP.
I DROP MY TOYS,
PICK 'EM UP, PICK 'EM UP,
AND PUT 'EM BACK IN THEIR PLACES.

I drop my candy
Pick it up, pick it up.
I drop my candy,
Pick it up, pick it up.
I drop my candy,
Pick it up, pick it up,
And throw it away in the garbage.

I drop my apple,
Pick it up, pick it up.
I drop my apple,
Pick it up, pick it up.
I drop my apple,
Pick it up, pick it up,
And wash it clean in the water.

I drop my dolly,
Pick it up, pick it up.
I drop my dolly,
Pick it up, pick it up.
I drop my dolly,
Pick it up, pick it up,
And lay her back in her cradle.

I drop my shoe,
Pick it up, pick it up.
I drop my shoe,
Pick it up, pick it up.
I drop my shoe,
Pick it up, pick it up,
And put it with my other shoe.

I drop my head,
Pick it up, pick it up.
I drop my head,
Pick it up, pick it up.
I drop my head,
Pick it up, pick it up,
And put it back on my shoulders.

PICK PICK PICK IT
PICK IT UP, PICK IT UP.
PICK, PICK, PICKIT,
PICK IT UP, PICK IT UP.
PICKA PICKA PICKY
PICK IT UP, PICK IT UP.
PICKA PICKA PICKA
PICK IT UP, PICK IT UP.

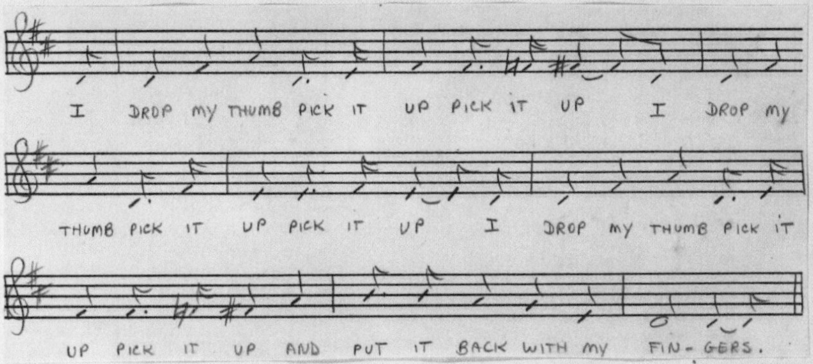
I DROP MY THUMB PICK IT UP PICK IT UP I DROP MY
THUMB PICK IT UP PICK IT UP I DROP MY THUMB PICK IT
UP PICK IT UP AND PUT IT BACK WITH MY FIN- GERS.

Okay, now, let's take turn about.
What do you want to drop and pick up?
It's your turn, now.
Loud. Louder. I want to hear you.

No. 13

8.

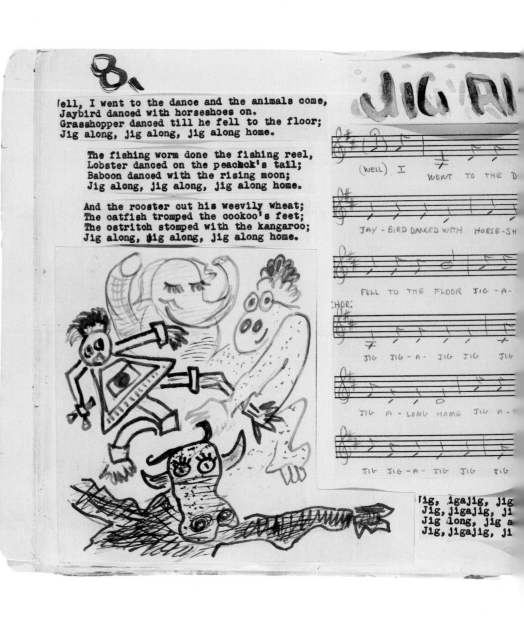

Well, I went to the dance and the animals come,
Jaybird danced with horseshoes on.
Grasshopper danced till he fell to the floor;
Jig along, jig along, jig along home.

The fishing worm done the fishing reel,
Lobster danced on the peacock's tail;
Baboon danced with the rising moon;
Jig along, jig along, jig along home.

And the rooster cut his weevily wheat;
The catfish tromped the cookoo's feet;
The ostritch stomped with the kangaroo;
Jig along, jig along, jig along home.

JIG A

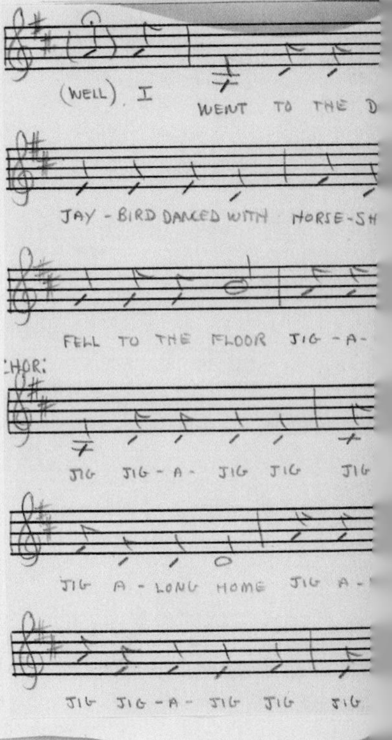
(WELL) I WENT TO THE D
JAY - BIRD DANCED WITH HORSE-SH
FELL TO THE FLOOR JIG - A -
CHOR:
JIG JIG - A - JIG JIG JIG
JIG A - LONG HOME JIG A -
JIG JIG - A - JIG JIG JIG

Jig, jigajig, jig
Jig, jigajig, ji
Jig along, jig a
Jig, jigajig, ji

...ong Home

And the an- i-mals come
...on grass-hop-per danced till he
jig-a-long jig-a-long home.
...long home jig jig-a- jig jig
jig-a-long jig a-long home
...long home.

...g along home,
...ig along home,
... jig along home,
...ig along home.

And the mama rat took off her hat,
Shook the house with the old tomcat;
Alligator beat his tail on the drum;
Jig along, jig along, jig along// home.

...e boards did rattle and the house did shake;
...he clouds they laughed and the world did quake;
...ew moon rattled some silver spoons;
...ig along, jig along, jig along home.

...he nails flew loose and the boards broke down;
Everybody danced around and around;
The house come down and the crowd went home;
Jig along, jig along, jig along home.

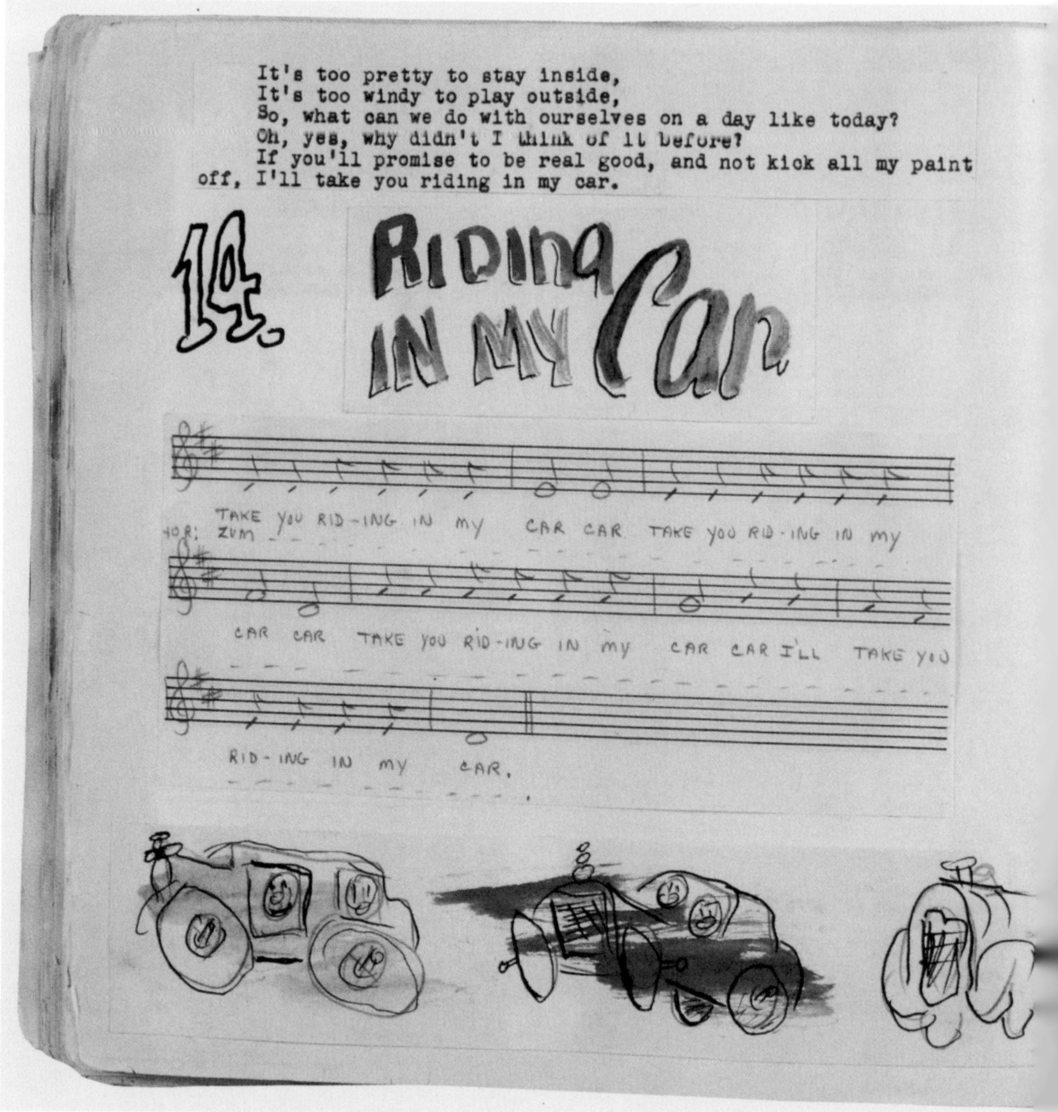

It's too pretty to stay inside,
It's too windy to play outside,
So, what can we do with ourselves on a day like today?
Oh, yes, why didn't I think of it before?
If you'll promise to be real good, and not kick all my paint off, I'll take you riding in my car.

14. RIDING IN MY CAR

TAKE YOU RID-ING IN MY CAR CAR TAKE YOU RID-ING IN MY
ZUM
CAR CAR TAKE YOU RID-ING IN MY CAR CAR I'LL TAKE YOU
RID-ING IN MY CAR.

254

TAKE YOU RIDING IN MY CAR, CAR,
TAKE YOU RIDING IN MY CAR, CAR,
TAKE YOU RIDING IN MY CAR, CAR,
I'LL TAKE YOU RIDING IN MY CAR.

CLICK CLAEK, OPEN UP A DOOR, GIRLS,
CLICK CLACK, OPEN UP A DOOR, BOYS,
FRONT DOOR, BACK DOOR, CLICKETY CLACK,
TAKE YOU RIDING IN MY CAR.

CLIMB CLIMB, RATTLE ON A FRONT SEAT,
SPREE I SPRADDLE ON A BACK SEAT,
TURN MY KEY, STEP ON MY STARTER,
TAKE YOU RIDING IN MY CAR.

ENGINE IT GOES, BRRM, BRRMM,
ENGINE IT GOES, BRRM, BRRM,
BRRM, BRRM, CHRRKA CHRRKA, BRRM, BRRM,
TAKE YOU RIDING IN MY CAR.

TREES AND HOUSES WALK ALONG,
TREES AND HOUSES WALK ALONG,
TRUCK AND A CAR, AND A GARBAGE CAN,
TAKE YOU RIDING IN MY CAR.

I'MA GONNA ROLL YOU HOME AGAIN,
I'MA GONNA ROLL YOU HOME AGAIN,
BRRM, BRRM, CHRRKA CHRRKA, ROLLY HOME,
TAKE YOU RIDING IN MY CAR.

I'MA GONNA LET YOU BLOW THE HORN,
I'MA GONNA LET YOU BLOW THE HORN,
OOORAH, OORAHH, OOGAH, OOOGAHH,
TAKE YOU RIDING IN MY CAR.

BRRM, BRRM, CHRRKA CHRRKA, BRRM, BRRM,
BRRM, BRRM, CHRRKA CHRRKA, BRRM, BRRM,
BRRM, BRRM, CHRRKA CHRRKA, BRRM, BRRM,
TAKE YOU RIDING IN MY CAR.

Woody Guthrie
Oct. 13
1948

The cover page of a letter written to Natanya Newman, Arlo Davy's babysitter, in January 1948. Woody imagines what his son will look like on his thirty-fifth birthday.

Woody writes using Arlo's persona, imagining how the six-month-old baby saw things.

3520 MERMAID AVENUE, BROOKLYN TWENTY FOUR NEW YORK CITY NEW YORK
[illegible] DAY OF [illegible] OF THE NEW YEAR OF NINETEEN AND FORTY EIGHT

MISS NATANYA NEWMAN
(I CALL YOU MISS BEFORE YOU GET A NEW MAN)

I GOT A GOOD LOOK AT THEM TWO SWEATERS WHICH YOU WENT DOWN TO THE STORE AND PICKED OUT FOR ME. I DIDNT KNOW THAT IT WAS YOU THAT PICKED THE SWEATERS OUT FOR ME TILL I HEARD MY DADDY WOODY AND MOMMY MARJORIE OUT HERE IN OUR BATHROOM HALL TALKING SO LOUD ABOUT THE SWEATERS. MY MAMA SAID THEY WAS A WONDERFUL COLOR, LIKE SOME KIND OF ICE CREAM WHICH YOU EAT WITH A SPOON. ALL I HEARD MY DAD SAY WAS THAT WASH THEM IN OUR KITCHEN SINK AND THEN POUR THE WATER OUT IN A WINEGLASS AND DRINK IT DOWN. IT WAS A HOUR OR SO BEFORE I GOT TO EVEN LOOK AT THE SWEATERS. AND, I JUST WANT TO LET YOU KNOW HOW PRETTY THEY BOTH LOOKED TO ME. TWO THE SAME COLOR, ONE WHICH I CAN BUTTON UP AND ONE WHICH I CAN RUN AND JUMP INSIDE OF.

ALL OF THE GOOD STUFF WHICH I DID HEAR MARJORIE AND WOODY SAY ABOUT THEM SWEATERS AND ABOUT YOU HAS SORT OF STUCK IN MY EARS LIKE FURNITURE WAX, AND I CAN'T SEEM TO SHAKE THE WORDS OUT. SO, ME BEING A GAY AND FAIRLY YOUNG BACHELOR WITH A LONG PARADE OF AWFUL GOOD LOOKING CLOTHINGS TO DECK OUT IN, AND YOU BEING, LIKE YOU SAY, MISS NATANIA, IN THE PLACE OF MRS. NATANIA, I GUESS IT'S OKAY BY ME IF YOU FINALLY DO COME AROUND TO THE FEELING THAT THIS LETTER IS PASSIONAL AND SEXUANATE. FLIRTY AND DIRTY, I GUESS OUR FOLKS WOULD CALL IT. I WAS BORN THIS WAY, FLIRTY, AND I CAN'T HELP THAT. I AM EITHER JUST ABOUT THE DIRTIEST MAN ON THE STREETS OR THE CLEANEST, I RUN SOMEWHERE IN BETWEEN THEM BOTH. I MUST BE QUITE A WOOER AND A SMOOTH OPERATOR, BECAUSE WOMEN AND GIRLS OF JUST ABOUT EVERY SIZE, SHAPE, FASHION, DESIGN, FORM, AGE, AND STATE OF GROWTH AND DEVELOPMENT ALL FALL UNDER THE LOOKS I SHOOT OUT OF MY EYES AT THEM. IF YOU COULD SEE HOW MANY OF THEM CROWD AROUND ME OUT HERE ON MY PASSION COUCH YOU'D GET WHAT I'M TRYING TO TELL YOU, WHAT I'M DRIVING AT, WHICH IS YOU.

YOU SEE, I GOT WAYS OF SEEING AND KNOWING STUFF WHICH NONE OF MY FOLKS KNOWS ABOUT. I GOT SEVEN HUNDRED AND SEVENTY SEVEN SENSES AND GIFTS OF MY MIND AND BRAIN WHICH THIS HUMAN RACE DIDN'T EVOLUTE UP TO, SO FAR, TILL NOW, YET, I MEAN. OH, I CAN'T EVEN WRITE ALL OF MY GIFTS DOWN HERE, BUT SINCE YOU DID FEEL THE URGE TO REACH OUT AND BUY ME THESE TWO PURPLISH SOUL COLORED COURTING SWEATERS, I FEEL LIKE I OWE YOU A SORT OF A SPECIAL DEBT, SO I'LL TELL YOU JUST HOW IT COME ABOUT THAT I AM FALLING SO FAST FOR YOU EVEN BEFORE, TO ALL OUTTER LOOKS AND APPEARANCES, I'VE GOT NO WAYS YET OF GETTING THE TOUCH ON YOU, OR, AS YOU WOULD SAY, GETTING IN TOUCH WITH YOU BY MALE NOR WIRE NOR WIRELESS. I GUESS YOU WANT TO KNOW, FIRST, AND HINDMOST, HOW IT WAS THAT I EVER DID GET MY SCREWS SO DEAD SET ON YOU AT SUCH A FAST RATE OF EARTHLY SPEED.

WELL. THIS IS BECAUSE YOU ARE A DANCER, SEE, A WHIRLER, A KICKER, A LOW BENDER AND A HIGH JUMPER. WELL, I'M ONE OF THESE THINGS, MY OWN SELF. I HAD A HECK OF A HARD TIME WAITING AROUND OUT YONDER IN THE WEEDS OF CREATION TILL I GOT A CHANCE TO BE BORN TO A PAIR OF DANCERS. I KNOW WHAT I WAS LOOKING FOR. I TOLD OLD PAPA CREATORE A HUNDRED TRIPS AND TIMES THAT I WAS WAITING FORTY THOUSAND CENTURIES IF I HAD TO WAIT THIS LONG TO GET BORN IN THE [illegible] A DANCER. MARJORIE SHE'S A DANCER, ONE OF THE BEST, [illegible] THE NICEST, AND PERTIEST TO LOOK AT. AND SO, WELL, THIS IS WHAT MAKES ME BY BLOOD AND CANDLEWAX BOUND AND EARMARKED TO BE BORN OUT HERE THROUGH THE EIGHTY SIX DOORS OF THE DANCING PLANETS. AND I'M HERE TO TELL YOU THAT YOU CAN'T DANCE YOUR DEEPEST DANCING TILL YOU SNATCH ONTO YOUR OTHER HALF, SEE, AND I'M TRYING TO TELL YOU, ALSO, TOO, ETC. THAT I AM HER. I MEAN, HIM. YOU'RE THE HER. [illegible] OF THIS, SEE, BECAUSE THE BIG FOLKS BACK OUT IN THE LANDS [illegible] MAKE DANCING BLOOD AND DANCING MUSLCES, IT'S ALL WROTE DOWN. I SEEN IT. I READ IT. I GOT THE SECRET COEDS RIGHT HERE IN MY FINGERPRINTS WHICH WILL UNRAVEL A LITTLE PLAINER FOR [illegible] TO SEE [illegible] DAY. YOU'D BE ABLE TO KNOW ALL OF THIS IF I COULD [illegible] A FEW CHANCES TO DANCE THE WORDS OUT FOR YOU.

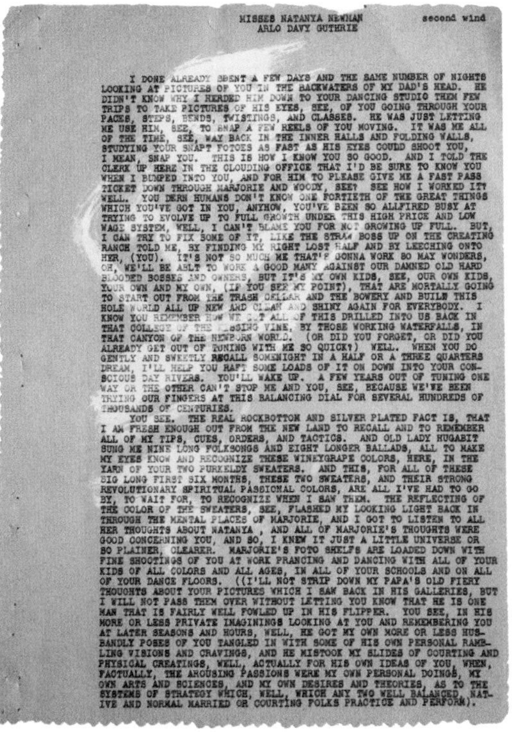

MISSES NATANYA NEWMAN — second wind
ARLO DAVY GUTHRIE

I DONE ALREADY SBENT A FEW DAYS AND THE SAME NUMBER OF NIGHTS LOOKING AT PICTURES OF YOU IN THE BACKWATERS OF MY DAD'S HEAD. HE DIDN'T KNOW WHY I HERDED HIM DOWN TO YOUR DANCING STUDIO THEM FEW TRIPS TO TAKE PICTURES OF HIS EYES, SEE, OF YOU GOING THROUGH YOUR PACES, STEPS, BENDS, TWISTINGS, AND CLASSES. HE WAS JUST LETTING ME USE HIM, SEE, TO SNAP A FEW REELS OF YOU MOVING. IT WAS ME ALL OF THE TIME, SEE, WAY BACK IN THE INNER HALLS AND FOLDING WALLS, STUDYING YOUR SNAPT FOTOES AS FAST AS HIS EYES COUDD SHOOT YOU, I MEAN, SNAP YOU. THIS IS HOW I KNOW YOU SO GOOD. AND I TOLD THE CLERK UP HERE IN THE CLOUDING OFFICE THAT I'D BE SURE TO KNOW YOU WHEN I BUMPED INTO YOU, AND FOR HIM TO PLEASE GIVE ME A FAST PASS TICKET DOWN THROUGH MARJORIE AND WOODY, SEE? SEE HOW I WORKED IT? WELL. YOU DERN HUMANS DON'T KNOW ONE FORTIETH OF THE GREAT THINGS WHICH YOU'VE GOT IN YOU, ANYHOW, YOU'VE BEEN SO ALLFIRED BUSY AT TRYING TO EVOLVE UP TO FULL GROWTH UNDER THIS HIGH PRICE AND LOW WAGE SYSTEM, WELL, I CAN'T BLAME YOU FOR NOT GROWING UP FULL. BUT, I CAN TRY TO FIX SOME OF IT, LIKE THE STRAW BOSS UP ON THE CREATING RANCH TOLD ME, BY FINDING MY RIGHT LOST HALF AND BY LEECHING ONTO HER, (YOU). IT'S NOT SO MUCH ME THAT'S GONNA WORK SO MAY WONDERS, OH, WE'LL BE ABLT TO WORK A GOOD MANY AGAINST OUR DAMNED OLD HARD BLOODED BOSSES AND OWNERS, BUT IT'S MY OWN KIDS, SEE, OUR OWN KIDS, YOUR OWN AND MY OWN, (IF YOU SEE MY POINT), THAT ARE MORTALLY GOING TO START OUT FROM THE TRASH CELLAR AND THE BOWERY AND BUILD THIS HOLE WORLD ALL UP NEW AND CLEAN AND SHINY AGAIN FOR EVERYBODY. I KNOW YOU REMEMBER HOW WE GOT ALL OF THIS DRILLED INTO US BACK IN THAT COLLEGE OF THE KISSING VINE, BY THOSE WORKING WATERFALLS, IN THAT CANYON OF THE NEWBORN WORLD. (OR DID YOU FORGET, OR DID YOU ALREADY GET OUT OF TUNING WITH ME SO QUICK?) WELL. WHEN YOU DO GENTLY AND SWEETLY RECALL SOMENIGHT IN A HALF OR A THREE QUARTERS DREAM, I'LL HELP YOU RAFT SOME LOADS OF IT ON DOWN INTO YOUR CONSCIOUS DAY RIVERS. YOU'LL WAKE UP. A FEW YEARS OUT OF TUNING ONE WAY OR THE OTHER CAN'T STOP ME AND YOU, SEE, BECAUSE WE'VE BEEN TRYING OUR FINGERS AT THIS BALANCING DIAL FOR SEVERAL HUNDREDS OF THOUSANDS OF CENTURIES.

YOU SEE. THE REAL ROCKBOTTOM AND SILVER PLATED FACT IS, THAT I AM FRESH ENOUGH OUT FROM THE NEW LAND TO RECALL AND TO REMEMBER ALL OF MY TIPS, CUES, ORDERS, AND TACTICS. AND OLD LADY HUGABIT SUNG ME NINE LONG FOLKSONGS AND EIGHT LONGER BALLADS, ALL TO MAKE MY EYES KNOW AND RECOGNIZE THESE WINEYGRAPE COLORS, HERE, IN THE YARN OF YOUR TWO PURKELDY SWEATERS. AND THIS, FOR ALL OF THESE BIG LONG FIRST SIX MONTHS, THESE TWO SWEATERS, AND THEIR STRONG REVOLUTIONARY SPIRITUAL PASSIONAL COLORS, ARE ALL I'VE HAD TO GO BY, TO WAIT FOR, TO RECOGNIZE WHEN I SAW THEM. THE REFLECTING OF THE COLOR OF THE SWEATERS, SEE, FLASHED MY LOOKING LIGHT BACK IN THROUGH THE MENTAL PLACES OF MARJORIE, AND I GOT TO LISTEN TO ALL HER THOUGHTS ABOUT NATANYA , AND ALL OF MARJORIE'S THOUGHTS WERE GOOD CONCERNING YOU, AND SO, I KNEW IT JUST A LITTLE UNIVERSE OR SO PLAINER, CLEARER. MARJORIE'S FOTO SHELFS ARE LOADED DOWN WITH FINE SHOOTINGS OF YOU AT WORK PRANCING AND DANCING WITH ALL OF YOUR KIDS OF ALL COLORS AND ALL AGES, IN ALL OF YOUR SCHOOLS AND ON ALL OF YOUR DANCE FLOORS. ((I'LL NOT STRIP DOWN MY PAPA'S OLD FIERY THOUGHTS ABOUT YOUR PICTURES WHICH I SAW BACK IN HIS GALLERIES, BUT I WILL NOT PASS THEM OVER WITHOUT LETTING YOU KNOW THAT HE IS ONE MAN THAT IS FAIRLY WELL FOWLED UP IN HIS FLIPPER. YOU SEE, IN HIS MORE OR LESS PRIVATE IMAGININGS LOOKING AT YOU AND REMEMBERING YOU AT LATER SEASONS AND HOURS, WELL, HE GOT MY OWN MORE OR LESS HUSBANDLY POSES OF YOU TANGLED IN WITH SOME OF HIS OWN PERSONAL RAMBLING VISIONS AND CRAVINGS, AND HE MISTOOK MY SLIDES OF COURTING AND PHYSICAL CREATINGS, WELL, ACTUALLY FOR HIS OWN IDEAS OF YOU, WHEN, FACTUALLY, THE AROUSING PASSIONS WERE MY OWN PERSONAL DOINGS, MY OWN ARTS AND SCIENCES, AND MY OWN DESIRES AND THEORIES, AS TO THE SYSTEMS OF STRATEGY WHICH, WELL, WHICH ANY TWO WELL BALANCED, NATIVE AND NORMAL MARRIED OR COURTING FOLKS PRACTICE AND PERFORM).

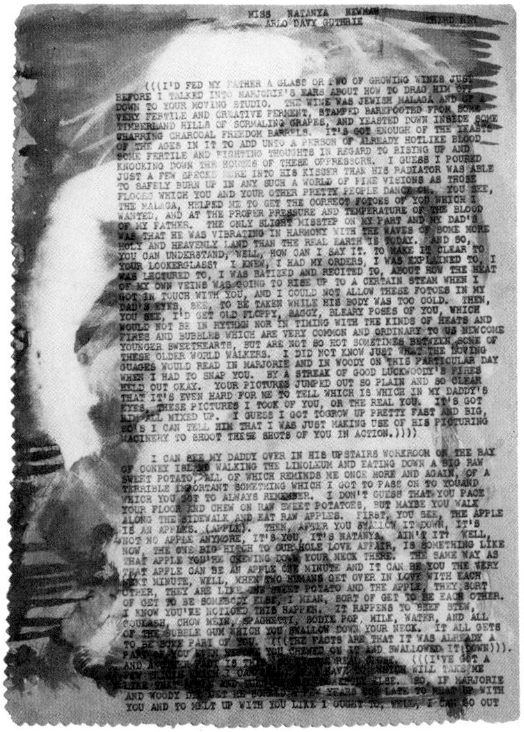

MISS NATANYA NEWMAN — THIRD [illegible]
ARLO DAVY GUTHRIE

(((I'D FED MY FATHER A GLASS OR TWO OF GROWING WINES JUST BEFORE I TALKED INTO MARJORIE'S EARS ABOUT HOW TO DRAG HIM OFF DOWN TO YOUR MOVING STUDIO. THE WINE WAS JEWISH MALAGA AND OF A VERY FERTILE AND CREATIVE FERMENT, STAMPED BAREFOOTED FROM SOME TIMBERLAND HILLS OF SCRMALING GRAPES, AND YEASTED DOWN INSIDE SOME CHARRING CHARCOAL FREEDOM BARRELS. IT'S GOT ENOUGH OF THE YEASTS OF THE AGES IN IT TO ADD UNTO A PERSON OF ALREADY HOTLIKE BLOOD SOME FERTILE AND FIGHTING THOUGHTS IN REGARD TO RISING UP AND KNOCKING DOWN THE HOUSES OF THESE OPPRESSORS. I GUESS I POURED JUST A FEW SPECKS MORE INTO HIS KISSER THAN HIS RADIATOR WAS ABLE TO SAFELY BURN UP IN ANY SUCH A WORLD OF FINE VISIONS AS THOSE FLOORS WHICH YOU AND YOUR OTHER PRETTY PEOPLE DANCE ON. YOU SEE, THE MALAGA, HELPED ME TO GET THE CORRECT FOTOES OF YOU WHICH I WANTED, AND AT THE PROPER PRESSURE AND TEMPERATURE OF THE BLOOD OF MY FATHER. THE ONLY SLIGHT MISSTEP ON MY PART AND MY DAD'S WAS THAT HE WAS VIBRATING IN HARMONY WITH THE WAVES OF SOME MORE HOLY AND HEAVENLY LAND THAN THE REAL EARTH IS TODAY. AND SO, YOU CAN UNDERSTAND, WELL, HOW CAN I SAY IT. TO MAKE IT CLEAR TO YOUR LOOKERGLASS? I KNEW, I HAD MY ORDERS, I WAS EXPLAINED TO, I WAS LECTURED TO, I WAS BATIZED AND RECITED TO, ABOUT HOW THE HEAT OF MY OWN VEINS WAS GOING TO RISE UP TO A CERTAIN STEAM WHEN I GOT IN TOUCH WITH YOU, AND I COULD NOT ALLOW THESE FOTOES IN MY DAD'S EYES, SEE, TO BE TAKEN WHILE HIS BODY WAS TOO COLD. THEN, YOU SEE, I'D GET OLD FLOPPY, SAGGY, BLEARY POSES OF YOU, WHICH WOULD NOT BE IN RYTHEM NOR IN TIMING WITH THE KINDS OF HEATS AND FIRES AND BUBBLES WHICH ARE VERY COMMON AND ORDINARY TO US NEWCOME YOUNGER SWEETHEARTS, BUT ARE NOT SO HOT SOMETIMES BETWEEN SOME OF THESE OLDER WORLD WALKERS. I DID NOT KNOW JUST WHAT THE LOVING GUAGES WOULD READ IN MARJORIE AND IN WOODY ON THIS PARTICULAR DAY WHEN I HAD TO SNAP YOU. BY A STREAK OF GOOD LUCKWOODY'S FIRES HELD OUT OKAY. YOUR PICTURES JUMPED OUT SO PLAIN AND SO CLEAR THAT IT'S EVEN HARD FOR ME TO TELL WHICH IS WHICH IN MY DADDY'S EYES, THESE PICTURES I TOOK OF YOU, OR THE REAL YOU. IT'S GOT HIM ALL MIXED UP. I GUESS I GOT TOGROW UP PRETTY FAST AND BIG, SO'S I CAN TELL HIM THAT I WAS JUST MAKING USE OF HIS PICTURING MACINERY TO SHOOT THESE SHOTS OF YOU IN ACTION.))))

I CAN SEE MY DADDY OVER IN HIS UPSTAIRS WORKROOM ON THE BAY OF CONEY ISLAND WALKING THE LINOLEUM AND EATING DOWN A BIG RAW SWEET POTATO, ALL OF WHICH REMINDS ME ONCE MORE AND AGAIN, OF A TERRIBLE IMPORTANT SOMETHING WHICH I GOT TO PASS ON TO YOUAND WHICH YOU GOT TO ALWAYS REMEMBER. I DON'T GUESS THAT YOU PACE YOUR FLOOR AND CHEW ON RAW SWEET POTATOES, BUT MAYBE YOU WALK ALONG THE SIDEWALK AND EAT RAW APPLES. FIRST, YOU SEE, THE APPLE IS AN APPLES. (APPLE). THEN, AFTER YOU SWALLOW IT DOWN, IT'S NOT NO APPLE ANYMORE, IT'S YOU, IT'S NATANYA. AIN'T IT? WELL, NOW, THE ONE BIG HITCH TO OUR HOLE LOVE AFFAIR, IS SOMETHING LIKE THAT APPLE YOU'RE CHEWING DOWN YOUR NECK THERE. THE SAME WAY AS THAT APPLE CAN BE AN APPLE ONE MINUTE AND IT CAN BE YOU THE VERY NEXT MINUTE, WELL, WHEN TWO HUMANS GET OVER IN LOVE WITH EACH OTHER, THEY ARE LIKE THE SWEET POTATO AND THE APPLE, THEY SORT OF GET TO BE SOMEBODY ELSE, I MEAN, SORT OF GET TO BE EACH OTHER. I KNOW YOU'VE NOTICED THIS HAPPEN. IT HAPPENS TO BEEF STEW, GOULASH, CHOW MEIN, SPAGHETTI, SODIE POP, MILK, WATER, AND ALL OF THE BUBBLE GUM WHICH YOU SWALLOW DOWN YOUR NECK. IT ALL GETS TO BE SOME PART OF YOU. (((THE FACTS ARE THAT IT WAS ALREADY A PART OF YOU [illegible] YOU CHEWED ON IT AND SWALLOWED IT DOWN))). AND [illegible] IS [illegible] (((I'VE GOT A [illegible] WHICH I CA[illegible] WILL TAKE ME [illegible] ELSE. SO, IF MARJORIE AND WOODY [illegible] YEARS [illegible] LATE TO [illegible] UP WITH YOU AND TO MELT UP WITH YOU LIKE I OUGHT TO, WELL, I CAN GO OUT

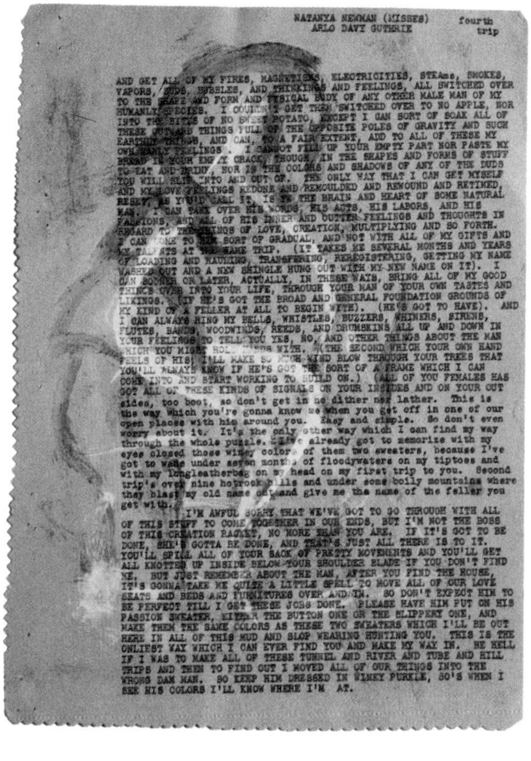

NATANYA NEWMAN (MISSES) — fourth trip
ARLO DAVY GUTHRIE

AND GET ALL OF MY FIRES, MAGNETISMS, ELECTRICITIES, STEAms, SMOKES, VAPORS, SUDS, BUBBLES, AND THINKINGS AND FEELINGS, ALL SWITCHED OVER TO THE SHAPE AND FORM AND PHYSICAL BODY OF ANY OTHER MALE MAN OF MY HUMANLY SPECIES. I COULDN'T GET THEM SWITCHED OVER TO NO APPLE, NOR INTO THE BITES OF NO SWEET POTATO, EXCEPT I CAN SORT OF SOAK ALL OF THESE OUTWARD THINGS FULL OF THE OPPOSITE POLES OF GRAVITY AND SUCH EARTHLY THINGS, AND CAN, TO A FAIR EXTENT, ADD TO ALL OF THESE MY OWN MANLY FEELINGS . I CANNOT FILL UP YOUR EMPTY PART NOR PASTE MY BREAD IN YOUR EMPTY CRACK, THOUGH, IN THE SHAPES AND FORMS OF STUFF TO EAT AND DRINK, NOR IN THE COLORS AND SHADOWS OF ANY OF THE DUDS YOU WILL SLIP INTO AND OUT OF. THE ONLY WAY THAT I CAN GET MYSELF AND MY LOVE FEELINGS REDONE AND REMOULDED AND REWOUND AND RETIMED, RESET, AS YOU'D CALL IT, IS IN THE BRAIN AND HEART OF SOME NATURAL MAN. I CAN TAKE OVER HIS WORDS, HIS ACTS, HIS LABORS, AND HIS PASSIONS, AND ALL OF HIS INNER AND OUTTER FEELINGS AND THOUGHTS IN REGARD TO THE THINGS OF LOVE, CREATION, MULTIPLYING AND SO FORTH. I CAN COME TO HIM SORT OF GRADUAL, AND NOT WITH ALL OF MY GIFTS AND MY TALENTS AT THE SAME TRIP. (IT TAKES ME SEVERAL MONTHS AND YEARS OF LOADING AND HAULING, TRANSFERING, REREGISTERING, GETTING MY NAME WASHED OUT AND A NEW SHINGLE HUNG OUT WITH MY NEW NAME ON IT). I CAN SOONER OR LATER, ACTUALLY, IN THESE WAYS, BRING ALL OF MY GOOD THINGS OVER INTO YOUR LIFE, THROUGH YOUR MAN OF YOUR OWN TASTES AND LIKINGS. (IF HE'S GOT THE BROAD AND GENERAL FOUNDATION GROUNDS OF MY KIND OF A FELLER AT ALL TO BEGIN WITH). (HE'S GOT TO HAVE). AND I CAN ALWAYS RING MY BELLS, WHISTLES, BUZZERS, WHINERS, SIRENS, FLUTES, BANDS, WOODWINDS, REEDS, AND DRUMSKINS ALL UP AND DOWN IN YOUR FEELINGS TO TELL YOU YES, NO, AND OTHER THINGS ABOUT THE MAN WHICH YOU MIGHT HOL[illegible] WITH. ((THE SECOND WHICH YOUR OWN HAND FEELS OF HIS, I'LL MAKE SO MUCH WIND BLOW THROUGH YOUR TREES THAT YOU'LL ALWAYS KNOW IF HE'S GOT THE SORT OF A FRAME WHICH I CAN COME INTO AND START WORKING TO BUILD ON.) (ALL OF YOU FEMALES HAS GOT ALL OF THESE KINDS OF SIGNALS ON YOUR INSIDES AND ON YOUR OUT sides, too boot, so don't get in no dither nor lather. This is the way which you're gonna know me when you get off in one of our open places with him around you. Easy and simple. So don't even worry about it. It's the only other way which I can find my way through the whole puzzle. I've already got to memorize with my eyes closed those winey colors of them two sweaters, because I've got to wade under seven months of floodywaters on my tiptoes and with my longleatherbag on my head on my first trip to you. Second trip's over nine hotrock hills and under some boily mountains where they blast my old name out and give me the name of the feller you get with.

I'M AWFUL SORRY THAT WE'VE GOT TO GO THROUGH WITH ALL OF THIS STUFF TO COME TOGETHER IN OUR ENDS, BUT I'M NOT THE BOSS OF THIS CREATION RACKET, NO MORE THAN YOU ARE. IF IT'S GOT TO BE DONE, SHE'S GOTTA BE DONE, AND THAT'S JUST ALL THERE IS TO IT. YOU'LL SPILL ALL OF YOUR BACK OF PRETTY MOVEMENTS AND YOU'LL GET ALL KNOTTED UP INSIDE BELOW YOUR SHOULDER BLADE IF YOU DON'T FIND ME. BUT JUST REMEMBER ABOUT THE MAN, AFTER YOU FIND THE HOUSE, IT'S GONNA TAKE ME QUITE A LITTLE SPELL TO MOVE ALL OF OUR LOVE SEATS AND BEDS AND FURNITURES OVER AND IN. SO DON'T EXPECT HIM TO BE PERFECT TILL I GET THESE JOBS DONE. PLEASE HAVE HIM PUT ON HIS PASSION SWEATER, EITHER THE BUTTON ONE OR THE SLIPPERY ONE, AND MAKE THEM THE SAME COLORS AS THESE TWO SWEATERS WHICH I'LL BE OUT HERE IN ALL OF THIS MUD AND SLOP WEARING HUNTING YOU. THIS IS THE ONLIEST WAY WHICH I CAN EVER FIND YOU AND MAKE MY WAY IN. BE HELL IF I WAS TO MAKE ALL OF THESE TUNNEL AND RIVER AND TUBE AND HILL TRIPS AND THEN TO FIND OUT I MOVED ALL OF OUR THINGS INTO THE WRONG DAM MAN. SO KEEP HIM DRESSED IN WINEY PURKLE, SO'S WHEN I SEE HIS COLORS I'LL KNOW WHERE I'M AT.

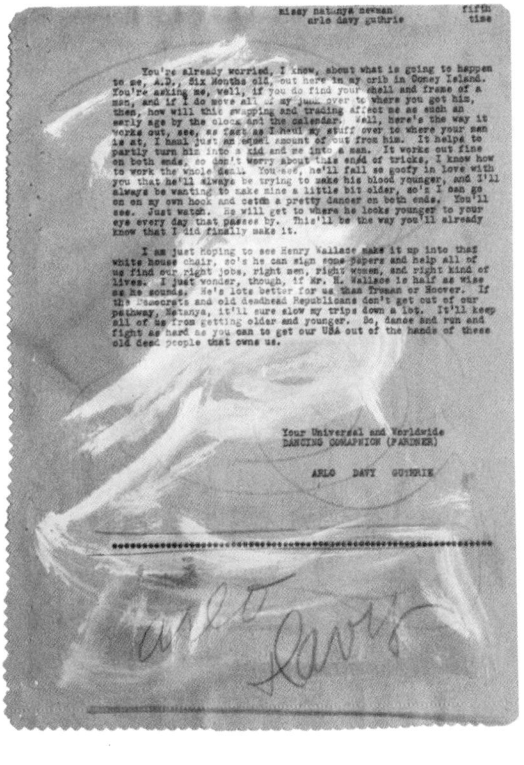

missy natanya newman — fifth time
arlo davy guthrie

You're already worried, I know, about what is going to happen to me, A.D., Six Months old, out here in my crib in Coney Island. You're asking me, well, if you do find your shell and frame of a man, and if I do move all of my junk over to where you got him, then, how will this swapping and trading affect me as such an early age by the clock and the calendar. Well, here's the way it works out, see, as fast as I haul my stuff over to where your man is at, I haul just an equal amount of out from him. It helps to partly turn him into a kid and me into a man. It works out fine on both ends, so don't worry about this end of tricks, I know how to work the whole deal. You see, he'll fall so goofy in love with you that he'll always be trying to make his blood younger, and I'll always be wanting to make mine a little bit older, so's I can go on on my own hook and catch a pretty dancer on both ends. You'll see. Just watch. He will get to where he looks younger to your eye every day that passes by. This'll be the way you'll already know that I did finally make it.

I am just hoping to see Henry Wallace make it up into that white house chair, so's he can sign some papers and help all of us find our right jobs, right men, right women, and right kind of lives. I just wonder, though, if Mr. H. Wallace is half as wise as he sounds. He's lots better for us than Truman or Hoover. If the Democrats and old deadhead Republicans don't get out of our pathway, Natanya, it'll sure slow my trips down a lot. It'll keep all of us from getting older and younger. So, dance and run and fight as hard as you can to get our USA out of the hands of these old dead people that owns us.

Your Universal and Worldwide
DANCING COMAPNION (PARDNER)

ARLO DAVY GUTHRIE

arlo davy

March 30th, 1948
old thoughts wash in
where new plans come to grow

A self-portrait in pencil, left, stands in contrast to an abstract portrait, across. Woody often worked in varying styles during the same periods, although there is a similarity in his curvilinear strokes.

"Cripple Annie" was most likely someone Woody actually knew from his Coney Island neighborhood. His portraits reflect his own sense of beauty, one that he saw daily in ordinary life, rather than a conventional ideal that doesn't actually exist.

Dear Henry
Thanks for your
big long letter asking
me for my autograph on a
foto of myself. I'm not
got any fotos. This is
more like me than any
foto I ever had.
You aim to have the
biggest foto collection in the
world, this one is
a good big one.
Hope you make
it.

your friend
Woody Guthrie
Feb. 14, 1948

A letter to a fan in response to a request
for a signed autograph on a photo.

239

UNPAID DEBTS ....
....
....
....
....
....

The air and the wind that I pull into my mouth tonight through the bowl and the stem pf my newly bought pipe has the taste and the feel of the late fall of the year about it.

The time & season is really the early part of the Month Of May. Rozzy is gone to plead her case around among her friends. Marjorie (and New Katie), are both over at Newark Y teaching more folks how to stand up good and live life goodly. I am here by my machine wondering which words of self defense I'll take in the Case of the Obscene Letters, (coming uply).

I can't claim to believe that Mary Ruth did wrong. She done just as right as she knew how. I'll not try to claim neither, that I did sadly nor badly wrong. I meant her no hurt. I meant to do her no harm. I meant, in my own ways, to bring some good things into her life. She used her womanly right to turn down all of my letters & all of my proposals. I see no fault nor blame in Mary Ruth.

I [illegible] this one word off my chest here tonight. I hope that someday, the whole round world will read these words and see the truth and facts of them. The sexual ignorance of all of us has already loaded our jailcells, our howling asylum walls, and our prison doors & windows full, doublefull, and overflowing. I'm not afraid of either one of the Three Places, nor all three of them. I can keep on writing my songs, my ballads, and my articles & stories, in all of these places. Some of my very best words can be written down behind the winding key. I just hope that Marjorie can sell a few of my writings to partly pay her and her people back for all of this unpaid debt I owe them.

Woody Guthrie

A pencil sketch of a man watching the Army Day Parade, New York, 1948.

Elvida B Lowsley
Rabbit Hopper
Husband
Woody Guthrie
April Firsto, 1948

Woody Guthrie

Another series of watercolors and text that fills an unlined marble notebook. It is a single letter to Marjorie in which Woody delves deeply into the restorative powers and meaning of family (in particular children) and the absence of these feelings in society. Recalling his unhappy time spent in the army, distanced from everything he loved and valued, he expressed himself in black and blue.

You never could
grow up here and
eat and drink our
things
without being born
a baby
and a little kid
first
Just like me and all of us

I know and see a
law above your
no kid law
a law that
says Before you can
be like a man
or be like a Woman
you've got to be
just like a little
Boy and a
little girl

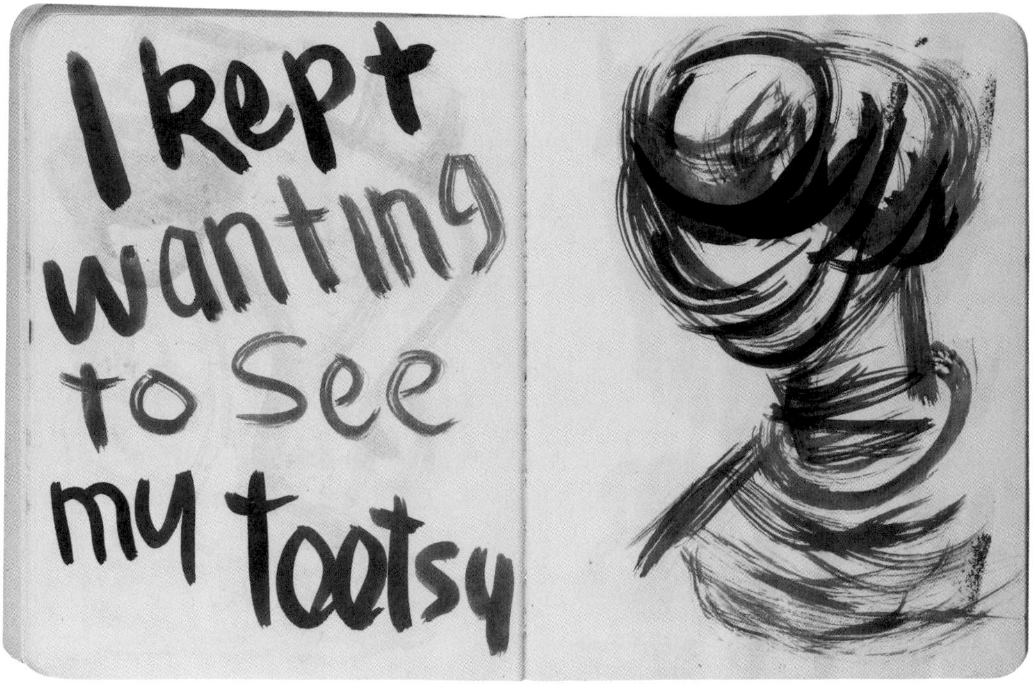
I kept
wanting
to See
my tootsy

the army camp was a crazy place
to ME

271

Where I didn't know a soul for 18 MONTHS

You've got to play
my Peekaboo game
and play my
hide & go seek game
my jumpy rope
game
Before you ever
get old enutt and
dead enough to
play this greedy
old landlord game
no Kids allowed

no children

I SAID TO
MY WIFE
I SURE DID
FEEL GLAD
that WE
Had OUR
KIDS

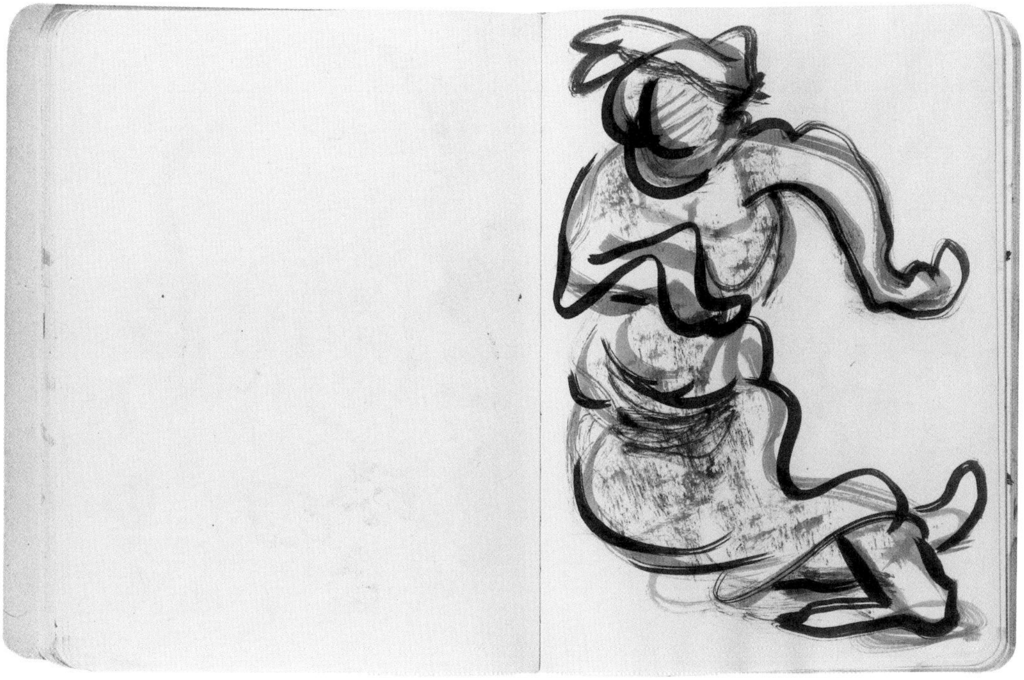

276

During the 1940s, Marjorie was touring with the Martha Graham Dance Company and teaching full-time at the Graham school in New York City. Woody was often left in charge of the children. Using inexpensive construction paper, watercolors, and colored chalks readily available at the corner store, Woody created artworks based on his daily life at home with the children. Sprawled out on the floor with records playing, his children created their own artwork alongside him. Taking an image, a phrase, or a rhyme from their spontaneous outpourings, Woody would expand the idea into a new song or painting. Conversely, new ideas for songs often evolved from these pictures, and he would quickly type a lyric line over it. Many of his children's songs, recorded on Folkways Records in the late 1940s, were created in this way.

atom
dance
Woody Guthrie
WG

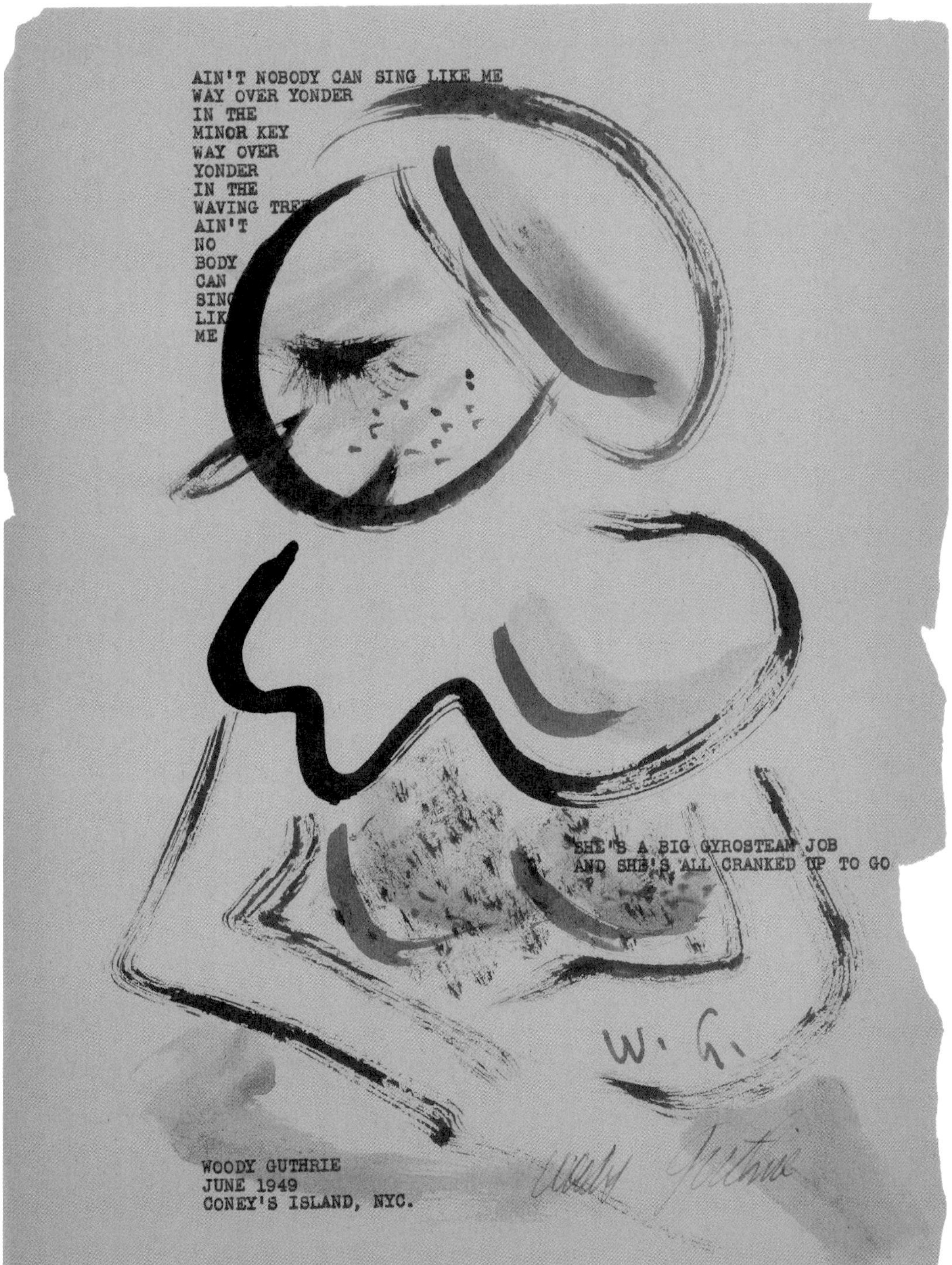
AIN'T NOBODY CAN SING LIKE ME
WAY OVER YONDER
IN THE
MINOR KEY
WAY OVER
YONDER
IN THE
WAVING TREE
AIN'T
NO
BODY
CAN
SING
LIKE
ME
SHE'S A BIG GYROSTEAM JOB
AND SHE'S ALL CRANKED UP TO GO
W. G.
WOODY GUTHRIE
JUNE 1949
CONEY'S ISLAND, NYC.
Woody Guthrie

Woody Guthrie

WG
Woody Guthrie

Woody Guthrie

WG
Woody Guthrie

why O why
W G
woody guthrie

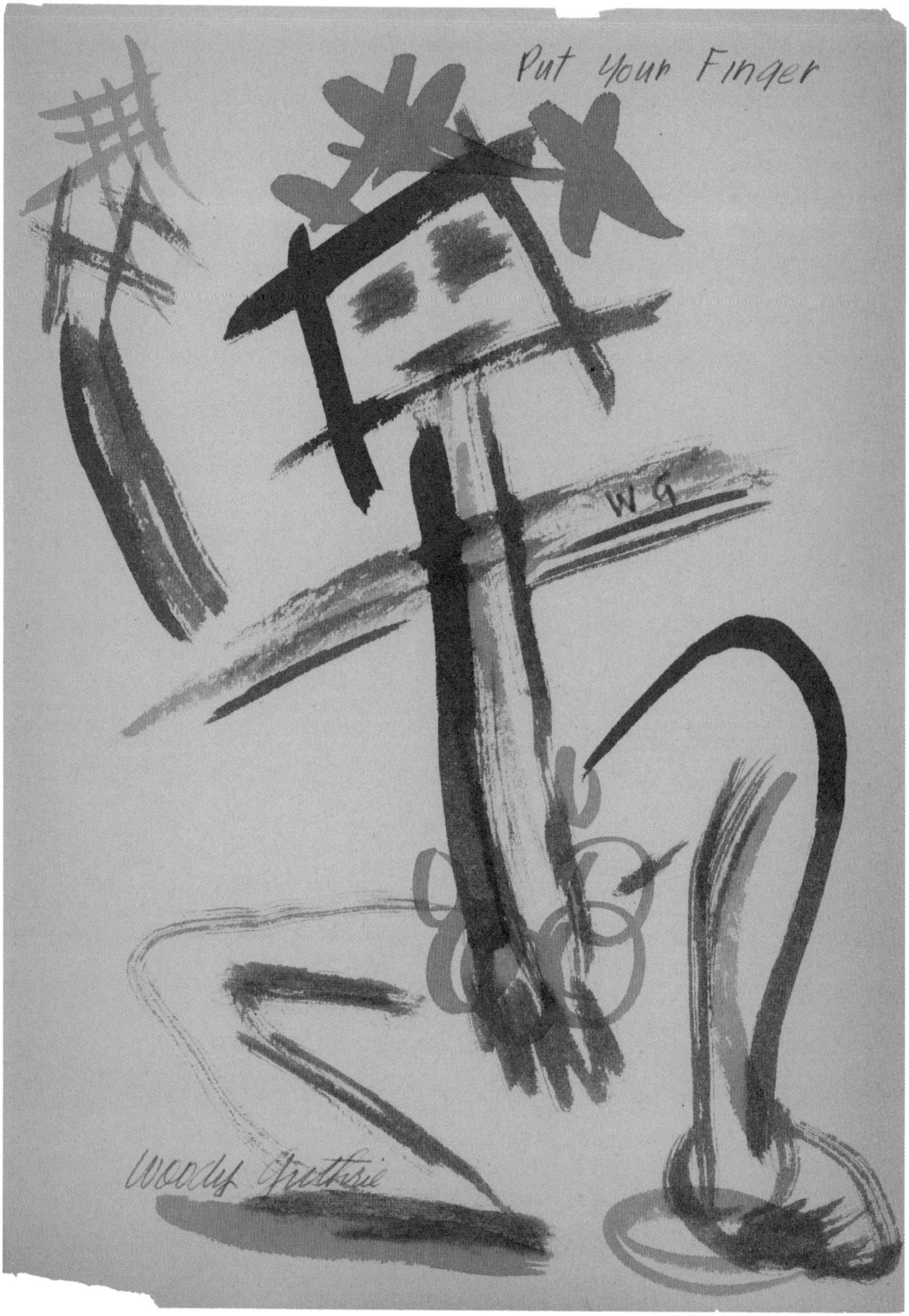
Put Your Finger
WG
Woody Guthrie

WG

288

289

OLDE MAN
ARLO DYBUCK DAVY
HE LOVES MEAT
HE LOVES GRAVY
SOMETIMES ONIONS
SOMETIMES 'TATERZ
OLDE MAN
ARLO
DYBUCK
DAVY ...
Woody Guthrie
WOODY GUTHRIE
JUNE 15th, 1949
Coney Highlands, NYCity

Woody Guthrie

WOODY GUTHRIE
3520 Mermaid Avenue
Brooklyn, 24, N.Y.
June 23rd, 1949
Woody Guthrie
I LIKE TO SWIM
IN MY WATER

WOODY GUTHRIE

Rare pastel portraits.

No Hand for trouble
Woody Guthrie
Coney Island
1949

DIRTY DISHES

I'VE SEEN MY SHARE
OF SAD & TERRIBLE THINGS
ON AND AROUND THIS WORLD
WHILST I MADE MY TRIP HERE
AND THE SADDEST
AND THE WORST THING
WHICH I'VE SO FAR SIGHTED
OR SEEN
WAS A SINK PILED UP FULL
OF OLD DIRTY DISHES
AFTER ALL OF THE DIRTIERS HAD GONE
TO LEAVE
THEIR LIPSTICK
AND THEIR HANDYMARKS
ON THE SINK FULL OF DIRTY DISHES
AND THE ONLY REAL GENIUS
OR THE ONLY WORKER
THE ONLY ARTIST
WORTH HIS OR HER FOOD AND SALTBLOCK
IS THE ONE
BIG OR LITTLE
THAT JUMPS INTO THAT SINK FULL
OF DIRTY DISHES
AND GETS THEM ALL PRETTY & SHINYOE
BY THE TIME THE SUN COMES IN
TO SHINE ON THEM.

SOCIALISM IS GOING TO DO AWAY
WITH SINKS PILED FULL OF VISITORS
THAT GO OFF HOME
AND LEAVE YOU NOTHING BUT
A HEADACHE & A HEARTACHE TO
GREET THE MORNING WITH.

OF THIS I'M SURE.

WOODY GUTHRIE
Corny Islande
May 16th, 1949

----- 30 30 -----

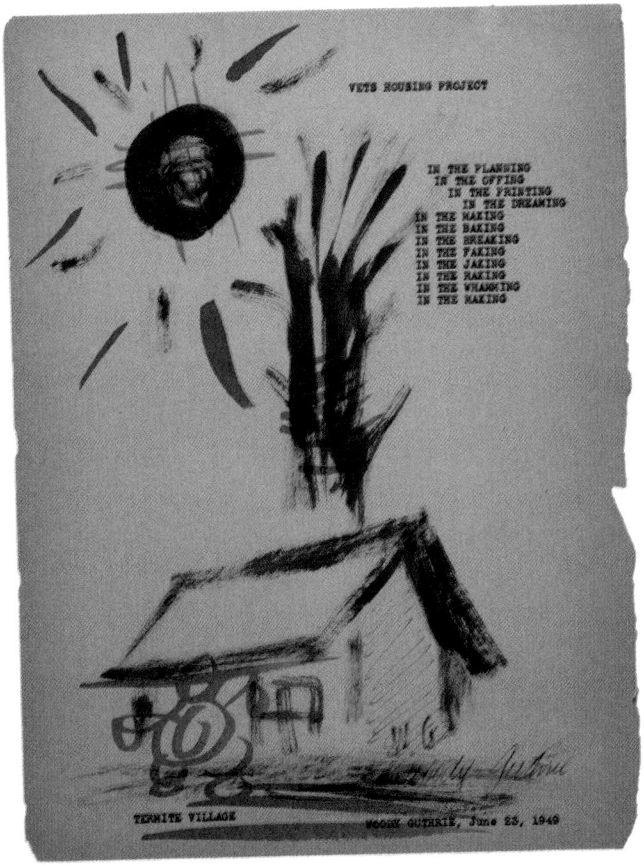
VETS HOUSING PROJECT
IN THE PLANNING
IN THE OFFING
IN THE PRINTING
IN THE DREAMING
IN THE MAKING
IN THE BAKING
IN THE BREAKING
IN THE FAKING
IN THE JAKING
IN THE RAKING
IN THE WHAMMING
IN THE MAKING
TERMITE VILLAGE
WOODY GUTHRIE, June 23, 1949

ACROSS: Consistent with his political beliefs, he connects his humanistic styled socialism to daily chores and home life. ABOVE: A brighter vision of Veteran's housing.

In the early 1950s, Woody took a ceramics class at Brooklyn College and created hot plates, tiles, and vases that he decorated with painted scenes and carved drawings and writings. During a stay with Pete and Toshi Seeger in Beacon, New York, he created free-form clay sculptures that remained on the shelf where he had placed them in 1951, and were retrieved in 2004. Only a handful of these ceramics survive. The family, however, still enjoys serving many dinners on this last hot plate.

Woody

The American Folksay Ballads and Dances album sent to Mary Guthrie and children Gwendolyn (Teeny), Sue, and Bill in 1949.

For Woody, any and all empty spaces were fair game to be used for art. "The pages that we left blank in this book are an insult to the human race," he wrote in a 1945 diary. Empty spaces in record albums were more opportunities for drawings, comments, and letters.

THIS IS TO MARY
AND TO EVERY BODY THAT HEARS IT !
from Woody and Marjorie and Cathy and
Coney Island

"Zibberzee," Woody's nickname for Arlo Davy Guthrie.

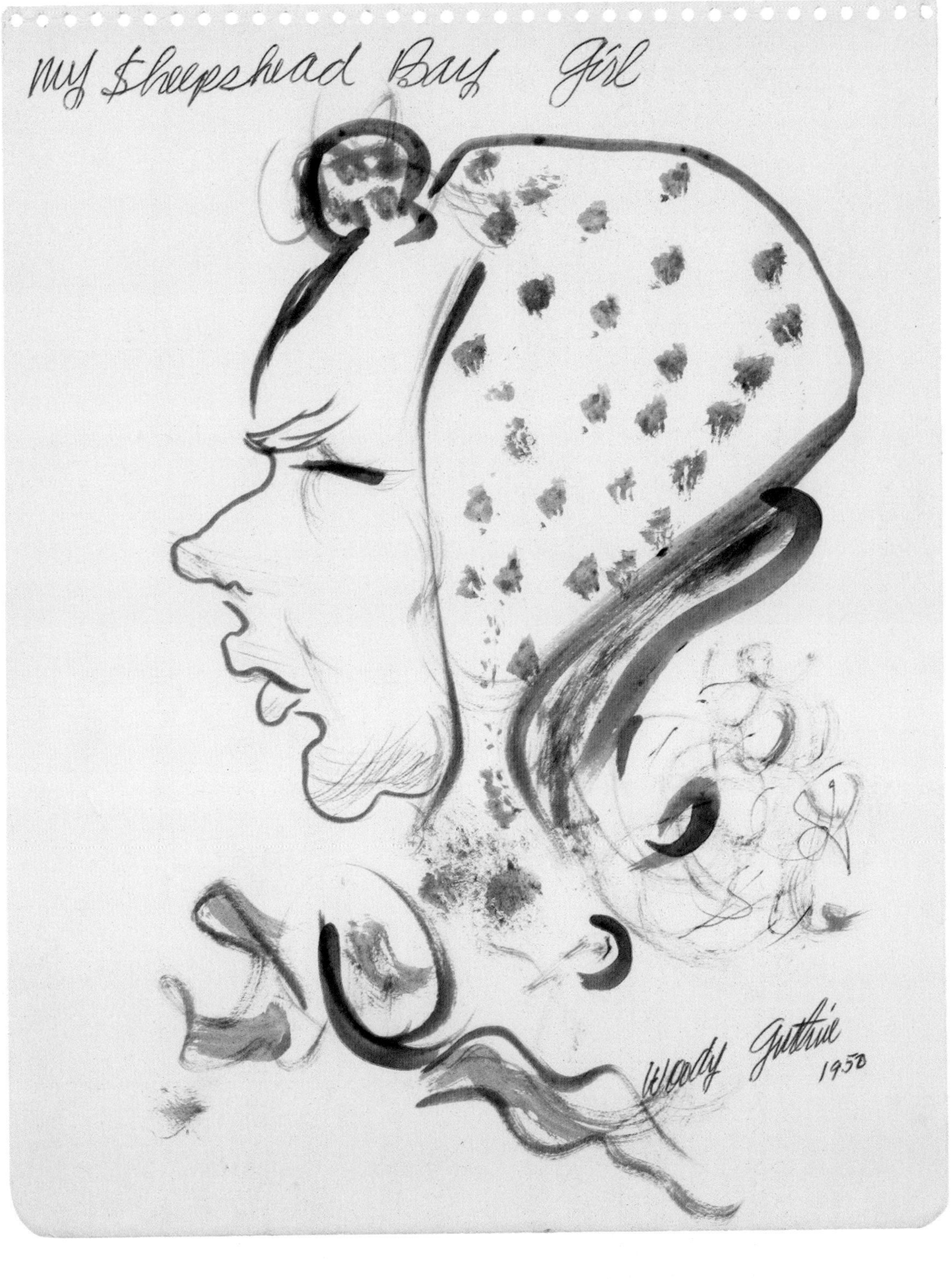

Marjorie's dancing school was in Sheepshead Bay, Brooklyn, from 1950 to 1978.

The Jolly Miner
Woody Guthrie
March 1951
Beach Haven

By 1951, it was clear that something was terribly wrong with Woody. He was unknowingly suffering the symptoms of Huntington's Disease: coming and going on impulse, appearing or not appearing at performances, showing lapses of coordination which were interpreted as alcoholism, and experiencing erratic emotional bouts. These works could mirror his condition; part here, part gone.

Looky Me
woody Guthrie
Brooklyn
march 1951

Conflicted expressions of war and love often appear as central themes during this period.

Low Lonesome
Woody Guthrie
March
1951

Woody traveled to Florida in 1951 to visit Stetson Kennedy, a writer and journalist who was actively fighting the Ku Klux Klan and Florida's racist policies of segregation. His novel, *Unmasked*, chronicles the activities of the Klan. Accompanying Woody was his young protégé, Ramblin' Jack Elliott, and Anneke Van Kirk, who became his third wife.

Angry and disgusted by what he saw, Woody created many notebooks filled with outrage: writings, lyrics, and art that dealt with Jim Crow politics, racist violence, and the "whites only" social order. These notebooks depict explicit scenes of lynchings and evidence of a vicious segregation policy, and KKK activities and hatred. The art is particularly eerie and introduces an element of sexual perversity and obscenity. At this time, Woody's own body was experiencing some of this; sexual fantasy and obscene behavior sometimes accompany symptoms of Huntington's Disease. Here he connects racism and sexual perversion, the former being the "obscenity" to be eradicated.

Mississippi
Woody Guthrie
3-31-'51

Southland Tourist
Woody Guthrie
down here on earth
March 1951

Back in New York, 1951. Beach Haven is the apartment complex where the family later moved, also in Coney Island, Brooklyn.

$tarvation disease
Woody Guthrie
April 1951
Beach Haven

Arlo's Funny Man
Woody Guthrie
April 1951
Beach Haven

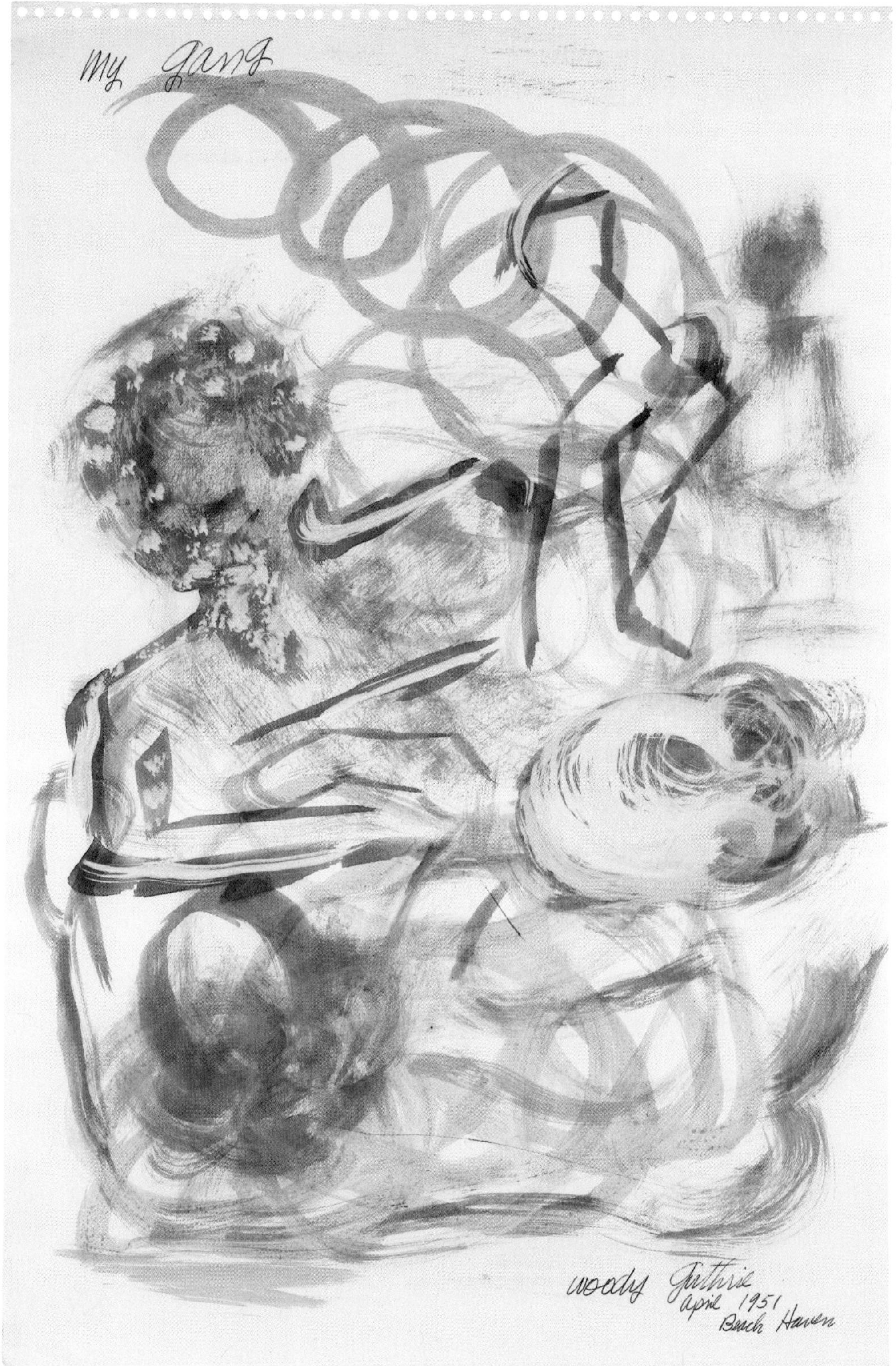

Woody's kids with Marjorie. *My Gang* now included Arlo, Joady, and Nora.

all work together
Woody Guthrie
1951

Unable to deal with Woody's increasingly erratic and often adulterous behavior, Marjorie encouraged a separation. Woody had to deal with many hard feelings and jealousy. So did she.

Pritty Near
Woody Guthrie
1951

Biggy Big Big
Woody Guthrie
1951

Woody typed an original song, *Hootenanny: My Hootenanny*, on wrapping paper, 1952.

By 1952, Woody was, for all intents and purposes, unable to continue his work as a performing folksinger. Ironically, he was unable to participate in the burgeoning folk music scene that was beginning to take form, and that he had partly inspired. Still struggling to stay connected, denying the effects that Huntington's Disease was having on him, he continued to write songs. This one is both nostalgic—reminiscent of his Almanac Days—and forward thinking: the Hootenannys of the next generation were just beginning.

My Hootenanny

MY HOOTENANNY

Woody Guthrie

Hootenanny! Hootenanny!
Hootin' Annie! Hotting Anny!
Long might you pull and take breath
Here in my midsts, Hootenanny! Sweet Hootennanny!
Sounding sweeter to me than any honey in any rock!
Sweet Hoot! Sweet Hoot! Sweet Hootin' Hootin' Hootin' Anny!
Hoot out to my world your clear young pretty voice
And sing to my scared and my neveous cowards
How easy is the union way of life
How nice and warm the union side of life;
How big and bright and sparkeldy is the lovingside
Of my big union world out freed from your fearful shadows;
Hootenanny Man! Holler these things to them!
Hottenanny Daddy! Hoot out at your greedy enemy
Greed itself, and shout and joke and sing
Down into the gutters and drains of history,
Down into the fires of old creation,
Down under, down in under, done done whittled on down;
Fiddled on down, all of my worst enemies
Riddled on down, all of my worst cowards;
Jazzed right on down, all of my old strangly notions!
I could call you my hottenanny,
Or I could call you my shootenanny, scootin' Anny,
Of my squirtin' Annie, or my squeekenanny,
Or my flirkinanny, flippinanny, shippinannie,
My flirtinanny, whoopinanny, scoopinanny,
And I'd still be okay as far as your name goes;
I did help to think up that namd, hootinanny
To mean the place where you could come to and to
Yell your head off about what's eatin' on you;
Tell who's beatin' on you, mistreatin' on ya;
Stoolin' on y', droolin' on ya, toadcoolerin on ya;
So's you'd have a good place to come sing and dance
About whoever it was that done you wrongly and howly;
Sing about who it was robbed you, ribbed you, gypped ya;
Rifled ya, stifled ya, pilfred ya, gyinnered ya;
Shot y', got y', whatnotted y', spotted y',
Goofed ya, spoofed ya, spondoolyxed ya, bamboozled ya;
Damffoozled ya, rubberhozed ya, bloodynozed ya;
Hyped ya, wheedled ya, needled ya, tweedled ya;
Hurt ya, scraped ya, raped ya, faked ya, trymaked ya;
Manhaided ya, eggscrambled ya, fandangled ya, misdone ya;
Badmanaged ya, hotcabbaged ya, booted ya, tooted ya, hotfooted ya
Insulted ya, curse ordled ya, bemuddle ya, muddled ya;
Unzippered ya, unlaced ya, traced ya, fast raced & fast talked ya
Bilked ya, badshowed ya, madroaded ya, throwed ya, blowed ya;
Badtimed ya, last dimed ya, frothyslimed ya;
Sweet Hootenanny girl, sweeter than all of these war shakers;
Sweeter to me than all of them quickers and takers and
Loosey tongued fakers; you are prittier than a million
Of their hippytwisters and greasy sisters twitching it for war;
You are pitching it for peace, Hootenanny Girl,
You are frailing it for friendship, Hootenanny Lady Fair;
Tossing it for the boss ain't your kind of a wine dance, is it ?
You do the fine dance about humanly sisterlyhood;
You do that finer dance about neighborly hippyloving;
Making love is ten zillions better than shaking up a war;
Making your peace is better than the wargirls crazy grease;
You'll forget more about pretty things than she ever will know;
Hootenanny Girly. Hootenanny Pearly. Hootenanny Maidela.
You can sing and talk all eternity about who treated your folks bad.
I was just born alistning to all of your hootenanny heartsongs,
And I was born here to listen, to finger and to lay and to
Play and to pray and to dance around my atom fire as much as I
Dang please while you're singing out the sounds of your
Hootennanny Song. We found toegether the only good way to
Spend the long and the short time of life, didn't we? Huhhh?
Didn't we, Sugar? Diddient we Babe Oh Bab?
Shootin' It At th' Hootenanny!
Bootin' it at th' Skootenanny!
Rakin' it at the Skweekinanny.
Takin' it at th' Bawlin' Squaller! Huh? Didn't we?
Us I mean, I mean, you and me here!
Us here hootin' it off together!
Hootin' it, rootin' it, knockin' it,
Rockin' it, sockin' it, boxin' it, anda foxxin' it;
Skippin' it, anda nippin' it here at our big loud hootenanny;
Hoofin' our hearts down to a nubb here at our Hoofinanny;
Hoopin' it, hopin' it, slappin' it, tappin' it,
Dreamin' it, schemin' it, fussin' it anda cussin' it,
Groovin' it, greazin' it, shovin' it, freezin' it,
Frettin' it anda sweatin' it out, here, here at this very hootenanny
Mopin' it anda hopin' it, softshoein' it, softsoapin' it;
Hopin' it, hopin' it, hopin' it, hoppin' it;
Hopin' this wole damn crazy warry world will drop
Down all of it's sad shooting irons and killing kannons
And come with you and me and slip it
Flip it over into that good groove that we love so well;
That good old groove of world work, world peace, woelrd kissing;
Worlds all hootin' it, hopin' it,
Dreamin' it, screamin' it, frimmin' it, frammin' it;
Whoppin' up a heaty pitch of firey kissfyrnaces which no
Uramyuuum stockypile could hit on in a trillion generations;
Me'n you's
Got the old world by the horn, ain't we, babeyy?
Didn't we grab things by the hot end, friend?
Huhhh? You an' me did, both did, diddle we?
Hippin' it here at my hootenanny?
Both of us, didn' we?
Hippin' it here;
Slippin' it here;
Drippen' it here at our hootenanny?!
I can't quite clear just quite remember how it went that other
Time
When we
Scooped it and that Heatin'anny,
Can you?
Not quite.
Not plumb quite.
I think we gotta go and try back over it
Once more,
Don't you?
Won't you?
Hittenanny?
Hootenanny?
Hooter
At our
Hootenanny?
Yeahhhhh!

Woody Guthrie

---------- END ------------

Woodrow Wilson Woody Guthrie
49 Murdock Court Apt 13
Bitchy Haven On Brighton
Brookelyne 23 New Yorke

Februarayyy 1952

From a notebook entitled *Chris Guthrie, Life and Times*. The entire notebook is a single epic illustrated letter to his newly born nephew, Christopher Guthrie, son of George Guthrie, Woody's younger brother.

23
knew how
to grow up here
to be

A painting of Anneke Van Kirk, Topanga Canyon, California. Temporarily living with actor Will Geer and family at their Topanga Canyon homestead, and now married to Anneke, Woody created notebooks filled with a freewheeling attitude that he often sent to Marjorie and the children to stay connected.

November went off over thattaway
some place I reckon
19*52
Perty good month
But coulda been lots better
without being any too good
Woody Guthrie
Geer Gardens
Topanga Canyon

I am that famious and well known lady by the farmous and well known name of anneke that said off down along a river bank one day back several years ago that it's harder to catch a worm than it is to catch a fish if you dont know just exactly which office to go dig in
December 1952
Woody Guthrie
Geers Garden
Topanga Canyon
but you call my good sunburn by that vulgar word of rude nudity

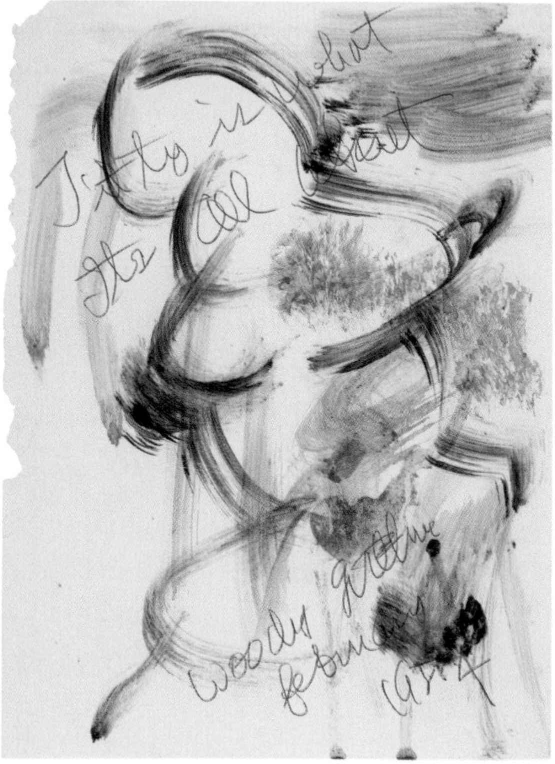

Which place
Is This ?
Woody Guthrie
Feb. 1952

A page from a collection of original songs, *Dustbowl Migratory Hobo Floods, etc. (Tragedy)*. Woody often worked in oversized accounting ledger books, which he discovered during his army training days. In the early 1950s, he often perused his original papers and lyrics, trying to collect and organize them into a single songbook. After pasting the original onto the current notebook, he might then paint over and reconstruct, as collage.

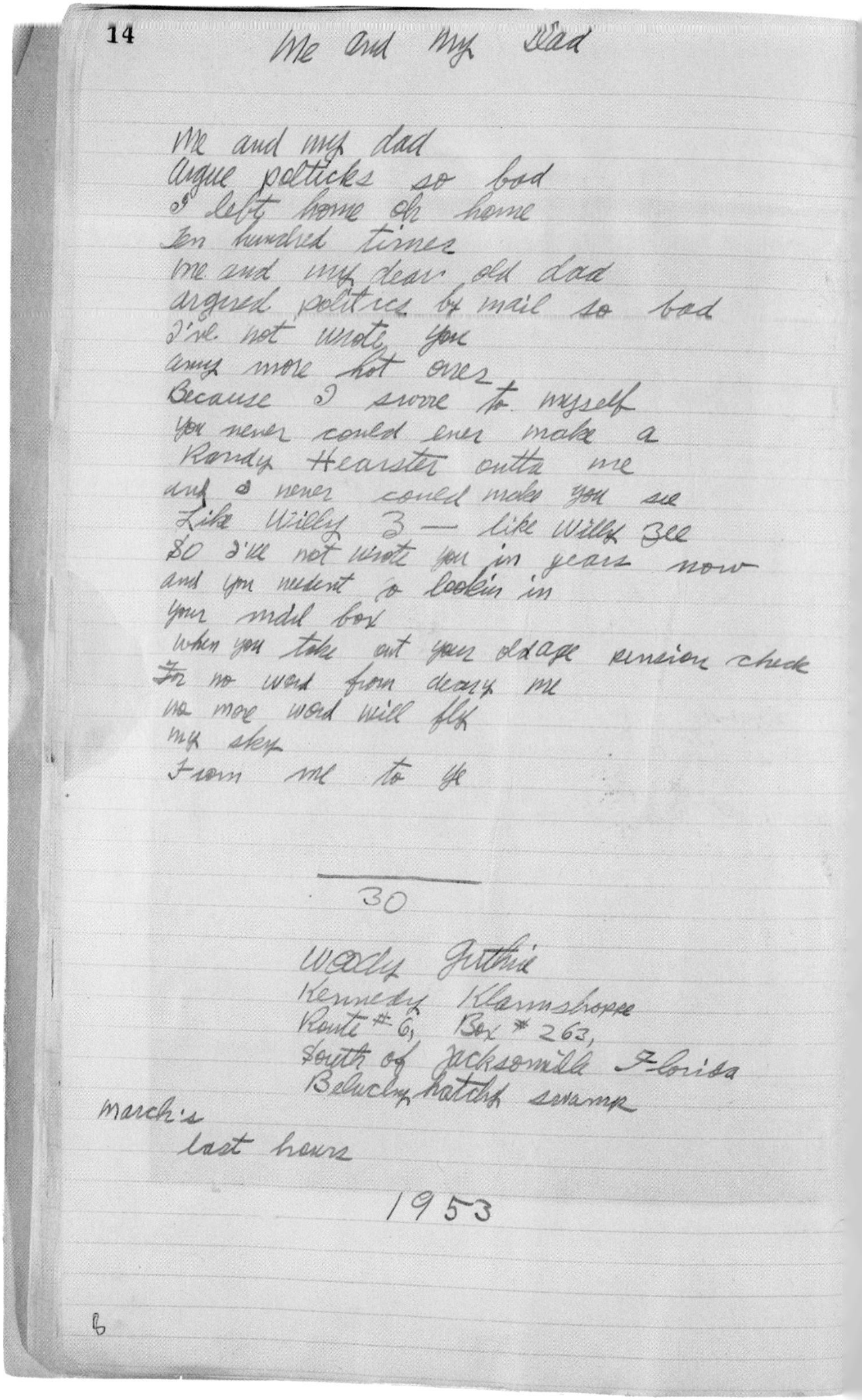
14

Me and My Dad

Me and my dad
Argue politicks so bad
I left home oh home
Ten hundred times
Me and my dear old dad
argued politics by mail so bad
I've not wrote you
any more hot ones
Because I swore to myself
You never could ever make a
Randy Hearster outta me
and I never could make you see
Like Willy Z — like Willy Zee
So I'll not wrote you in years now
and you needent go lookin in
your mail box
when you take out your oldage pension check
For no word from deary me
no more word will fly
my sky
From me to ye

30

Woody Guthrie
Kennedy Klarmshoppe
Route #6, Box #263,
South of Jacksonville Florida
Beluthy hatchy swamp
March's
last hours

1953

6

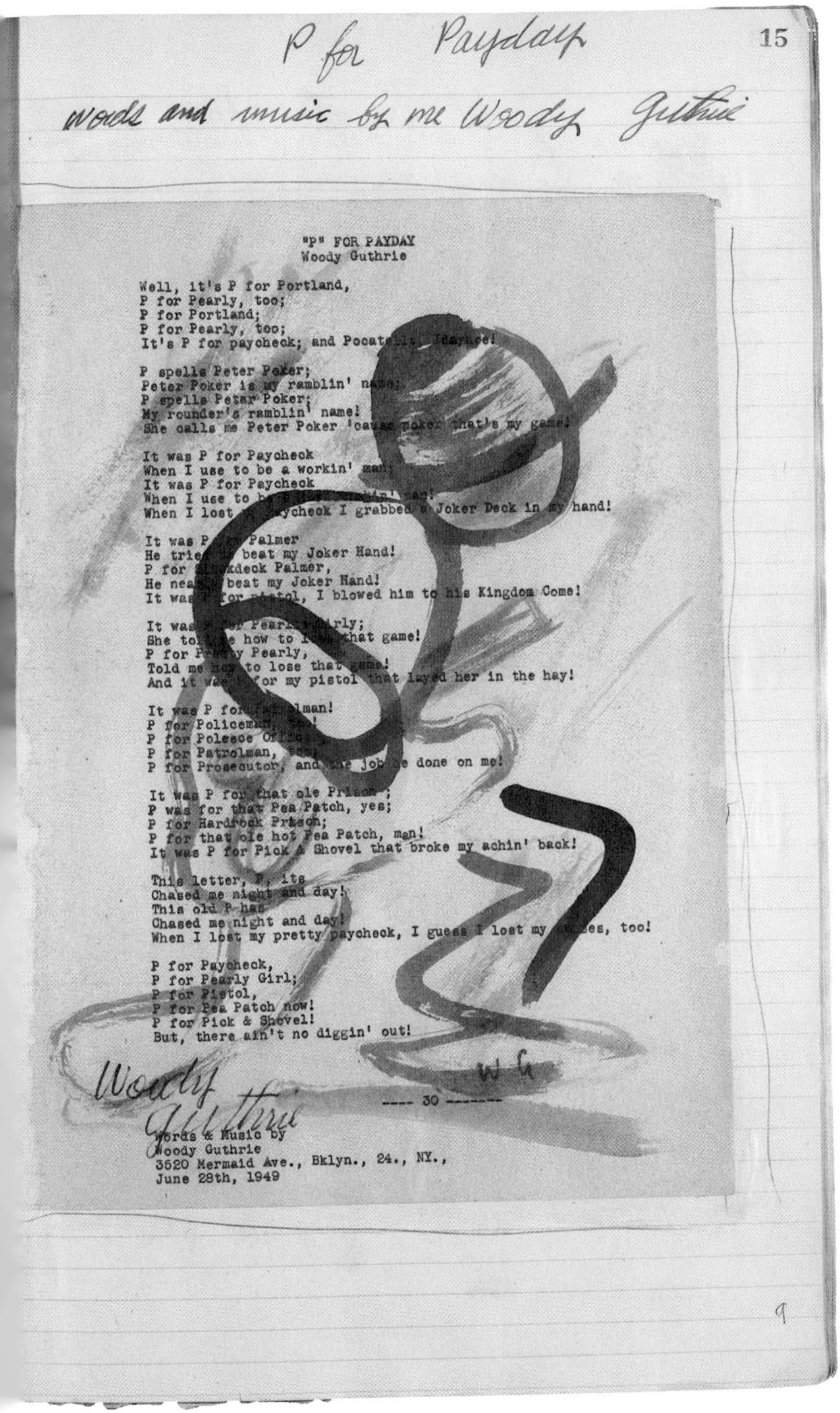

P for Payday

15

words and music by me Woody Guthrie

"P" FOR PAYDAY
Woody Guthrie

Well, it's P for Portland,
P for Pearly, too;
P for Portland;
P for Pearly, too;
It's P for paycheck; and Pocat[illegible]!

P spells Peter Poker;
Peter Poker is my ramblin' name;
P spells Petar Poker;
My rounder's ramblin' name!
She calls me Peter Poker 'cause poker that's my game!

It was P for Paycheck
When I use to be a workin' man;
It was P for Paycheck
When I use to b[illegible]kin' man!
When I lost [illegible]aycheck I grabbed a Joker Deck in my hand!

It was P [illegible] Palmer
He trie[illegible] beat my Joker Hand!
P for [illegible]kdeck Palmer,
He nea[illegible] beat my Joker Hand!
It was [illegible] pistol, I blowed him to his Kingdom Come!

It was [illegible] Pearl[illegible]rly;
She to[illegible] how to [illegible] that game!
P for P[illegible]y Pearly,
Told me [illegible] to lose that game!
And it wa[illegible] for my pistol that layed her in the hay!

It was P for [illegible]lman!
P for Policeman, [illegible]!
P for Poleece O[illegible]
P for Patrolman, [illegible];
P for Prosecutor, and [illegible] job [illegible] done on me!

It was P for that ole Prison;
P was for that Pea Patch, yes;
P for Hardrock Prison;
P for that ole hot Pea Patch, man!
It was P for Pick & Shovel that broke my achin' back!

This letter, P, its
Chased me night and day!
This old P has
Chased me night and day!
When I lost my pretty paycheck, I guess I lost my [illegible]es, too!

P for Paycheck,
P for Pearly Girl;
P for Pistol,
P for Pea Patch now!
P for Pick & Shovel!
But, there ain't no diggin' out!

W G

Woody Guthrie

---- 30 -------

Words & Music by
Woody Guthrie
3520 Mermaid Ave., Bklyn., 24., NY.,
June 28th, 1949

9

Spontaneous and forceful, his rough-hewn scrawl predates graffiti art by several decades. These images come from a 1953 notebook created on a return visit to Stetson Kennedy in Florida.

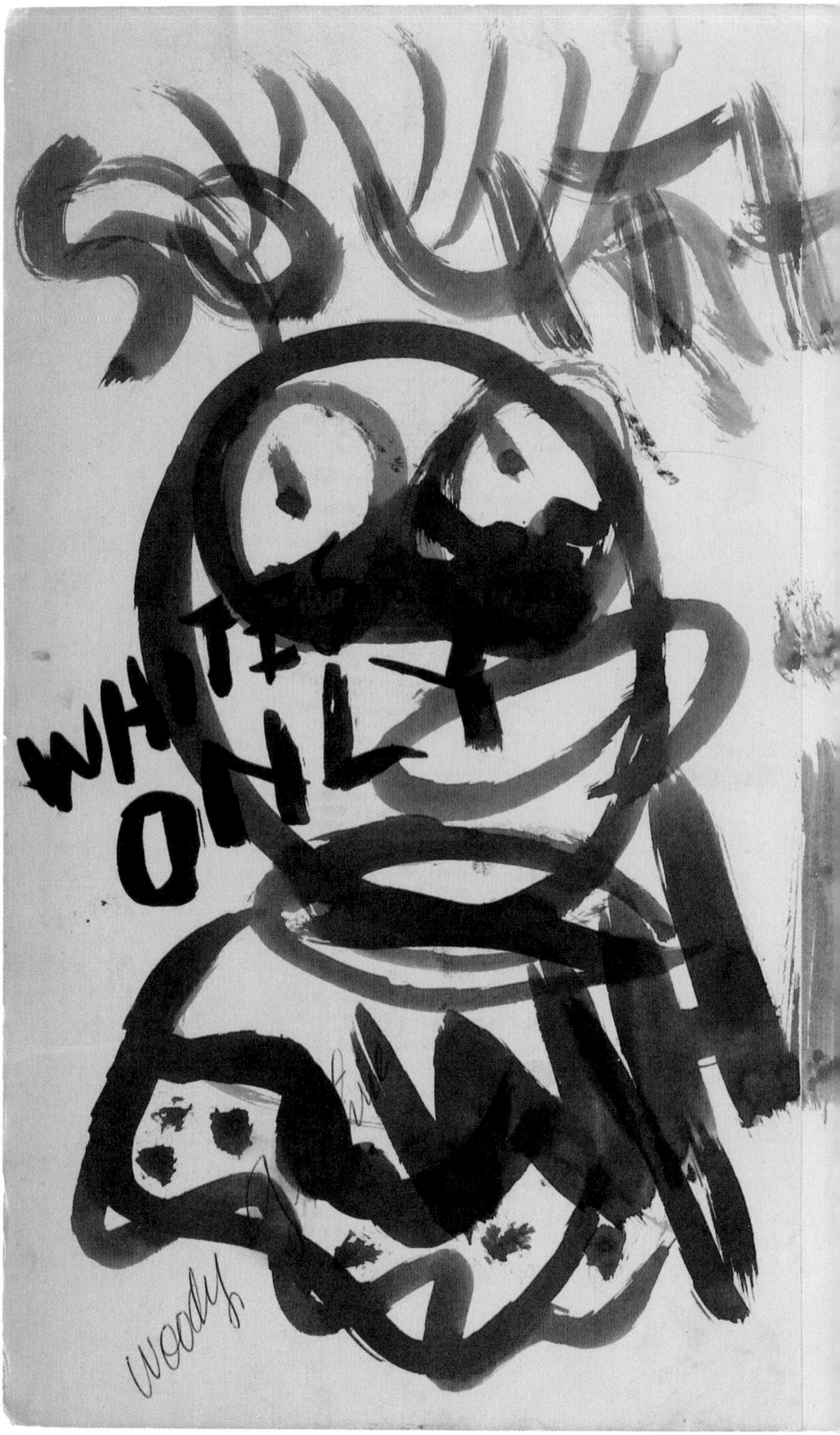

Southern
WHITE
CAT
Swamp Hats
FLORIDA
June 4th 1953

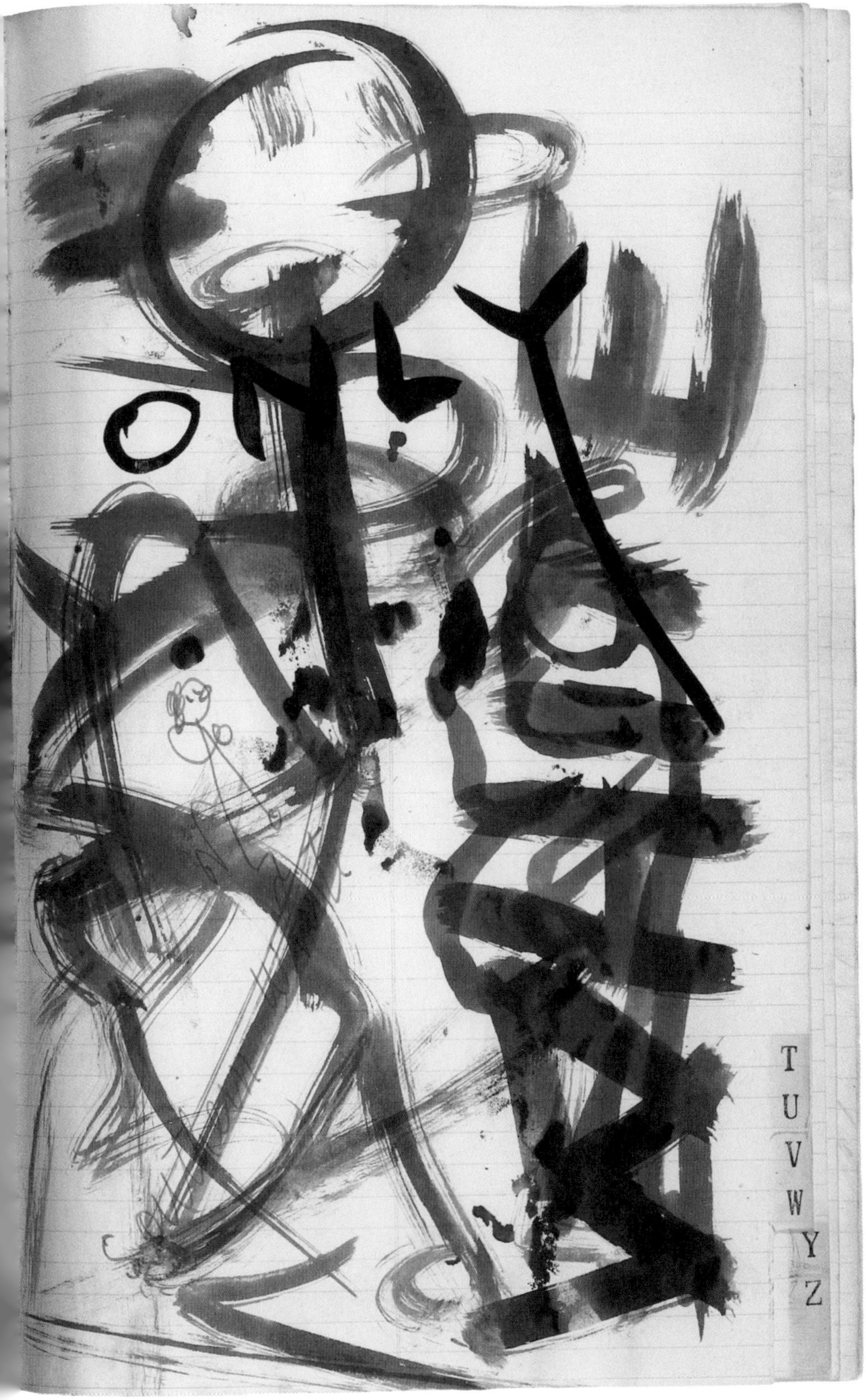
ONLY
T
U
V
W
Y
Z

"Every living song I've ever made up is a hard times song of protest.—Woody Guthrie, NYC on the move, 1954."

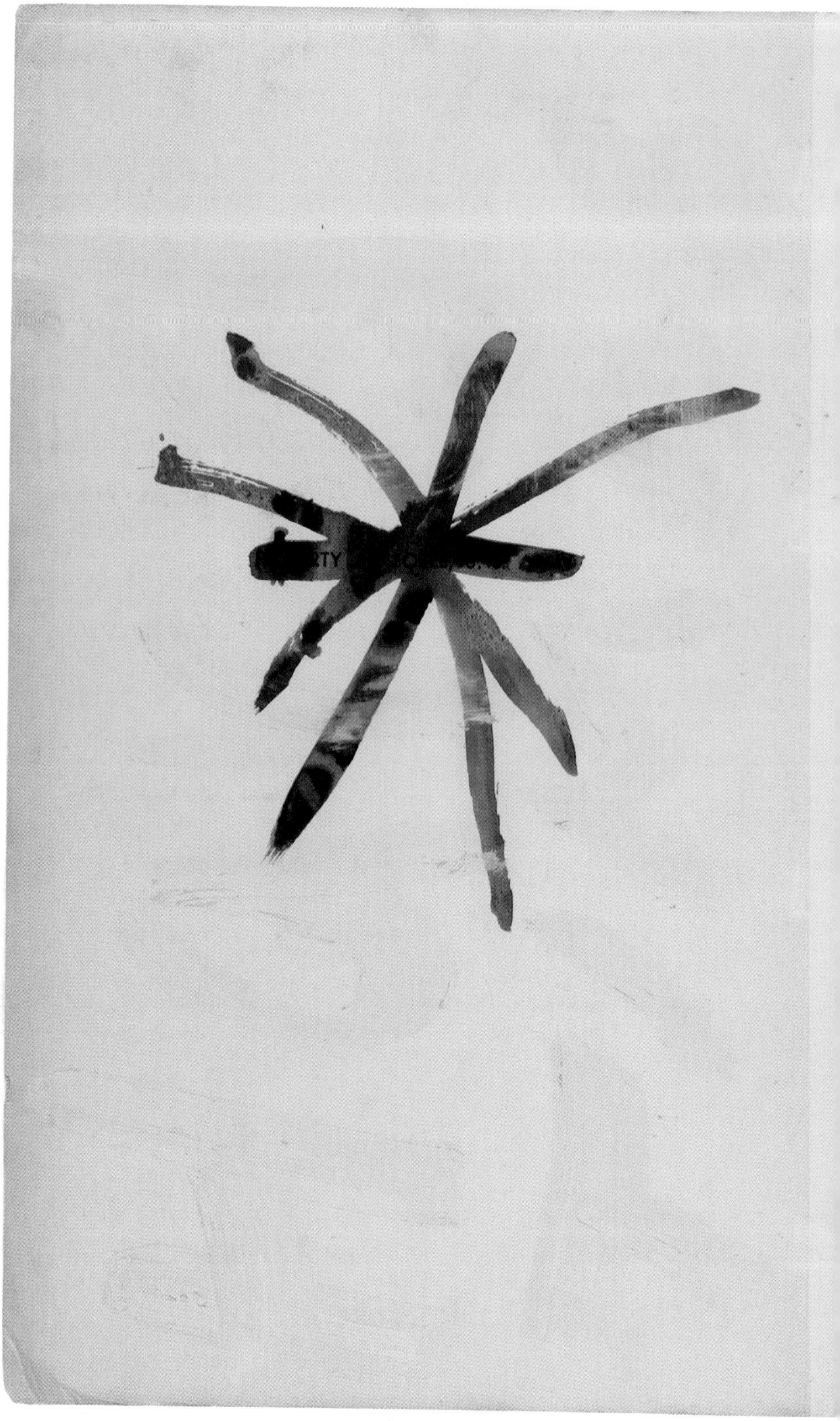

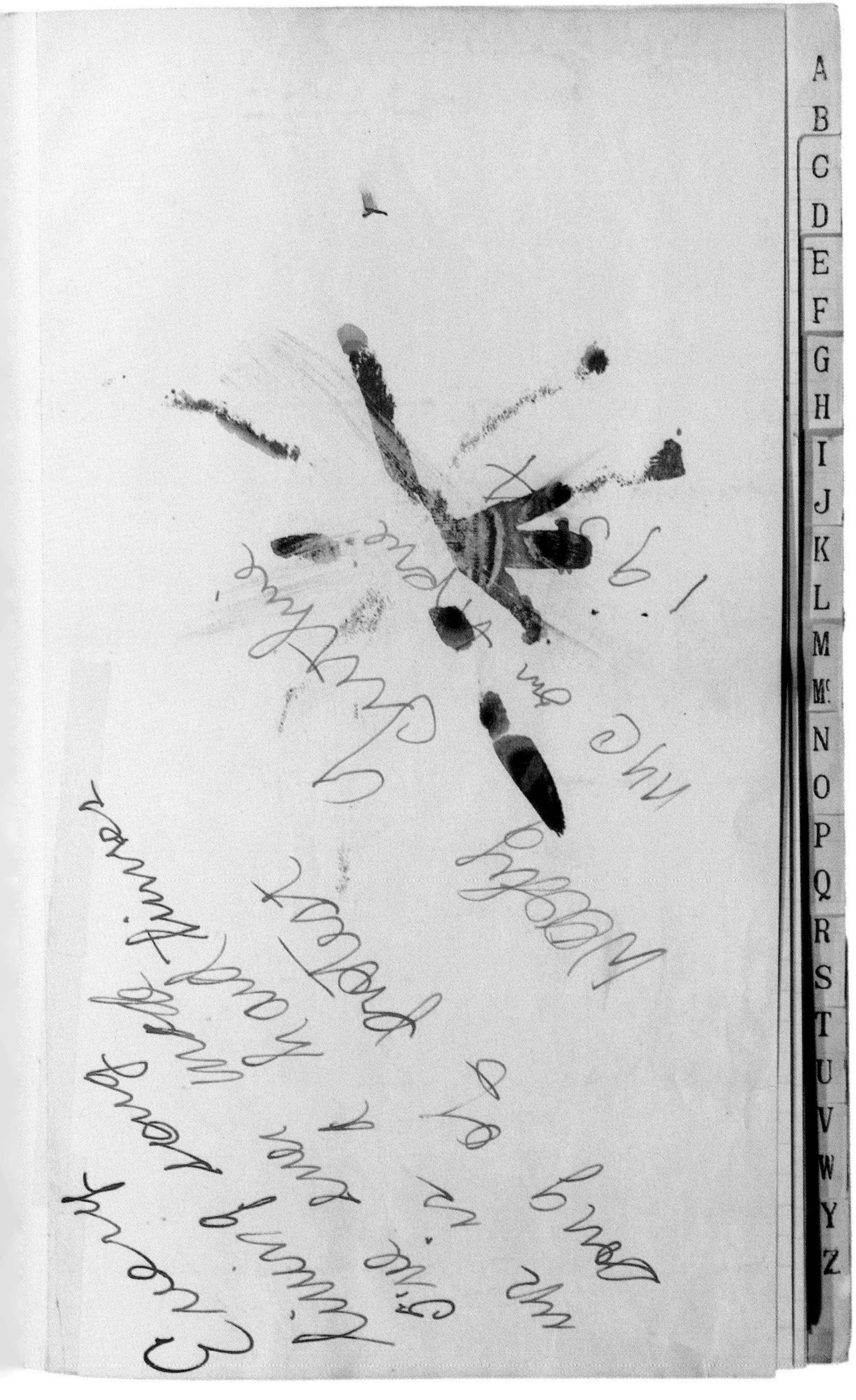
Woody Guthrie

Woody was permanently hospitalized with Huntington's Disease in 1954. He spent Sundays with Marjorie and their children, and other close friends who continued to care for him throughout the years. He continued to write and draw, now with much broader, circular lines, until he was no longer able to control his movements. His family and friends supplied him with pens, pencils, and hundreds of notebooks and, as time went on, legal pads, which provided a larger space for him to work on. When he did run out of paper he would turn the notebook upside down and begin again, working backward from the end of the notebook to the beginning, drawing over the previous piece.

Many of his drawings took on spiritual themes with stars, planets, angels, Jesus, and otherworldly figures appearing or disappearing. His songs, too, reflected an association with spiritual matters. In one of his final (legible) songs, the phrase "Oh God" appears continuously, used as both verse and chorus. Structured on the page this way, the lyrics themselves almost make us experience text as art.

In the early 1960s, Woody was visited in the hospital by many young musicians who were beginning to follow the path he had cleared for them, that of a "socially conscious" songwriter. They were eager to be near him, to bring their recordings of his songs for him to hear, and to play music for him.

Woody's song lyrics, artworks, essays, poetry, manuscripts, and letters were collected and saved by his wife, Marjorie, who went on to found the Huntington's Disease Society of America, the Woody Guthrie Archives, and the Woody Guthrie Foundation

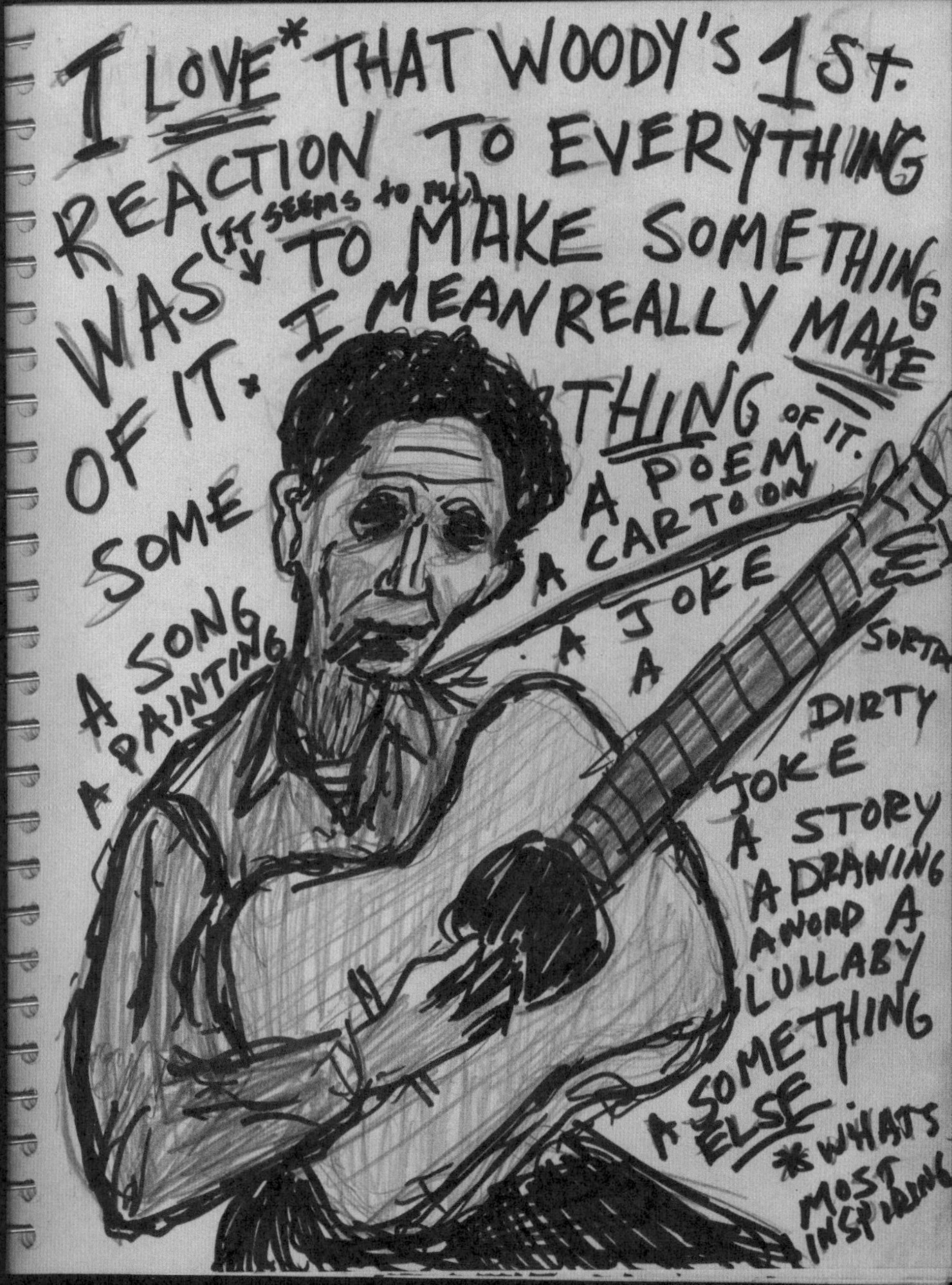
I LOVE* THAT WOODY'S 1st.
REACTION TO EVERYTHING
WAS (it seems to me) TO MAKE SOMETHING
OF IT. I MEAN REALLY MAKE
SOME THING OF IT.
A POEM
A CARTOON
A JOKE
A SONG
A PAINTING
A
A
A SORTA DIRTY JOKE
A STORY
A DRAWING
A WORD
A LULLABY
A SOMETHING ELSE
*WHAT'S MOST INSPIRING

ACKNOWLEDGMENTS

This book could not have been done without the hearts, minds, and hands of the following people:

Harold Leventhal and Jorge Arevalo, who first created the Woody Guthrie Archives with me in 1994 and continue to work daily to maintain and preserve Woody's legacy in every possible way; Felicia Katz-Harris, archivist, who helped us throughout this project, handling original materials and reproductions, researching, providing endnote information, and contributing both historic and personal insights—all with a smile; The Smithsonian Folkways organization and the Asch Family, who made their entire, brilliant collection available to us; Barry Ollman, who made his unique and historic collection available to us; The entire Rizzoli staff and especially Charles Miers, Ellen Nidy, Eva Prinz, Anet Sirna-Bruder, and Alex Tart, who created this vision with us and became part of our tribe as well as our friends; Sandy Choron for bringing us together; my Mermaid Avenue brothers Billy Bragg and Jeff Tweedy, who continuously give their profound and lasting insights into Woody's works, words, and life; "Cripple Annie" and everyone whose likeness appears and prevails in this book; Mary Guthrie Boyle, Gwen, Sue, and Bill Guthrie, whose shared lives are at the core of, and live on in, Woody's songs, creative works, and this book; Michael Kleff, who nurtured me with the line, "Wow, this is really gonna be great"; Michael Smith and Anna Canoni, who always do whatever needs to be done, whenever it needs to be done, and get everything done. Without them, nothing would get done.

And finally, to Steven Brower for his enormous insight, creativity, endurance, and ultimate professionalism. By taking on this task, he has given American culture and the entire world a fundamental and essential chapter in Woody Guthrie's life story and artistic legacy.

—Nora Guthrie

To learn more about Woody Guthrie please visit:
www.woodyguthrie.org

Little did I know when I entered the Museum of the City of New York back in 2000 to see a Woody Guthrie exhibit that I would be embarking on a journey, although when I arrived at the Woody Guthrie Archives for the first time shortly afterward I knew it had begun. I am forever indebted to Nora Guthrie for her incredible generosity, wisdom, guidance, support, and candor. Working with her made this project a true labor of love.

At the archives a special thank you to Harold for his acumen and enthusiasm, and to his lovely wife, Natalie. To Felicia for her patience and perseverance in undertaking what might have seemed like an insurmountable task and Jorge for his support and knowledge; likewise Michael and Anna.

To Stephanie Smith at the Smithsonian Folkways Archives for all her help, and to Barry for his willingness to allow us to use his private collection. At Rizzoli a very special thanks to Eva, who shared our passion from the beginning, for her guidance. Likewise Charles, Ellen, Anet, and especially Alex, for keeping us on track and making us look good. To Sandy, who brought all of us together and her husband, Harry, who came along for the ride.

Behind the scenes a special thanks to Martin Fox, for his friendship and helping me dot my T's and cross my I's. To Arnold and David Katz and Anthony Loew for their photography and willingness to help; to Toni Caron and Deb Lee at John K. King Book Store in Detroit for helping find that lost book, and to my sister Susan's friend of long ago, Rima Rosenthal, who played a Woody Guthrie record for me for the very first time.

To Anne Pae and David Sachs at the Huntington's Program, Terence Cardinal Care Center for their willingness to share with me the incredible work they do, and to Dr. Michael Hayden of the Centre for Molecular Medicine and Therapeutics, who has dedicated his life to finding a cure. For more information contact the Huntington's Disease Society of America National headquarters at 1-800-345-HDSA (1-800-345-4372).

And, finally, to Kati and Janna, lights of my life, who have to put up with all my obsessions. —*Steven Brower*

Endnotes

WGA – Woody Guthrie Archives

Page 10: "I knew that my trail would be a story . . ." *American Folksong*, 13.

Page 11: "The hard-working people just stumbling about . . ." Guthrie, *Bound for Glory*, 231–33.

"I scratched around in the books . . . ." Guthrie, *Bound for Glory*, 226.

"I wanted to be my own boss. . . ." Guthrie, *Bound for Glory*, 226.

Page 12: "For the next few months . . . putting it down on something."

"I painted cheap signs and pictures . . . a thousand years." Guthrie, *Bound for Glory*, 230–31.

Page 14: "I got to going out . . . " Guthrie, *Bound for Glory*, 231–32.

"Yes, I'll go. . . . highway leading west." Guthrie, *Bound for Glory*, 249.

Page 15: "I heard one of them holler . . . " Guthrie, *Bound for Glory*, 259.

Page 21: "A Photographer Without a Camera." Guthrie, *Born to Win*, 19.

"I would like to paint you a picture with strokes of electricity." Guthrie to Thayer, no date.

Page 23: "The thousands of days . . . " Marsh and Leventhal, *Pastures of Plenty*, 139.

Page 25: "New York is a big town for painting pictures." Marjorie Guthrie, *Woody Sez,* 114.

"God, I wish we could go on some kind of trip together. . ." Postcards, 9/23/44, WGA.

Page 26: "My sketch on the other side of this sheet is one of my proudest and most original." Guthrie to Marjorie Guthrie, 8/29/42.

Page 28: "Marjorie and me said when Stacky . . ." Marsh and Leventhal, *Pastures of Plenty*, 177.

"And it flew across my mind . . ." "Three Year Old" letter, 3/16/1946, Smithsonian Folkways Collection.

"To just sorta halfway give you a rough idea of the Peakly Pinnacle . . ."
Guthrie to Alan Lomax, May 2, 1950.

Page 29: "Not a table was set up . . ." Longhi, *Woody, Cisco, & Me*, 54.

Page 30: "All art and all industry and all work and all play." Marsh and Leventhal, *Pastures of Plenty*, 91.

"A Hoodis goes to show you that you can take all of your ugliest things . . ." Manuscripts Box 4, folder 36, WGA.

Page 34: "How He Looks at Things." Marjorie Guthrie, *Woody Sez*, XIX.

"You know what a artist is don't you . . ." Marjorie Guthrie, *Woody Sez*, 133.

Page 35 "This is adobe art, painted of open air, clay and sky . . ." Inscription courtesy of the Collection of Barry and Judith Ollman.

"As I was walking that ribbon of highway . . . " *This Land is Your Land*, Songs 1, WGA.

"In the world's mighty gallery of pictures . . . " Traditional.

Page 36: "Woodrow Guthrie or just plain Woody . . ." *Woody Sez,* XIX

"Stayed a few nights with a artist . . ." Marjorie Guthrie, *Woody Sez*, 165.

Page 37: "Life has got a habit of not standing hitched." Marjorie Guthrie, *Woody Sez,* 166.

Page 82: "When I first got to New York . . ." Marsh and Leventhal, *Pastures of Plenty*, 141.

Page 83: "Now if people who read books and go around making speeches . . ." All Artists, 11/29/43, NB 1 #19, WGA.

Page 77. "Bleed one inch . . ." Artwork Series 13 #1, WGA.

Page 243: "And I've Got to Be Drifting Along." Guthrie, Song, WGA.

"One day we'll all find out that all of our songs . . ." Carty, *A World of Wisdom, Quotations for Enlightenment.*

Page 244: "Love is all force. Love is all power." Marsh and Leventhal, *Pastures of Plenty*, 233.

Page 245: "Gonna tell y' what t'do if y' wanta win some peace . . ." Notebook 2-9, WGA.

"Woody Adversity Guthrie." Cray, *Ramblin' Man*, 371.

"This world it's hit me in my face . . ." Klein, *Woody Guthrie*, 386.

"Worth Quoting." Guthrie, Library of Congress Recordings, Elektra Records.

Illustration Credits

WGA =Woody Guthrie Archives
NB= notebooks

Endpapers: Diary, New York, NY, 1942. NB-1 #10 (inside cover), WGA. When Woody returned to New York in 1942, following his job writing songs for the Bonneville Power Administration in 1941, he went to live with the Almanac singers. The Almanacs were a group of folk singers whose mission was to use traditional music, along with cowritten topical compositions, to advocate for progressive political issues. Woody joined the group, which included Millard Lampell, Lee Hayes, Bess Lomax, Agnes "Sis" Cunningham, Arthur Stern, and Pete Seeger.

Years later, some of these musicians regrouped as the Weavers, the first folk group to land a #1 hit song on the Billboard charts with Leadbelly's "Goodnight Irene." The group was soon blacklisted, but appeared in a defiant 1955 concert at Carnegie Hall. This historic night marked the beginning of the folk revival, from which emerged Peter, Paul & Mary and hundreds of other musicians who continued to combine folk music with a political message.

This photograph is from Woody's travels along the Oregon coast in 1941. The caricature of Woody is by Gordon Freison, who published *Broadside* in the 1950s, the first folk music publication to feature new songs by up-and-coming writers. Bob Dylan and Phil Ochs were first published in *Broadside* in the 1960s.

Page 1: NB 2 #2, WGA

Page 2: Marjorie and Cathy Ann, Coney Island, 1947. Courtesy the collection of Nora Guthrie.

Page 3: Woody en route to Florida, 1951, NB 2 #5, WGA.

Page 4: Woody outside the *People's World* office, Los Angeles, 1939, 1 #4, WGA.

Page 6: *Before*, Akron, Ohio, 10/22/44, in a store-bought cardboard frame. Courtesy the collection of Nora Guthrie.

Page 7: Woody, *Hear My Banjo Play* publicity photo, 1 #49, 1941, WGA.

Page 9: Woody in Pampa, 1929, 2 #1, WGA.

Page 10: Courtesy the collection of Nora Guthrie, 1951.

Page 11: NB 1 #1, Series 8 #5-back, WGA.

Page 18: Woody in 1953, NB 2 #5, WGA.

Page 19: NB 1 #10, WGA.

Page 20: Self-portrait, 1944. Dry brush and ink on onionskin paper, 27.8 x 21.5 cm. Artwork Series 9, #6a, WGA.

Page 21: Top: Correspondence Box 2, Folder 7, 1945, WGA.

Page 21: Bottom: Series 10 #1-back, WGA.

Page 26: Art Series 15 #1, WGA.

Page 30: Courtesy the collection of Nora Guthrie.

Page 31: *Ballads of Sacco & Vanzetti*, Smithsonian Folkways Records.

Page 32: Tissue over cardstock, 1947, Series 15 # 11, WGA.

Page 33: *IF I WAS EVERYTHING ON EARTH*, May 1935. Crayon on loose-leaf paper with type script. Alonzo Zilch Songbook, NB-1 #87(1), WGA.

Page 38: Santa Fe, NM, 1936. Oil on canvas, 44 cm. X 61cm. Courtesy the collection of Barry and Judith Ollman.

Page 39: Untitled (Lincoln portrait), 1937. Oil on canvas, Courtesy of Smithsonian Folkways Records.

Page 40: *Maggie Mozella McGee*, Pampa, TX, Feb. 10, 1935. Crayon on loose-leaf paper with type script. Alonzo Zilch Songbook, NB-1 #87(2), WGA.

Page 41: *Nobody's Darling*, Los Angeles, CA, 1938. Pen on loose-leaf paper with type script. NB-1 #5(181), WGA.

Pages 42–60/Facsimile: Los Angeles, CA, 1938. Pen and colored ink with crayon in Progress brand composition notebook. Single panel and sequential cartoon art, 20 x 25.5 cm. Daily Record series, NB-1 #1, NB-1 #2, WGA.

Pages 61–63: "Woody Sez" cartoon series, Los Angeles, CA, 1939. Brushed ink on vellum, 27.5 x 22.5 cm. Artwork Series 1 #1 & 2, WGA.

Pages 64–65: *Don't Let Anything Keep You from Registering* (from *Voter Registration* series), 1939. Brush and pen ink on onionskin paper, 28 x 21.6 cm. Artwork Series 3 #3. WGA.

Pages 66–71: *This is the hand cartoon series*, Los Angeles, CA, 1939. Series 2, brush and pen, brown ink on onionskin paper, 28 x 21.6 cm. Artwork Series 2, WGA.

Page 72: Untitled (from *Work Songs to Grow On* covers series), ca. 1941. Brush and ink on Dance Center of Philadelphia stationery, 22.5 x 30.2 cm. Artwork Series 15 #2. WGA.

Page 73: Untitled portrait (from *Portraits and Caricatures* series), New York, NY, Sept. 1942. Ink and colored pencil on paper, 33 x 21.5 cm. Artwork Series 6 #8, WGA.

Pages 74–79: Sketches of various Almanac Singers (from *Portraits and Caricatures* series), 1941. Pencil and pen on paper. Series 6, WGA.

Pages 80–81: Untitled. Crayon on paper. Artwork Series 20, #2, WGA.

Page 84: *Woody Guthrie's 25 cent Songbooks*, mimeographed songbook covers, 1945. Songbooks, WGA.

Page 85: *What a Beautiful World* cover art. Series 25, #1, 1940, WGA.

Pages 86–103: *Bound for Glory* illustrations, New York, NY, 1942. Ink on poster board, 28 x 36 cm. Artwork Series 7, WGA.

Pages 104–5: Letter to Marjorie Guthrie, August 29, 1942. Correspondences-2, Box 2, Folder 8, WGA.

Pages 106–15: NB-1 #10, 1942, WGA.

Page 116–17: *Railroad Pete* (from 1942 diary), New York, NY. NB-1 #10, Correspondences-4 (1942 postcards), WGA.

Page 118: *Cathy Rooney* (from *Drawings of Family* series), Sept. 11, 1944. Pencil on newsprint paper. Artwork Series 24 #4, WGA.

Page 119: Postcards from 1941–44 written to Marjorie and Cathy Ann.

Page 120: *Cathy* (from 1943–44 journal). Watercolor. NB-1 #18 (cover and edge), WGA.
Page 121: New York, NY, 1942. Notebooks 1, 42.

Page 122: *We're back and will sing you some seaman songs* (from *Illustrations for Sea Manuscripts* series), 1944. Pen and ink on onionskin paper, 27.8 x 21.5 cm. Artwork Series 9 #1, WGA.

Page 123: *I WANNA COME HOME* (from *Illustrations for Sea Manuscripts* series), 1944. Pen and ink on onionskin paper, 27.8 x 21.5 cm. Artwork Series 9 #3, WGA.

Page 124: *Slim, Tough Guy!* (from *Illustrations for Sea Manuscripts* series), 1944. Pen and ink on onionskin paper, 27.8 x 21.5 cm. Artwork Series 9 #1, WGA.

Page 125: *Dollar Limit* (from *Illustrations for Sea Manuscripts* series), 1944. Pen and ink on onionskin paper, 27.8 x 21.5 cm. Artwork Series 9 #7, WGA.

Page 126: *Coffee Time* (from *Illustrations for Sea Manuscripts* series), 1944. Pen and ink on onionskin paper, 27.8 x 21.5 cm. Artwork Series 9 #10, WGA.

Page 127: Untitled (figure in helmet from *Illustrations for Sea Manuscripts* series), 1944. Pencil on newsprint, 28 x 21.5 cm. Artwork Series 9 #30, WGA.

Page 128: *Are you calling me into your picture, daddy?* (from *Drawings of Family* series), 1946. Practical drawing tablet. Series 18 #6, WGA.

Page 129: *Miss Stackabones,* (from *Drawings of Family* series), 1946. Practical drawing tablet. Series 17 #4, WGA.

Page 130: *I put my ribbon in your hair,* (from *Drawings of Family* series), 1946. Practical drawing tablet. Series 17 #7, WGA.

Page 131: Top: *The deepest conflicts of the running day, Drawings of Family* series, 1946. Practical drawing tablet. Series 17 #10, WGA.

Page 131: Bottom right: Untitled, 1946. Practical drawing tablet. Series 18 #5, WGA.

Pages 132–33: Some of Woody's hand-painted notebook covers, 1940s.

Pages 134–35: *Work Songs to Grow On,* drafts for album covers for Folkways Records, 1946. Artwork Series 13, #1-4, WGA. Smithsonian Folkways Collection, WG-3-05-18-C2, WG-D2-08.

Page 136: Art Series 24 #7, pencil, WGA.

Page 137: Art Series 24 #14, ink on onionskin, WGA.

Pages 138–43: *Woody Guthrie's 25 cent Songbooks*, 1945. Watercolor on mimeographed songbook covers. Songbooks, WGA.

Page 144: *Group Count*, September 13, 1945. Pen on loose-leaf paper, 26.5 x 20 cm. Artwork Series 11 #5, WGA.

Page 145: Narratives and Quotes, Merchant Marines, Oct. 24, 1946, NB-1 #51.

Pages 146–49: Selected untitled drawings from the notebook titled *Sterling*, 1946. NB-1, #49, WGA.

Pages 150–56: Selected untitled drawings from the notebook titled *The Faulks: an Epistle...* October 21, 1946. Dry brush and ink and wash. NB-1 #50, WGA.

Pages 157–59: Selected works, April 19–23, 1946. Pen and ink, brush and ink on paper. BOX 3, FOLDERS 1.2 3, Smithsonian Folkways Collection.

Page 157: *Aint no use*, Smithsonian, Box 3, folder 3.

Page 158: Smithsonian, Box 3, Folder 1

Page 159: Smithsonian, 3-04-04.

Pages 160–63: Selected works, April 21–23, 1946. Brush and ink on paper. Smithsonian Folkways Collection, WG-3-02-05, WG-3-01-30, WG-3-04-10, WG-3-02-12.

Page 160: *Wish I were a single girl again*, Smithsonian, 3-03-04.

Page 161: *I took in some washing*, Smithsonian, 3-03-05

Page 161: *Jig along home*, Smithsonian, 3-04-12.

Page 164: *Bitter Fruit.* Pencil and pen and ink on paper. Smithsonian Folkways Collection,WG-3-01-11.

Page 165: Untitled, April 22, 1946, pen and ink on paper . Smithsonian Folkways Collection, WG-3-03-26.

Page 166: *New Morning Sun*, April 23, 1946. Brush and ink on paper. Smithsonian Folkways Collection, WG-3-02-06.

Page 167: Untitled, no date. Brush and pen and ink on paper. Smithsonian Folkways Collection, WG-Box 3, Folder 1.

Page 168: Untitled, no date. Brush on paper. Smithsonian Folkways Collection, WG-3-03-06.

Page 169: Untitled, April 23, 1946. Brush on paper. Smithsonian Folkways Collection, WG-3-02-24.

Page 170: *These Mountains*, April 22, 1946. Pencil and brush on paper. Smithsonian Folkways Collection, WG-3-03-17.

Page 171: Top: *I know I'm Getting Home*, April 22, 1946. Pencil and brush and ink on paper. Smithsonian Folkways Collection, WG-3-01-19.

Page 171: Bottom: *Your clothes don't fit you right*, April 22, 1946. Pencil and brush and ink on paper. Smithsonian Folkways Collection, WG-3-03-22.

Page 172: Top: *New Morning*, April 23, 1946. Brush and dry brush on ledger paper. Smithsonian Folkways Collection, WG-3-02-14.

Page 173: Bottom: *You woke up my neighborhood*, April 23, 1946. Brush and dry brush on ledger paper. Smithsonian Folkways Collection, WG-3-02-14.

Page 173: *Suki jump*, April 23, 1946. Brush and dry brush on ledger paper. Smithsonian Folkways Collection, WG-3-03-33.

Page 174: *Late last night*, April 20, 1946. Pencil and pen and ink on paper. Smithsonian Folkways Collection, WG-3-03-08.

Page 175: Pencil and pen and ink on paper. Smithsonian Folkways Collection, WG-3-04-20, WG-3-03-19, WG-3-04-08, WG-D2-25.

Page 176: *Pretty and Shinyo.* Ink on smooth board. Smithsonian Folkways Collection, WG-D2-25.

Page 177: Brush ink on paper. Smithsonian Folkways Collection, WG-D2-42.

Page 178: Paper, watercolor, ink/pen. Smithsonian Folkways Collection, WG-D1-10.

Page 179: *Rope Dance.* Smithsonian Folkways Collection, WG-D2-36.

Pages 180–83: *So Long, It's Been Good to Know You* lyric series, 1945. Watercolor and fountain pen on construction paper, 30.5 x 22.5 cm. Artwork Series 12 #1-20, WGA.

Page 184: *All Work Together.* Ink on smooth board, Smithsonian Folkways Collection, WG-D2-24.

Page 185: Pen/ink, bond. Smithsonian Folkways Collection, WG 3-01-08.

Page 186: *The blues is made out of trouble*, April 23, 1946. Dry brush on ledger paper. Smithsonian Folkways Collection, WG-3-03-28.

Page 187: *Looking for a woman that's hard to find*, April 23, 1946. Brush and dry brush on paper. Smithsonian Folkways Collection, WG-3-01-02.

Page 188: *Slipknot.* Pencil and pen and ink on paper. Smithsonian Folkways Collection, WG-3-04-21.

Page 189: *Stay gone*, April 23, 1946. Dry brush on ledger paper. Smithsonian Folkways Collection, WG-3-04-22.

Page 190: Top: *Lady of the train*, Coney Island, NY, Oct. 31, 1946. Pencil and pen on stenographer's notepad. NB-1, #54, WGA.

Page 190: Bottom: *Twice I Fell Down Once*, Coney Island, NY, August 7, 1947. Pencil and pen on stenographer's notepad. NB-1, #54, WGA.

Page 191: Untitled (from pencil drawings and ink drawings series), 1946. Brush and ink on cardboard, 36.2 x 27.5 cm. Artwork Series 16 #4, WGA.

Page 192: *I Couldn't Say* (from *Sacco & Vanzetti Drawings* series), 1946. Series 14, #5, pencil on paper, WGA.

Page 193: Top left: *Judge Thayer* (from *Sacco & Vanzetti Drawings* series), 1946. Dry brush, ink, and watercolor on construction paper, 30.5 x 23 cm. Artwork Series 14 #1, WGA.

Page 193: Top right: *Consciousness of guilt, to the jury* (from *Sacco & Vanzetti Drawings* series), 1946. Pencil on construction paper, 30.5 x 23 cm. Artwork Series 14 #6, WGA.

Page 193: Bottom: *Salloon close to Suassos Lane, Plymouth, Massachussets*, (from *Sacco & Vanzetti Drawings* series), 1946. Pencil, ink, watercolor on construction paper, 30.5 x 23 cm. Artwork Series 14 #4, WGA.

Pages 194–97: Untitled, 1946 Diary. Watercolor. NB-1, #52, WGA.

Pages 198-203: Selected works from *What a Beautiful World* (1) series, 1947. Brush and dry brush in artist's sketchbook, 35.5 x 25 cm. Artwork Series 25, WGA.

Pages 204–13: Selected works from *What a Beautiful World* (2) series, 1947. Brush and dry brush and ink in artist's sketchbook, 42.7 x 35 cm. Artwork Series 26,

Pages 214–19: Selected works from *Short Hauls* journal, August 9, 1947. Watercolor on lined notebook paper. NB-1 #57, WGA.

Pages 220–27: Selected works from *Cathy* journal, 1947. Watercolor on notebook paper. NB-1, #58, WGA.

Pages 228–41: Selected works from *Short Ones* journal, Nov. 9, 1947. Watercolor. Letter to Marjorie, Notebooks 1, #62, WGA.

Page 242: *Cathy Says* journal notebook cover, 1947. Brush on paper. NB-1 #56, WGA.

Page 243: Arlo birth announcement. Watercolor on cardstock. Aliza Greenblatt correspondence Series 1, Box 1, Folder 24, 1947, WGA.

Page 243: Photograph courtesy of Nora Guthrie.

Page 244: Correspondence 1, Box 3, Folder 5, WGA.

Page 245: NB 2 #5, 1953, WGA.

Pages 246–55: *Woody's 20 Grow Big Songs*, New York, NY, 1948–49. NB-1 #86, WGA.

Page 256: Watercolor, 1948. Smithsonian, WG-D1-06.

Page 257: *Arlo Guthrie on his thirty-fifth birthday*, ink on paper. Courtesy of the Collection of Barry and Judith Ollman.

Pages 258–59: *Miss Natanya Newman*, Jan. 12, 1948. Watercolor on paper. Courtesy of the Collection of Barry and Judith Ollman.

Page 260: *Old thoughts wash in*, March 30, 1948. Brush and ink on bond paper, 18 x 13 cm. Artwork Series 15 #12, WGA.

Page 261: Self-portrait (from *Drawings,*

Coney Island, NYC series), undated. Pencil on paper, 35.5 x 21.5 cm. Artwork Series 23 #5, WGA.

Page 262: *Cripple Annie* (from *Drawings, Coney Island, NYC* series), April 12, 1948. Pencil, pen and ink on construction paper, 35.5 x 21.5 cm. Artwork Series 23 #2, WGA.

Page 263: *Dear Henry*, Feb. 14, 1948. Pen and wash on paper. Courtesy of the Collection of Barry and Judith Ollman.

Page 264: *Unpaid Debts* (from watercolor/constr. paper/no date series), May 1948. Brush and ink, type script on construction paper, 30.3 x 23 cm. Artwork Series 21 #1, WGA.

Page 265: *a 59th St. gent watches army day parade* (from *Drawings, Coney Island, NYC* series), April 10, 1948. Pencil on lined yellow paper, 35.5 x 21.5 cm. Artwork Series 23, #6, WGA.

Page 266: Elvida B. Lousley (from *Drawings, Coney Island, NYC* series), April 1, 1948. Pen and ink on lined yellow paper, 31.5 x 20.2 cm. Artwork Series 23 #7, WGA.

Page 267: Ink on paper, Courtesy of the Collection of Barry and Judith Ollman.

Pages 268–76: Selected artwork from *No kids allowed* journal, 1948. Watercolor and dry brush. NB-1 #66, WGA.

Page 277: Top: *Lost John* (from watercolor/constr. paper/dated series), Coney Island, NY, 1949. Ink, watercolor on construction paper, 30.2 x 22.7 cm. Artwork Series 22 #15, WGA.

Page 277: Bottom left: *Sweetie oh sweetie come smella me now, Don't I smell nice and clean.....ohhh?* (from watercolor/constr. paper/dated series), Coney Island, NY, June, 1949. Watercolor on construction paper, 30.2 x 22.7 cm. Artwork Series 22 #20, WGA.

Page 277: Bottom right: *No girl* (from watercolor/constr. paper/dated series), Coney Island, NY, June 21, 1949. Watercolor on construction paper, 30.2 x 22.7 cm. Artwork Series 22 #23, WGA.

Page 278: *Atom dance* (from watercolor/constr. paper/no date series), no date. Watercolor on construction paper, 30 x 22.7 cm. Artwork Series 21 #9, WGA.

Page 279: *She's a big gyrosteam job and she's all cranked up to go* (from watercolor/constr. paper/dated series), 1949. Watercolor on construction paper, 30.1 x 22.5 cm. Artwork Series 22 #19, WGA.

Page 280: Untitled (from watercolor/constr. paper/no date series), no date. Watercolor on construction paper, 30.2 x 22.6 cm. Artwork Series 21 #12, WGA.

Page 281: Watercolor on construction paper. Series 21, # 2, WGA.

Page 282: Untitled (from watercolor/constr. paper/no date series), no date. Watercolor on construction paper, 30.2 x 22.7 cm. Artwork Series 21 #16, WGA.

Page 283: Untitled (from watercolor/constr. paper/no date series), no date. Watercolor on construction paper, 30.2 x 22.6 cm. Artwork Series 21 #13, WGA.

Page 284: Untitled, (from watercolor/constr. paper/no date series), no date. Watercolor on construction paper. Artwork Series 21 #14, WGA.

Page 285: *Why O Why* (from watercolor/constr.paper/no date series), no date. Watercolor on construction paper, 30.2 x 22.7 cm. Artwork Series 21 #21, WGA.

Page 286: *Put your finger* (from watercolor/constr. paper/no date series). Watercolor on construction paper, 30.2 x 22.7 cm. Artwork Series 21, #23, WGA.

Pages 287: Watercolor, dry brush. Smithsonian Folkways collection, WG-D1-05, WG-D1-03, WG-D2-44.

Page 288: Watercolor. Smithsonian Folkways collection, WG-D1-07.

Page 289: *I got tears in both eyes* (from watercolor/constr. paper/dated series), Coney Island, NY, 1949. Ink and watercolor on construction paper, 30.2 x 22.7 cm. Artwork Series 22 #13, WGA.

Page 290: *Olde Man, Arlo Dybuck Davy* (from watercolor/constr. paper/dated series), June 15, 1949. Watercolor on construction paper, 30.2 x 22.7 cm. Artwork Series 22 #21, WGA.

Page 291: Untitled (from watercolor/constr. paper/no date series), 1949. Watercolor on construction paper, 30.3 x 22.7 cm. Artwork Series 21 #7, WGA.

Page 292: *I like to swim in my water* (from watercolor/constr. paper/dated series), June 23, 1949. Watercolor on construction paper, 30.2 x 22.7 cm. Artwork Series 22 #25, WGA.

Page 293: Smithsonian Folkways collection, WG-D1-02.

Page 294: *Atoms can't hurt me* (from Crayons and pastels on construction paper series), Coney Island, NY, 1949. Pastel on construction paper, 30.5 x 22.8 cm. Artwork Series 20 #5, WGA.

Page 295: *No hand for trouble* (from Crayons and pastels on construction paper series), Coney Island, NY, 1949. Pastel on construction paper, 30.5 x 22.8 cm. Artwork Series 20 #6, WGA.

Page 296: *Dirty dishes*, May 16, 1949. Watercolor on construction paper. Manuscripts-1, Box 7, Folder 21, WGA.

Page 297: Top left: *Vet's Housing Project*, May 16, 1949. Watercolor on construction paper. Manuscripts-

1, Box 7, Folder 23, WGA.
Page 297: Sculpture and ceramic tile with glaze. Courtesy Nora Guthrie.

Page 298-99: Inside *American Folksay Ballads and Dances* recording, Asch Records, Nov. 8, 1949. Pen and ink. Courtesy of the Collection of Barry and Judith Ollman.

Page 300: Top: Untitled (from Art Work (Rich Art sketch book) series), 1950. Brush and ink on artist's sketch pad, 35.2 x 27.9 cm. Artwork Series 29 #4, WGA.

Page 300: Bottom: *Zibberzee* (from *Drawings of Family* series), Feb. 16, 1950. Watercolor and pencil on construction paper, 30.5 x 22.7 cm. Artwork Series 24 #17, WGA.

Page 301: *My Sheepshead Bay Girl* (from Art Work (Rich Art sketch book) series), 1950. Watercolor and ink on artist's pad, 35.2 x 27.9 cm. Artwork Series 29 #12, WGA.

Page 302: Jolly Miner (from Art Works [Tablet] series), Beach Haven, NY, March 1951. Dry brush, ink, watercolor on artist's pad, 45 x 30 cm. Artwork Series 30, #7, WGA.

Page 303: *Washington Breakdown* (from Art Works [Tablet] series), March 1951. Dry brush, watercolor on artist's pad, 45 x 30 cm. Artwork Series 30, #8, WGA.

Page 304: *Looky Me* (from Art Works [Tablet] series), March 1951. Watercolor on artist's pad, 45 x 30 cm. Artwork Series 30, #11, WGA.

Page 305: *The Draft Age* (from Art Works [Tablet] series), Beach Haven, NY, March 1951. Dry brush and pen on artist's pad, 45 x 30 cm. Artwork Series 30, #13, WGA.

Page 306: *Low Lonesome* (from Art Works [Tablet] series), Beach Haven, NY, March 1951. Watercolor, ink, on artist's pad, 45 x 30 cm. Artwork Series 30 #15, WGA.

Page 307: *These Ones Have Won Out* (from Art Works [Tablet] series), Beach Haven, NY, 1951. Watercolor on drawing paper, 45 x 30 cm. Artwork Series 30, #16, WGA.

Page 308: *Mississippi* (from Art Works [Tablet] series), March 31, 1951. Watercolor and dry brush on drawing paper, 45 x 30 cm. Artwork Series 30, #17, WGA.

Page 309: *Southland Tourist* (from Art Works [Tablet] series), March 1951. Watercolor, pen and colored pencil on artist's pad, 45 x 30 cm. Artwork Series 30 #18, WGA.

Page 310: *Tourist Look Good* (from Art Works [Tablet] series), Beach Haven, NY, April 1, 1951. Dry brush and pen, watercolor on artist's pad, 45 x 30 cm. Artwork Series 30 #19, WGA.

Page 311: *Starvation Disease* (from Art Works [Tablet] series), Beach Haven, NY, April 1951. Watercolor and dry brush on artist's pad, 45 x 30 cm. Artwork Series 30 #22, WGA.

Page 312: *Arlo's Funny Man* (from Art Works [Tablet] series), Beach Haven, NY, April 1951. Watercolor and dry brush on artist's pad, 45 x 30 cm. Artwork Series 30 #27, WGA.

Page 313: *My Gang* (from Art Works [Tablet] series), Beach Haven, NY, April 1951. Watercolor on artist's pad, 45 x 30 cm. Artwork Series 30 #28, WGA.

Page 314: Untitled (from Art Works [Tablet] series), Beach Haven, NY, April 1951. Watercolor on artist's pad, 45 x 30 cm. Artwork Series 30 #29, WGA.

Page 315: *All Work Together* (from Kids songs illustrations series), 1951. Brush and ink, watercolor on artist's pad, 42.8 x 35. Artwork Series 31 #8, WGA.

Page 316: *Jealous Love* (from Art Works [Tablet] series), Beach Haven, NY, April 1951. Watercolor, ink, and pen on artist's pad, 45 x 30 cm. Artwork Series 30 #26, WGA.
Page 317: *Pritty Near* (from Kids songs illustrations series), 1951. Watercolor on artist's pad, 42.8 x 35 cm. Artwork Series 31 #2, WGA.

Page 318: *Biggy Big Big* (from Drawings and Watercolors series), 1951. Watercolor on artist's paper. Artwork Series 15, #17, WGA.

Page 319: *Hootenanny: My Hootenanny*, 1952, Typescript on wrapping paper. Smithsonian, WG-D2-48.

Pages 320–21: Selected artwork, 1952. Watercolor in ledger book. NB-2, #8(53, 54), WGA.

Pages 322–23: Selected artwork, November 1952. Watercolor and crayon in ledger book. NB-2, #9 (pages 133-134). WGA.

Page 324: Top: *Bite [hell] out [of] her* (from [finger paint?] series), February 1954. Paint on glossy paper, 30.5 x 22.7 cm. Artwork Series 33 #4. WGA.

Page 324: Bottom: *Titty is what it is all about*, February 1954. Paint on glossy paper, 30.5 x 22.7 cm. Artwork Series 33 #3, WGA.

Page 325: *Which place is this?*, paint and pastel on glossy paper, 1952, Series 22 # 32, WGA.

Pages 326–27: *P for Payday*, Coney Island, NY, June 26, 1949. Watercolor on construction paper glued in notebook. NB-2, #2, WGA.

Pages 328–29: *Southern White*, June 4, 1953. Watercolor. NB-2, #11(inside cover). WGA.

Pages 330–31: *South White*, June 1953. Watercolor. NB-2, #11. WGA.

Pages 332–33: NB 2 # 12, 1954. WGA.

Page 334: Selected artwork, 1957. Pen and pencil in composition book. NB-1, #75(13). WGA.

Closing endpapers: *Peace*, an illustration for the song "Talking World Peace" in a collection of songs, 1952. NB 2 # 9, WGA.

Photography Credits:

Arnold and David Katz: Pages 1, 5, 37, 65, 88, 94-95, 97-98, 100, 102-103, 119, 120–21, 128–31, 181–82, 191,

193, 195–241, 244, 247, 250–53, 269–76, 297, 301–18, 320–33, endpapers.
Anthony Loew: 38, 257–59, 263, 267, 299.

Bibliography

Asch, Moe, ed. *American Folksong.* DISC Record Company, 1947.

Blum, Geoffrey. *The Unexpurgated Carl Barks.* Prescott, Ariz.: Hamilton Comics, 1997.

Carty, Donald G. *A World of Wisdom: Quotations for Enlightenment.* The Library for Higher Learning, 2002.

Coyle, William. *From Scatology to Social History: Captain Billy's Whiz Bang, Studies in American Humor,* Vol. III, No. 3, January 1977.

Cray, Edward. *Ramblin' Man: The Life and Times of Woody Guthrie.* New York: W. W. Norton & Company, 2004.

Guthrie, Marjorie, Harold Leventhal, Terry Sullivan, and Sheldon Patinkin, eds. *Woody Sez.* New York: Grosset & Dunlap, 1975.
Guthrie, Woody. *Bound for Glory.* New York: E. P. Dutton & Company, 1943. New edition, 1968.

Guthrie, Woody. *Seeds of Man.* University of Nebraska, 1995.

Woody Guthrie to Marjorie Guthrie, 8/29/42. Correspondence 2, Box 2, Folder 8, WPA.

Woody Guthrie to Alan Lomax, May 2, 1950, Accessions 2004. 90.1, WGA.

Woody Guthrie to Judger Thayer, no date. Smithsonian Folkways Archives, BOX 3, FOLDER 8, WG-3-08.

Woody Guthrie, Library of Congress Recordings, Elektra Records.

Woody Guthrie, Notebook 2-9, WPA.

Woody Guthrie, Postcards, 9/23/44, WGA.

Ketchum, Richard M. *Will Rogers: The Man and His Times.* Touchstone, 1973.

Klein, Joe. *Woody Guthrie: A Life.* New York: Knopf, 1980.

Landau, Ellen. "The Art of Woody Guthrie." *Hard Travelin': The Life and Legacy of Woody Guthrie,* edited by Robert Santelli and Emily Davidson. Middletown, Conn.: Wesleyan University Press, 1999.

Longhi, Jim. *Woody, Cisco, & Me.* Chicago: University of Illinois Press, 1997.

Mandell, Jonathan. "Guthrie's First Bid for Glory: With a Paintbrush." *The New York Times,* January 30, 2000.

Marsh, Dave, and Harold Leventhal, eds. *Pastures of Plenty: A Self Portrait.* New York: Harper Perennial, 1990.

Masterpieces in the Art Institute of Chicago. Chicago: The Art Institute of Chicago, 1952.

Maxton, John. *The Art Institute of Chicago.* London and New York: Thames and Hudson, 1970. Reprinted 1977.

Rogers, Will. *The Illiterate Digest.* A. L. Burt Company, 1924. Republished by Gale Research Company, 1974.

Rosen, Michael J., ed. *People Have More Fun Than Anybody: A Centennial Celebration of Drawings and Writings by James Thurber.* New York: Harcourt Brace & Company, 1994.

Thurber, James and E. B. White. *Is Sex Necessary?* New York: Harper & Row, 1929. Reprinted 1957.

Yagoda, Ben. *Will Rogers: A Biography.* New York: Alfred A. Knopf, 1993.

ABOUT THE AUTHORS:

Steven Brower is an award-winning graphic designer and writer working in New York City. He teaches at the School of Visual Arts in New York City, Kean University in New Jersey, and Marywood University in Pennsylvania. He resides in Matawan, New Jersey, with his wife and daughter and their six cats.

Nora Guthrie is the cofounder and director of the Woody Guthrie Archives in New York City. Over the years, she has collaborated with many artists and organizations to create new projects using Guthrie's previously unknown and unpublished works, among them, the Smithsonian Institution's traveling exhibition *The Life and Legacy of Woody Guthrie,* Billy Bragg and Wilco's *Mermaid Avenue* CDs, and The Klezmatics: *Woody Guthrie's Happy Joyous Hanuka.*

faces
and pretty
looks on
pretty
and
look too
too mad
and too
ugly
to suit
me
Take it easy
But take it.

P
Q
R
S
T
U
V
W
Y

PEACE